CHAPTERS

ACKNOWLEDGEMENTS

To Ken Doyle, Liam Reilly, and the late John O'Brien for sharing their memories with me over the last 42 years. I extend that to other members of the group through the years who have played in Bagatelle and contributed to this book all of whom, I hope, I have mentioned. If I have left anyone out my sincere apologies but fear not as when it becomes No.1 on the New York Times Best Sellers List, I will make sure your names will be put in the reprint!

To Dave Keegan for his unselfish help in giving me the use of some of his simply wonderful photographs to which of course he remains copyright. It has made a big change to the book. I am delighted to have them displayed within these pages.

Many thanks to Gerry Gallagher at www.irishshowbands.com and the Reynolds family for the use of some of the group photographs. To Shea Tomkins from Ireland's Own for the use of the Bagatelle cover picture (issue 5,449.) The picture remains the subject of copyright.
To Amanda Horan for the superb cover to this book.

John Kennedy O'Connor for the dramatic detail and quotes from the 1990 Eurovision in his book, The Eurovision Song Contest; 50 Years Official History.

To Jim McQuillan for his photographs, knowledge, and inside information on the band. I'm pretty sure every phone call we've had was at least 7 hours long and I could probably pay for Bagatelle to do a gig in my sitting room such were the bills I had to pay to Virgin Mobile!

My partner Samantha for always being there for me, keeping me sane and the support you continue to give me. Likewise, to the man above. My mum. Though you are not here in body, you remain within me in spirit. Can you tell Elvis he is missed badly down here? You get to listen to him in concert behind those pearly gates every night while we are stuck with that God-awful Bon Jovi down here!

Finally. For Choo Choo.

All rights reserved.
Published by Zesty Thorndyke Publishing.
Printed in Ireland by Modern Printers, Co. Kilkenny.
A catalogue record of this book is available from the British Library.

Copyright; Brian Kennedy
Back cover photograph; Dave Keegan Photography.
Cover Design: Amanda Horan

Why not follow me on www.briankennedywriter.com

INTRODUCTION

There's a good chance Bagatelle might not have made it to celebrate their 40th anniversary in 2018. I'm pretty certain the band would have to call it quits after Liam Reilly had his life flash before him at a gig in the South East of Ireland as they celebrated bringing in the New Year.

And that's all down to yours truly.

The Olympia Ballroom. Waterford. December 31st, 1997. Bagatelle are playing a New Year's Eve gig in the soon to be destroyed ballroom of yesteryear.

Bagatelle had been part of my life's timeline. I met my wife on a blind date at one of their gigs. Broke up with her several years later, and too much Jack Daniels, at one of their gigs.

I then found my partner Samantha after I won two tickets to one of their gigs, plucking up the courage to ask her out after a year of awkward shyness.

We love Bagatelle and have no plans to break up, Jack Daniels related or not.

Back to the scene of my crime.

I was ushering in the New Year with a group of friends. By this stage the band where about to enter 1998, the 20th anniversary of a Bray/Dundalk connection which had broken onto the Irish scene scoring a huge hit with a now iconic song that would embed the innocent 46A bus to Dun Laoghaire, and any drunk that rode it, into the hearts of an entire nation. Whilst my friends struggled with some of the set-list, opting safely for a couple of old favourites like "Trump Card" and "Second Violin," I was howling out every word of every song in a tone that sounded like a bag of cats being strangled.

With 30 seconds of 1997 left I decided I had to be the first person to welcome the group into 1998 so I quickly barged my way through the crowd, taking out four pints of Harp on a small table, which I'm sure was also filled with glasses of assorted whiskey, before I reached my target – Liam Reilly.

With a beaming smile in a drunken haze I reached out to shake his hand. I muttered something along the lines of "Happy New Year, Christ your f****** brilliant!" and proceeded to pull Bagatelle's frontman to the precipice of the stage. Now this would have been a hefty drop for the Dundalk man, ten feet at least, so fearing for his health I let go, sending me hurtling backwards onto a strangers table and covering myself, and the angry occupants, in what tasted like Guinness, but I could also vaguely make out a Rum & Black on my shirt as well.

I offered a thousand apologies and a round of drinks as Mr. Reilly emerged unscathed in time to launch into "Rock & Roll Fantasy."

The band continued to rock the house as my friend Damien, who was not a massive fan, but knew they were popular, asked why they hadn't "made it" in English or international waters.

It was a fair question, one to which I have scratched my head at least a thousand times.

You see Bagatelle have always been something of a wonderful mystery. A sort of enigma with a stigma. Success on a national scale, gold and platinum albums and a dedicated fan base who have worshipped at the altar of the group, some for almost five decades now, yet critical acclaim eluded them, having to content themselves with begrudging comments in some music magazines and tabloids that were happy to promote other artists, some without an ounce of originality.

It was the steadfast , stick to your guns, originality that ran through the spine of the group as they emerged from cover version dancehall days and a decaying showband scene to huge success at the turn of an economically depressed eighties, in turn producing a colossal hit in "Summer in Dublin" that has not only stood the test of time over 40 years later but became an anthem for the Irish diaspora all across the globe.

Their radio friendly sound seemed distinctively American. You could close your eyes during "Love is the Reason", "Trump Card" or "Rock 'n' Roll Fantasy" and think it was Bob Seger, or the Steve Miller Band singing it back to you.

In Liam Reilly the group had a storyteller. A musician whose song-writing capabilities, often outstripping his achievements with Bagatelle, writing songs of emigration like "The Streets of New York" and "The Flight of Earls" and imbedding those tunes in the minds of a generation. A man who almost had Europe in the palm of his hands as international stardom beckoned only to be denied in front of an audience of 600 million watching the Eurovision Song Contest.

Bagatelle were and remain a group of superb originality.

A band that U2 wanted to be when they were still playing the Dandelion Market in Dublin for free and trying to coax Polydor Records to sign them like they had Bagatelle.

A group whose songs had been covered and often referenced in the annals of Irish music.

Those songs are still relevant to many Irish artists that came after Bagatelle. There would be no new school without the old school.

Back to the Olympia, as I'd ushered in the New Year by almost taking a life and paying a hefty £52.98 for a round of drinks that I had utterly decimated, my crime hadn't gone unnoticed.

From nowhere two hefty bouncers, who looked like they'd been lured down a mountain for a piece of meat, caught a hold of me and carried me through the exit door by using my head as a battering ram.

Left alone outside on the pavement with the remains of a cold taco chip and the sting of what should be severe brain damage kicking in, I was left to lament what an utter clown I had been.

As the third encore of "Summer in Dublin" is struck up and sung with vigour back into the night I was left licking my wounds outside but safe in the knowledge that I would never have to regale my story of almost killing Liam Reilly to his face.

That was until I started to write this book!

FOREWORD BY EAMON CARR

Even back then, Bagatelle were celebrating an era that had already passed. And when "Summer in Dublin" hit the airwaves in 1980, the nation embraced this ration of instant nostalgia like pilgrims clasping a sacred relic.

Liam Reilly's song clearly had what music industry moguls call the X factor. It affected people in ways most disposable pop songs didn't come near. Within weeks of its release, "Summer in Dublin" had become more than a mega-hit. It became an anthem.

Reilly was a piano player who knew his way around the Elton John songbook. His mates had served their apprenticeship in bar bands. Together they'd been schlepping around for a couple of years before "Summer in Dublin" transformed their fortunes.

The song opened doors to major venues and the group quickly became the envy of ambitious young local bands, including U2, whose Larry Mullen Jr would later quip that he'd referred to them as "Bag-a-money".

Liam Reilly's song was the modern pop equivalent of Pete St John's "Dublin In the Rare Auld Times".

Instead of vanished landmarks such as the Pillar, the Met and the Royal, Bagatelle invoked sights, sounds and smells we were all too familiar with. The 46a bus, noisy jet planes, a crowded Grafton Street and the open sewer that was the river Liffey. But just like childhood holidays, the picture conjured up was of a bright, warm summer's day. The river was particularly odious on hot days.

No doubt when we hear the song's singalong cadences, we imagine a rose-tinted capital city. Not the dilapidated, economically mismanaged dump it was in 1980, when Charlie Haughey warned us to tighten our belts as the dole queues grew longer and school leavers had little option but to go abroad in search of work.

Forty years later, you might believe the old French saying: "The more things change, the more they stay the same."

The beggars are still on horseback as the country is saddled with unimaginable debt and the prospect of another wave of mass emigration. The skyline has changed of course. The Liffey has a few more bridges over it. And much of the docklands is covered in shiny big buildings that will be keeping NAMA busy for a while.

But being Irish, no matter how bleak things get, we'll still have a song in our hearts. And Bagatelle's "Summer in Dublin" is one of those timeless, feelgood jingles that brightens the mood.

Curiously, the lyric tells the story of someone who wants to get out of the city, to a place where there isn't much traffic. A place where you can hear the wind, the birds and the sea. It's a yearning for the kind of peaceful retreat that Charlie Haughey found when he acquired Inishvickillane.

When Bagatelle released their song on a 7" black vinyl single (207811 Irl) in 1980, it was to a world of pirate radio and Radio 2 "Comin'atcha!"

It was an era before downloads, ringtones and even CDs.

Punk rock had come and gone. New Wave bands were mutating. And the New Romantics were getting into their stride.

In this environment, safe, unthreatening Bagatelle were never likely to challenge The Blades, Microdisney or The Virgin Prunes in the affections of the critical elite.

As Ken Doyle of Bagatelle once remarked, "The song is everywhere. Like Kellogg's Cornflakes, it's in everybody's home. But no one is raving about it."

Yet "Summer in Dublin" now ranks alongside The Pogues "Fairytale of New York" and "One" by U2 as one of the best loved Irish pop songs ever. And that's its own just reward.

Because Bagatelle were maverick Rock 'n' rollers at heart. There's a clue in the song's narrative.

When Reilly sings *"I was singing a song I heard somewhere, called Rock 'n' 'Roll Never Forgets",* he was referencing Bob Seger, the no-nonsense American rocker whose song "Rosalie" Thin Lizzy recorded.

It is tempting to think that "the drunk on the bus" who told Reilly "how to get rich", has bought the song and contributed to the band's royalties. It's the stuff of pop dreams. Whatever the weather, we will always have Summer in Dublin.

Eamon Carr (credit; Evening Herald).

ONE

WELCOME TO THE REST OF YOUR LIFE

"In music I found something I loved and went after it with all my heart. There was no plan B in my life after that. Never."

JOHN O'BRIEN

Ireland in 1953.

De Valera was leader of Fianna Fail, having just led his party through a successful general election. Sean T. O'Kelly was President and there were less than three million people on the Emerald Isle.

The depressing emigration rates of the Fifties continued. 60,000 left our land for foreign shores in 1953 alone and the sexually liberated Sixties that followed seemed unthinkable.

Bad days still existed. Over 2,000 children in Industrial schools and the shameful secrets that would go unnoticed until a new century.

In Bray, 20,000 resided by a seafront that brought visitors aplenty. The town even had a rather unique tourist attraction, an aerial chairlift that would whisk passengers up to the Eagle's Nest on the heights of Bray Head. So popular indeed you had to stand in line at 9am during the scorching hot summers of the early Fifties just to get a ride.

October 4th, 1953 saw the Doyle family welcome their son Ken into the fold. He would be a welcome third addition to the household. Before then the Doyle's had been blessed by daughter Rosemary and son Martin. Both would excel in their vocations.

Rosemary would go on to work for Air France and is a degree student from the Open University having studied at Oxford University while brother Martin had become a world-renowned flute maker and highly respected musician.

The Doyle's beginnings were humble to say the least. They lived in a small two bedroomed house in Michael's Villas in Bray which was actually a converted stable. In Ken's own words *"So you see we share something in common with the big JC from Galilee!"*

Ken idolised his dad George. A talented man who built his own wood-turning lathe and a great carpenter to boot. Times were hard in the Fifties, but he managed to secure a job as a bus driver at a time they were one of the lowest paid professions in Ireland. The Emerald Isle had become a ghost town with successful industries far and few between. Many had opted for Ellis Island again. Two decades on from the Great Depression it seemed nothing had changed.

Though Ken's father wasn't a musical man he did like to sing a song and would normally exercise his vocal cords after a session in the local pub. Songs like " Steady Boys and Step Together" or "A Nation Once Again" would become his party pieces.

It would also bring back memories of his military service days during World War II as he was General Hugo McNeill's driver throughout the war. O'Neill always wanted him by his side, no matter how tired he was, but always made sure Private George Doyle was well fed and fortified in a quiet corner of the Officer's Mess.

His mum Rosalene (affectionately known as "Roly") was a tremendous singer and a great cook. She was the conventional stay at home mother looking after her brood (another son Gerry arrived five years after Ken) though she became involved in amateur dramatics when she could find the time. She had an incredible repertoire of songs, singing everything from Irish acts like Gilbert O' Sullivan, through Rock & Roll, Gospel and standards of the day.

"One day my father brought me with him to give a hand cleaning the garden for a nearby elderly couple called the Emerson's on New Court Road. When we had finished and put the tools away, I spotted a piano in the corner of this tiny garage. It wasn't long before I was playing some clumsy kind of melody on it when in walked Mr. Emerson. I remember my father apologising to him for me having the tenacity to go near it, but Mr. Emerson just laughed. The fact I was 7 years of age might just have helped me!" **Ken Doyle**

However, Mr. Emerson thought the music that had emerged from his tiny garage wasn't half bad. *"You know that young lad of yours is very musical. I've been looking for a good home for that piano for a while now so you can have it if you want"* he remarked.

George didn't need to hesitate for a moment.

The very next day the piano was collected and brought home with the help of a family friend and his van. Ken wouldn't sleep a wink the night before. The sheer excitement kept him up all night. That piano and a crackly old radio the family kept in the front room would be the starting point of a musical journey that the Bray native is still on. Many a tune was bashed out on that old Joanna.

School would be a brutal regime. The Christian Brothers ran the order of the day and certainly didn't hold back when it came to brutality.

Ken had seen it first-hand.

The terror they put into every boy's mind with their long black cassocks, half white collars and leather straps. The sheer panic if they had done something wrong. The ignominy of a beating in front of their classmates.

Ken couldn't wait to walk away from it. Once he fell on the wrong side of one particularly sadistic Brother who beat him severely, leaving him dizzy and vomiting uncontrollably. Even at the tender age of ten his mind was made up. He needed to leave that institution. Skipping school would become the order of the day. A young Ken would befriend the nearby Walshe family, bringing their dogs on long walks on days he should have been in school. The day he was released from the brutal state sponsored school felt like a bird being released from a cage.

Missing school would come at a price. 10 shillings to be exact for not attending.

Living in a seaside town there would always be jobs found at the local amusements. Places like the Fun Palace, Dawson's and the Casino run by the Arcari family proved popular.

It was at Dawson's Amusements he secured his first job earning £3.10 shillings a week. He recalls happy marching up to the local Garda Station and gleefully paying the fine from the school and getting a receipt.

Happier times came when he worked in Killiney Railway Station where Mr.Benville, who knew Ken from the time he worked at a local garage, took him onboard – pardon the pun. Those perfect manners instilled from his mother came in handy where he got on well with all the passengers, some of them are still friends to this day. The only thing Ken despised was the awful black wool uniform he was made to wear. At the time, fourteen-year-old boys were very fashion conscious and appearance was everything so Mr. Benville let him have it for the many times he went on board without it.

He could never stay angry at him though.

Here was this very keen and motivated young teenage kid working on a railway line when most boys were still at school not knowing what they wanted to do with their life. But Ken knew what he wanted. It would always be music. Afternoon matinees, keeping a close ear on soundtracks (with a particular interest in James Bond themes) where Doyle discovered the genius of the late John Barry who fuelled his fire. With the lack of trains in Ken's normal shift, the morning train departed at 9am with the next at 2pm, there was plenty of time to practice music.

He ended up working there for six years before he finally decided to pursue a career in music. When push came to shove it wasn't an easy decision. The railway was a pensionable job for life, but he took a leap of faith to follow his dream. It may have been the equivalent of being blindfolded and hopping off a cliff, but the 21-year-old was headstrong.

He found out a short time later Mr. Benville had kept young Doyle on the books for six months, just in case the music didn't work out. "*What a heart of gold he had,*" remarked Ken.

Inspiration for a career in music always started from home.

"There was always music in the house. I remember my brother Martin bringing home a little banjo and before long he was knocking out tunes on it. He played everything from the banjo to the tin whistle in school and had a knack of picking up tunes fast. He could knock a tune out of anything. He was the Einstein of the house. Me and my younger brother Gerry would accompany Martin to various small pubs which held sessions with every form of instrument: flutes, tin whistles, accordions, bodhrans, concertina spoons, sheep bones and mandolins. The first time I heard him play the mandolin I had to get one. I scoured the streets of Dublin looking for one, but most people had not heard of a mandolin. I was making my way back to Connolly station when I spotted an old pawn shop on Gardner Street. The shop was called Godwins (no longer standing) so I asked the owner had he got one.

"What in the name of Christ is that?" came the reply. He pondered for a while and had a look in the back of the shop. I heard him say "I have a queer looking thing here, but I don't know what it is" before bringing out a small black case with an inch of dust on it. He used a damp cloth to wipe it down and when he cracked it open there sat a beautiful round black mandolin with three strings left. We settled on a price of £20. I stopped at O'Neill's in Capel Street to buy a set of strings. I was absolutely made up! From there I learned a host of traditional Irish songs and would accompany Martin to the sessions along with Gerry, who was not playing at the time but listening and learning to play the mandolin."
Ken Doyle

Though he would master the old piano from Mr. Emerson and do his best with the mandolin, it would be bass and guitar that Ken would perfect. Little did he know where this would all lead. By chance, a visiting American called Bob Denton was travelling around Ireland, learning all about Irish music to add to his repertoire. At the time he had his trusty D35 acoustic guitar along with a Vega five string banjo, Gibson teardrop flatback mandolin and Ovation guitar. Ken was immediately interested.

"Even though I played the mandolin, Gerry had put in a savage amount of time practicing on it as well and had overtaken me, so I set my sights on a guitar instead. That's when I ran into Bob. What a happy accident that was! Bob was selling his Ovation guitar but wanted £80, a large sum of money at the time. At the time I earned just £6 in wages. I had around £40 saved and Christ that was a struggle, and never thought I would have enough. Thankfully, Bob took pity on this sorrowful heartbroken Irish boy and said he'd take £40 now and to send the other £40 to America as he was going back there." **Ken Doyle**

True to his word, Ken would mail over the extra £40 and to this day still has the guitar in his seaside house in Bray.

With the deal done he quickly learned the chords and rhythms for backing tunes and along with Martin on banjo and Gerry on mandolin the trio had a band.

Enter the Doyle's!

Another hobby for Doyle growing up was frequenting the local dump, which he did on almost a daily basis! There Ken and Gerry used to go and collect old brass bells and picture frames and sell them on to a junk man for 'a couple of bob' so they could buy sweets and ice cream. It was on one visit the brothers accidentally came across an old record player and a glut of old 45 singles. Naturally the free purchase was taken home and with a little bit of persistence Gerry managed to get the battered old player working and in no time, they were introduced to Fats Domino, the Everly Brothers, Johnny Cash, and Tony Bennett to name but a few.

In the late sixties a massive tax rebate of £100 came Ken's way from CIE. After contributing £50 to his beloved mother to keep the house going, he caught the train from Bray and headed to the relatively near big smoke of Dublin. Being a man of considerable means now, Ken strolled around looking for something to spend his vast fortune on. Nothing seemed to catch his eye at first, but eventually as he headed back to Tara Street to catch the train home, he clocked a closing down sale at a music shop which boasted a fine array of bass guitars. Doyle finally settled on one cherry red and cream binding bass which he purchased for £20.

And with that Ken Doyle's ride on the musical rollercoaster began with that bass. In early 1977 he would join a four-piece band that lasted about as long as a chocolate fireguard.

"I think every musician who has been successful can remember their very first band. I joined a group with Ned Teehan & Brian Baynes and a drummer called Richie which was called Butch (it was named after a Christian brother from Presentation college in Bray that we knew.) I was younger than the boys and extremely inexperienced. Ned would say stuff like "Let's jam in a 12 Bar A" and I'd think "what in the name of Christ is he on about! What's a 12 Bar A?" But over time we clicked I suppose. I had to learn quickly. I joined the band on a Monday and by Thursday I had the bones of 20 songs learned on my bass. On Friday they said, "Oh by the way you are playing a gig with us in the Woodlands Hotel in Greystones tonight!" I was scared shitless!" **Ken Doyle**

The band would last that one solitary gig.

"It was so funny. I remember halfway through the gig, Ned the singer looking at Baynsey and pointing at his neck. I thought it meant his voice

had gone so I moved across the stage to investigate, only to hear Ned say "Do you see a knob there?" to which Baynsey shook his head in a confused manner and said "No, why?" to which Ned replied "Then turn it fucking down!" We called it a night after that!" **Ken Doyle**

That old chestnut "reconcilable differences" (namely the three boys wanting to kill each other) was named as the reason the group folded. There are no plans of a reunion and world domination for Butch as I write this book. Sadly, the late great Brian Baynes passed away some years ago in San Diego, but his daughter Jessica carries on the family music tradition. It took two months for Ken to make up with Ned and Brian. Putting their disastrous hotel gig behind them, the boys thought another shot at stardom was probably worth a go. This would come in the shape of The Elastic Band, a group comprising the three boys but adding drummer Paul Fairclough and Marian Byrne on vocals.

Being a guy who never rested on the laurels of the instrument he was playing, Doyle swapped his beloved cherry red bass for an old sixties Fender Jazz bass which he secured for £100, and still has it to this day.

However, there seemed to be something still missing. That's when the group got wind of a great rhythm guitarist called John O'Brien who had been playing the pub circuit locally. Not only could he play, he was extremely knowledgeable of the music business and was also a terrific songwriter. Ken approached the group's new would-be guitarist, and immediately struck up a chemistry between both men that would last over 40 years.

"John was like a second father to me. Even his daughter has always regarded me as her big brother. He was so knowledgeable. About everything. Before Google there was John! I learned so much from him. We called him the oracle. I always used to say to John Alphonsus Mario Valentine O'Brien (to give him his full title) that he was over-designed for Rock & Roll as he had so many strings to his bow. And I was right. There would never have been a Bagatelle were it not for the vision and dream of John O'Brien." **Ken Doyle**

Even by 1977 John O'Brien had some serious musical chops and a wealth of experience.

He got his very first guitar in 1953, the year Ken Doyle was born, and had played in a host of Rock & Roll bands.

"I remember getting my first guitar in 1953. It was Merle Travis that I had heard on the radio that first influenced me. I had a birthday and Christmas coming up and I was delighted to receive a guitar as a present. To be honest it wasn't great, it was almost an unplayable lump of wood,

but it was a start! All my family had been very musical so were naturally supportive which reassured me." **John O'Brien**

At the time the guitar seemed to be a symbol of the Antichrist if you ever went to church. You see the Catholic church did not take too kindly to Rock & Roll and vilified the music each Sunday from the Pulpit. When a certain dark-haired boy from Tupelo, Mississippi gyrated his way into the living rooms of millions after an appearance on the Ed Sullivan Show in 1956, Elvis Presley would become the living embodiment of Satan himself. That and for some reason nylon blouses! Your regular priest would have gone as far as saying if you turned up in church with an inch of a blouse sporting nylon, you'd have to face the wrath of him, the church goers and possibly the town!

O'Brien had left Ireland in a cattle-boat in 1959 for a happening, vibrant London where he spent a decade, playing in four bands whilst there. He came back looking for success in Ireland and was happy to link up with Elastic Band. His father figure influence would become a reassuring aspect, especially for Ken who would follow him onto greater things.

The group gigged on a regular basis. Drummer Paul Fairclough, who had joined from the Alias B Band, another local group, used to have an entertaining and novel way of interacting with the crowd.

"It was a fun time to be in the band. I had this small set of drums but no actual hardware, so we would weld together a grey shelving angle and towards the end of the gig , when the band was cooking, the weld would break and the Tom-Toms would roll down off the stage onto the dancefloor. We were a dangerous band to see as you could end up getting flattened by them! The audience loved it and thought it was part of the act, but it was pure necessity." **Paul Fairclough**

"We used to run gigs in places like the Holyrood Hotel with a group of different bands from Dublin. One day Ned said to me "I've just booked a band called the Boomtown Rats. I've been dealing with a guy called Bob Geldof and from what I heard a few people said he's an awful bollocks but sure I suppose we will have to wait and see." I remember that first gig we saw them. They arrived on a Saturday night; Geldof stormed around like a General with military precision making sure there was only one door in so nobody could get in for free. He was wearing the big trademark hat. The group got up on the stage, put on the sunglasses, turned their backs to the audience and remained quiet and motionless for about 30 seconds, then spun around, hit it and practically blew the place away. Everybody in the room knew the band was special and going places." **Ken Doyle**

Geldof would go on to orchestrate a band who topped the English charts, had 12 Top 40 hits, six well received albums and 40 million records sold. He went on to champion 'Live Aid' and though he's become a royal pain in the arse to some of recent times, back then he was a maverick. And we all embraced him as one of our own.

Sadly, there were a few rock & roll egos and petty squabbling within The Elastic Band and their fate was sealed a couple of months later and a split. They had lasted for five gigs.

After all this was 1977. Punk had landed, kicking down the doors of the musical establishment and upsetting the applecart. Nobody had heard a sound like this before. And the Elastic Band certainly hadn't been the Sex Pistols. Many young bands would take up Punk as it was the hip movement at the time. It would prove a temporary setback for guitarist John O'Brien. But he could see a bigger picture.

"The breakup of the band did not phase me. I was used to the music scene and it was part of the territory. I had a good cabaret band before it called Hussle. We were based in Lexlip and played 5,6, even 7 nights a week. I took the Elastic Band slot to try something different having been in so many bands. My old Beetle car did a fair bit of travelling in those days. I had a target with these bands that I never really achieved. I remember telling Marian Byrne I wanted a band consisting of lead guitar with double bass, acoustic guitar, electric guitar and drums. I'm sure that would have given us a sound like no other band in Ireland."
John O'Brien

By now Ken Doyle was extremely pissed off. What had looked promising had fallen apart. Though he had a background of traditional Irish music he had embraced the hippie lifestyle that went with the Elastic Band. He needed a new fix, a new band. Until then, his Fender jazz bass went under the bed and rapidly gathered dust.

By late 1977 John O'Brien had started to put together a new band to take on the world. It would be a venture the guitarist had Ken Doyle in mind and John would head hunt him for a time, repeatedly calling to Doyle's door five Sunday's in a row. By the time he knocked for a sixth time, Ken was ready to tell him to fuck off to high heaven but eventually gave in to O'Brien's soft demeanour.

"I remember opening the door and was just about to deliver my two-word symphony, but John was very perceptive. He said, "Look I know what you are about to say but all I ask for old times' sake is to give it a go. If you don't like it, I'll drop you straight back. No questions asked." So, I agreed and that brought an end to it." **Ken Doyle**

Apart from being a highly intelligent man and a great musician, O'Brien was a dogged determined individual. Like a Canadian Mountie, he always got his man.

The Boulder Band in 1977 (L-R;) Marian Byrne, Paul Fairclough, Ken Doyle with Bree Harris and John O'Brien in front. Pic courtesy of Bree Harris.

John had arrived in his green VW Beetle , affectionately known as Jezebel as her registration included JZL, to collect Ken and both made their way to Silverpine Studios, a small studio run by the Stapleton family, a kind clan who were willing to help out and it was here John and Ken were reunited with Marian Byrne and Paul Fairclough, both of the Elastic Band and another girl, Bree Harris. Bree had been part of the Alias B Band along with Paul Fairclough, a band that had solid reviews in the now legendary Mississippi Rooms in Bray. Bree was a confident, brassy girl who could sing the phonebook and added more eye candy to the punters. Doyle liked the vibe straight away, even without a note being played.

The first song attempted together was the Hank Williams Classic "Tonight The Bottle Let Me Down" (you can always be reassured of a country song lamenting a lost love while drinking half a bottle of Jack Daniels) and as soon as the girls started to sing the hair would stand on the back of the necks of the men. The vocal blend was heavenly. Ken looked at John and Paul and cracked a big smile. Bingo.

After the gig Ken shook John's hand thanking him for this opportunity.

"I remember him saying that he loved the fire inside me when I was playing. He must have seen or heard something I was not aware of, bless him! I used to get up to all sorts as a child which would make my

mum laugh. She always said "Blessed are the cracked for they let the light shine in." I think I was about 10 when I understood what she meant. I think maybe John spotted some of that in me." **Ken Doyle**

The result of this would be The Boulder Band, a group which lasted around two years playing covers by the likes of Hank Williams, Janis Joplin, Fats Waller, Lou Harris and Joni Mitchell among others, but also chipped in with a lot of originals.

"The band had a certain magic that connected with the punters. I think the combination of the two girls, Marian and Bree, is what attracted me to the band and those who came to see us. They really sounded great together. We did half a mix of originals and covers. Two of our originals, "Ocean" and "Elmira" became real crowd favourites. The lyrics were written by Mike Maher, Bree's husband at the time." **Paul Fairclough**

"We were a blend of Country, Blues and Soft Rock with two women up front. The blend of music felt really special and soon people started to compare us to Fleetwood Mac with Christine McVie and Stevie Nicks. John O'Brien had heard me sing one night and said he was putting a band together and I trusted John. He had such knowledge on music and what worked. I had gigged before this with the Alias B Band, but this was different. We knew we had something." **Bree Harris**

"Bree and I loved working together and writing original music for The Boulder Band. In fact, nearly everyone brought something to the table when it came to writing songs. I penned two songs called "Love Letters" and "Tell the Truth", Bree wrote "Back on the Juice" and "Levee Lady" and John O'Brien would write "Say Goodbye" and "Love Is the Reason". Of course, those two songs became Bagatelle classics." **Paul Fairclough**

Three months of rehearsal , mainly at Silverpine Studios , with the odd acoustic session at John O'Brien's house at 100 Sugarloaf Crescent, a house that became central to the early days of Bagatelle, gave way to the Boulder Band's first gig, organised by Ray Dicker, whose parents owned Dicker Electrical shop on Main Street in Bray. When Silverpine was no longer an option the group went to Galtrim Lodge where Bree lived with her ex-husband at the time, often rehearsing outside on hot sunny days. With Molly's bakery on one side and the post office buildings on the other side, there would be no problem from those neighbours. It became a regular occurrence of post office workers sticking their heads over the wall to see what was going on. Many stuck around for the band's sessions. An early fanbase had been made!

Soon the group began making waves locally and gained a following. Determined to succeed where the Elastic Band had failed the Boulder Band gigged constantly, sometimes four nights a week. They honed a tight sound and started a residency in a local haunt, the Mississippi Rooms.

"The Mississippi Rooms just got better and better as a venue. We started Sunday afternoons there and would pack them in and began a Monday night residency there for a while. We gigged in places like The Holyrood or the Eagle House which were both on the seafront in Bray. Sometimes we would go to Dublin and play The Merrion Inn and pack them in. The punters used to be literally hanging from the rafters. We had worked so hard in getting our name out there that it started to pay off. We even had a Friday night residency in Murphy's in Phibsborough. The fact that most of our stuff was original made us unique. It was something that also made Bagatelle stand out when they started gigging. Putting across original material is hard and risky, but it worked well for them" **Bree Harris**

After a few months gigging the band copped a fair-haired guy in the crowd who had popped along to a few of their gigs. He always seemed interested in what was going on up on stage and seemed to be at any gig the band played locally. At one of the very last Boulder Band gigs the group asked him if he played anything. He said piano and he filled in on a few songs from the set that night.
His name was Liam Gerrard Reilly.

"I used to go see them in a place called The Magnet in Dublin with a friend of mine. I always loved what they played. Their music. One night after a few jars I was invited on stage, so I started to play this piano that was on the side of the stage. It was my first real introduction to the band." **Liam Reilly**

Little was it known then that the Dundalk native would play an instrumental part in the history of not just an impromptu gig with the Boulder Band but as the driving force behind the group that would become Bagatelle.
As for the Boulder Band? A close but no cigar effort if ever there was one. Despite all the hard work and gigs tensions would come to the surface once too often. After a productive couple of years together the group would disband. But their place in what would become Bagatelle's history was confirmed. A local band playing original music and making a name for themselves. Had the Boulder Band settled their differences and continued in the same vein it is quite possible they could have achieved what Bagatelle were about to.

"It was sad when the band broke up, but of my time with them I wouldn't change a thing. It was the most fun ever. A time in my life although it was a short spell, I will never forget. If we had changed our goal and done cover versions, it never would have happened. We would not have stood out and The Boulder Band would just be another small group playing local bars. We achieved more than that, so it was a shame when we split." **Bree Harris**

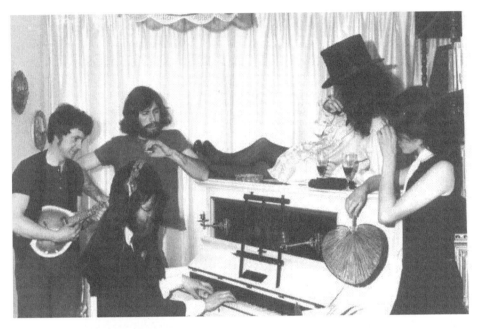

The Boulder Band larking about. They would split in 1978, making way for Bagatelle. Above, Bagatelle's first gig outside Bray at The Beechmount Hotel in Navan. Admission £2.

"It started as a fun band and we all enjoyed the music we made. And for a while, things really began to look up. The more gigs we did, the more venues we played, the popularity of the group grew. People really got to know us. Alas it wasn't to be. I think we were frustrated by the way it had to end. But it was lovely being part of the Boulder Band" **Paul Fairclough**

By this stage Ken Doyle must have thought there was either an Indian sign, a hex or someone with a voodoo doll of him poking it with needles as the Bray native was having a really bad run of luck. He had only been playing a couple of years and this was the third band he had been in that went tits up. However, that would change in a way the then 24-year-old could never imagine.

By now it was 1978. Ireland was entering a deep recession. Unemployment was rife, and those that did work paid 60p of £1 in tax.

Just think about that. 60p of your £1 going on tax. It was a time of strikes from banks, trains, and post offices. Oil was scarce and petrol even more so. It was a time of Fianna Fail and a man who came on our television set telling us to tighten our belts whilst he was off buying an island and wearing silk shirts.

Music was an outlet that could take you away from it, for however briefly. Being in a band had been something to look forward to. To rise above the dole queues, burdening bills, and shit that we inherited. Ireland was a third world country. Ken Doyle and John O'Brien knew music was something to channel their positive energy into. To get away from the bollocks surrounding them.

Music was something the Dole, the Taxman or Charles J. Haughey couldn't take away from them. It was here Bagatelle was born.

TWO

DOING BUSINESS IN BURGERLAND

"Some bands sign million-pound contracts in huge offices with marble tables and record producers smoking a fine Cuban cigar. We signed ours over seven cheeseburgers, five packets of chips and a couple of fish fillets."

KEN DOYLE

Ken Doyle did not need much persuasion in joining this new group, hoping it could kick on past what the Boulder Band achieved. Even at this young age it had still been a steep learning curve towards any form of success for Doyle, but he lived forever in hope. Sure, he quizzed John about everything this band would or could be, but there was a calm assurance from O'Brien that maybe this band could be different. That maybe this was the shot they had been looking for. Marian Byrne had joined from the Boulder Band, but a drummer was still needed. At the time there wasn't a large group of drummers knocking about.

"I remember striking up a conversation with a guy I met by chance at a petrol station one day and he actually played drums. He warmed to the conversation and I thought I was onto something. That was until I asked him who do you listen to and what his musical influences were only for him to reply "Barry Manilow. Look I could drum anything!" That was the end of his audition!" **Ken Doyle**

Another piece of the Bagatelle puzzle was briefly filled in when Joe Bollard came in on keyboards. A terrific musician in his own right he had cycled across America in tandem, done several radio documentaries and even wrote his own autobiography.
Not bad for a blind man.
Joe's involvement was brief – three gigs – so Mick McNally took over the reins soon after, again just for a short time. From there the late Brian Molloy from Westland Studios had heard of a promising drummer who had a good rep having drummed for many bands by the name of Wally McConville.
Wally auditioned at 100 Sugarloaf Crescent with "Sweet Georgia Brown" being the first song he played along to. He was an instant success and joined the band that afternoon. The last place needed filling now was on

keyboards. With Joe Bollard and Mick McNally vacating that position the group steadied themselves for what they thought might be a long and possibly fruitless exercise.

Thankfully, word of mouth had come to them about a guy in Dundalk that had become available after recently splitting up from a local band. Word filtered through his keyboard playing was excellent and his vocals "sounded like Leo Sayer."

"I knew John Woods of Polydor Records from my time in the Boulder Band and wondered would he be interested in this new band we were putting together as I reckoned there could have been a record deal in it. But we desperately needed to find a keyboard player. Then we heard of a guy from Dundalk who had won a song contest somewhere who also played piano and guitar and could hold a note. So, we brought this guy, Liam Reilly, to the house in Sugarloaf Crescent where his first choice of song was "Goodbye Yellow Brick Road". It wasn't until Ken Doyle came in the room that he twigged that it was the same Liam Reilly who had played that one gig with the Boulder Band. "Jesus Christ it's you" – said Ken (or words to that effect!) **John O'Brien**

The Dundalk man was the final piece of the puzzle. Liam Reilly's inclusion in the band would go on to have a massive influence on Bagatelle and their success. His songwriting ability would be second to none, penning hit after hit with the group and achieving huge success outside the band as a songwriter for others.

Born January 29, 1955 and living in a council estate in Fatima, Dundalk, Liam had early contact with the piano as a small kid, stretching himself up to tinkle the ivories of his father's piano in the house. He quickly learned harmonica, took up accordion which his father played while Liam's mum sang with a choir which she still does as a youthful 88-year-old!

In 1967 he won his first award on accordion in a Ceoltas Ceoltoiri Eireann event at the age of 14 in Enniscorthy. When he was 17, he won the senior piano event in Buncrana. This boy was going places! Not long after he helped to form a local band.

"We called the group Changes and were an original band. We got the name from the Bowie classic "Changes" which soon became our signature tune. The group was me, Kevin McCourt and John Jordan and we used to gig regularly in Dundalk. Kevin is an accountant, a great guitar player and a lifelong friend. John actually passed away some time ago in Cape Town. It was my first experience in a band setting, and we had a lot of fun." **Liam Reilly**

Liam would move to a new house built by his father in Dundalk later and though music would ultimately be his living, Liam's initial background suggested his real vocation would be elsewhere. He trained to be a teacher at St Patrick's College (which didn't work out after he was caught by a priest with a six pack and playing "Whiter Shade of Pale" on the organ one night) so then took a job with a computer company in Dundalk while also driving to Dublin three nights a week to earn a diploma in foreign trade. The computer company finished shortly after, but the astute young Reilly wasn't long in finding paid employment – taking a job with BP Chemicals as Shipping Manager with the company.

"On Independence Day, July 4th, 1978 I left my job, just as Bagatelle were about to hit it big. I told my boss, frankly I could not do this anymore. Yes, it paid the bills, but I had zero interest in the job. I auditioned for the band and shortly after Marian Byrne, who had been fronting the group, left and emigrated to America so the spotlight sort of fell on me. By this stage I had already penned "Summer in Dublin" a tune which I had won a song contest in Dundalk that John Woods (who would become instrumental in granting Bagatelle a record contract) had been a judge of that night. I had been living in a flat at no.2 Leeson Street when I wrote it. I performed the song that evening with guitar and thought nothing more of it until Bagatelle came together. It was then the group found out about the song. The rest is history I suppose!" **Liam Reilly**

Everything was now in place. Except for one crucial element.
The name of the band.

"It was a chore naming the band. I remember going through about 50 names with Marian and still not getting an agreement. We got a gig in Dublin at The Baggot Inn and Charlie the manager of the pub said he wanted to book the band and he would advertise this by putting a big sign in the window of our name. He asked, "What's the name of the band?"
I went "Oh Bollocks!" The next day he rang again pestering me. I had picked up my telephone, knowing I had avoided the issue too long now, but I didn't have a clue what to do. Suddenly inspiration came in the shape of my local postman. He put a letter through the mailbox, and it was a mailshot, advertising cheap Beethoven recordings – "buy one get one free." One of them was called the Bagatelle recordings so I went with that.
Charlie asked me to spell it, which I did, he paused then said, "That's a stupid fuckin' name, you won't be using that in a year's time." What more can I say? **John O'Brien**

As for a manager? Well for a fleeting moment in time one man took over the reins and let them go just as quick. That man was Larry Flood.

"I had played with John for a couple of years and enjoyed it. We became good friends and I managed a couple of cabaret acts along the way. I briefly took the job as manager of the group, but I really didn't have enough experience in the type of management Bagatelle needed at the time. They were very eager to get on the scene and make an impact. Even at that point I knew they had huge potential, so because of managing just cabaret acts I was sort of the weakest link so to speak. They were and still are a great band and it's nice to have been part of their history."
Larry Flood

By now Bagatelle were using John O'Brien's rented house at 100 Sugarloaf Crescent in Bray to practice. It had been advertised as a three bedroomed house, but you would have done well to fit a person standing up in the third room, let alone a bed. If you tried to swing a cat around the room, he would have been killed from hitting all the four walls. It was that tiny. However, it was the front room which was the epicentre of things. A small sitting room area which doubled as a part time rehearsal room with an old piano, a stack of amps, and several other pieces of paraphernalia. Abbey Studios it was not but every band had to start somewhere.

O'Brien had moved in there in 1976, playing for the house by gigging all the hours God gave him while surviving on a paltry existence. However, driven by the love of his craft, the Bray native never dwelled on where the next meal was coming from. He was so immersed in music nothing else really mattered.

"Sugarloaf gave us a start. It was a time of no money for us. I remember the first day I spent in the house we had a helping of cucumber sandwiches. It wasn't posh. We were broke! But I hung in there. To me John O'Brien was a genius that I looked up to, so I knew we were going places." **Liam Reilly**

From humble beginnings began greatness. Every group member brought something to the party. Wally McConville's vibrancy on drums, Ken Doyle's charisma and deft bass playing. The song writing ability of both Reilly and O'Brien with the latter, now almost a veteran, adding his musical knowledge, sensibility and guitar playing. John's father figure status within the band was crucial to Bagatelle's success. His organisation and arrangements of the tunes he wrote and co-wrote. Without John O' Brien there would be no Bagatelle story to tell.

Outside of the house the group needed to get a few gigs.

Local haunts in Bray would be the obvious choice, but they would also look further afield.

On Friday October 20th, 1978, in the Nationalist & Leinster Times, an advert was listed in the paper's entertainment section which read; BAGATELLE (Ex- Boulder Band featuring Marian Byrne.)

The gig was for the El Ruedo Club in Carlow. Small the venue may have been, but it did not matter a jot to the lads.

They were in print and it was a start.

However, it would be the Mississippi Rooms in Bray which became a real home from home. A place synonymous with the early days of Bagatelle and before that the Boulder Band. A venue constantly used by the group to help give them the exposure they needed. Mind you it took a while to get bodies in to hear them play. Stephen Reynolds, who ran the venue, used to bring people in off the street to hear Bagatelle play.

I remember the first night we played the Mississippi Rooms. We got the gig through a friend of mine, a saxophone player named Joe McIntyre, who thought that venue would be perfect for us. When we walked in there was a bartender, two guys at the counter and us. So, OK we didn't fill the place on our opening night! That first gig attracted about 12 people. I know this as I counted them during one of our songs. Every night Stephen Reynolds who owned the place would go out and bring people off the street to listen to us. He was utterly determined God bless him. The next night we played to 40, then 80. By that Sunday we completely packed the place out. I cannot begin to tell you how important that venue was to us in the early years. It really kept us alive." **Ken Doyle**

There would be strong competition from local bands. Acts like The Bogey Boys, FBI, Time Machine all who also played the venue. Much like the famed Troubadour Bar in Hollywood, the Mississippi Rooms became the place to be seen and play. While Glen Frey and Don Henley, Elton John, Joni Mitchell and Carole King played regularly at the superb West Hollywood Troubadour in Los Angeles, Bray's finest and beyond made the Mississippi Rooms the happening place to be.

"It's lovely reminiscing about some of the old haunts we played in. Sadly, most have gone or changed names. The Mississippi Rooms in now The Hibernian. We rocked places like The Merrion Inn, The Magnet, The Summerhill Hotel and Tom Lyons Pub in Carrick on Suir. Then there was The Cellar in Dundalk and the Baggot Inn. Toners of Baggot Street was a classic as well. It was there I met three members of ABBA who were playing the RDS the next day. They loved our music and introduced themselves to us, warmly shaking my hand and shooting the breeze. It felt surreal. I was meeting one of my bass playing heroes, the late great Rutger Gunnerson from ABBA. All those great lines, like "Dancing Queen" for example" **Ken Doyle**

With the band slowly establishing themselves in Bray, thoughts turned to Dublin and different venues with a vibe and possibly a record deal. At the time Irish bands weren't pinning down three album deals and scoring hits across the water in the United Kingdom except for a couple of notable acts. They included The Boomtown Rats who had managed to get out of Dublin and score big with songs like "Rat Trap", "Someone Looking at You" and the UK number 1 "I Don't Like Mondays", whilst a charismatic bass player from West Bromwich who grew up in Dublin named Philip Parris Lynott had earlier launched Thin Lizzy into the stratosphere with hits like "Whiskey In The Jar" "Jailbreak" and "The Boys Are Back In Town" – that latter which went Top 10 in the Billboard charts in the US.

It was a time when punk was in and the melancholy Beatlesque tunes of Gilbert O' Sullivan along with the laid-back tones of Val Doonican who both had huge success in the early seventies had long gone. Despite having Irish acts of quality like Horslips, Planxty, Paul Brady and Rory Gallagher, none could make an impact on the English singles charts.

Before that there had been the odd one hit wonder. Mullingar's finest Joe Dolan charted at Number 3 in the UK with "Make Me an Island" a song that sold half a million copies in 1968 while The Dubliners sold around 250,000 copies of 'Seven Drunken Nights' on its way to Number 7 in the UK a year earlier in 1967. The early eighties also threw up some strange Irish entries like Foster & Allen reaching Number 18 in 1982 with "A Bunch of Thyme". Their debut appearance on Top of The Pops mortified me as they looked like they were dressed as a pair of middle-aged Leprechauns. Sweet Lamb of Christ.

Fast forward 40 years and Irish acts like U2, Enya, Kodaline, Snow Patrol, Divine Comedy, even Jedward and Westlife had put that wrong to right (alarmingly Westlife had over 15 chart-toppers) as Irish acts regularly charted well in England.

The Holy Grail of course was to land a record deal, release a few singles and get yourself on the Rock & Roll rollercoaster that could see you hit the highs or crash and burn over a few months, years, or if you are lucky, maybe a decade or two.

The late Lemmy Kilmister of Motorhead once said *"It doesn't matter how good you are, how well you play or how much you're liked. If you are not in the right place at the right time, then it's never going to happen for you"*.

Every band needed that break.

Luckily for Bagatelle it soon came.

And it was playing in one of their favourite venues they were first sussed out. The late John Woods of Polydor Records, who was well known to John O'Brien, would eventually send an A&R man along to watch a Bagatelle gig in Toners of Baggot Street, a small venue with a small stone walled cellar with a great vibe the band loved playing in.

"It was always handy knowing someone like John Woods at Polydor. As it turns out he knew Liam, having judged him in a singing contest that Liam won before he joined Bagatelle. I knew he was impressed with him and I'm sure would want him to front the group. We had put in the hours travelling and playing anywhere anyone wanted us and I felt the timing was right. We also had Marian Byrne and though she would leave shortly after she had a great voice and she looked fabulous as well. We were all hopeful we might see John at that gig in Toners" **John O'Brien**

By this stage Bagatelle had a new manager. Gerry Madigan had taken on the group with dreams of the band cracking it, getting a record deal and making it big, not only in Ireland but far beyond. In the history of the group his inclusion is rather short and sweet but nonetheless important. He had been amazed at the quality of the original material the group were writing (which he encouraged more of as the band also did a lot of rhythm & blues numbers.) Here was this new untapped resourceful band straight out of Bray and rocking the house, who with some fine tuning may have stood a chance of making the big time.

"My dream and vision for Bagatelle from the beginning was to play almost a full repertoire of all original music, and aim directly for the global market, using their success in Ireland to finance that campaign. The lads were extremely talented. I always encouraged them to play their original music. We also knew John Woods from Polydor was interested in the band. I believed the groups market could have been to eventually

embark on a strong offensive of the United States market on the same circuit and public that would attend Billy Joel and similar sort of middle of the road acts. You may recall how U2 did not have very much success in Ireland at the beginning but hit it big in Sweden with Sonnet Records. However, with their success there, they focused solidly on the US market and it generated their ultimate global success." **Gerry Madigan**

Having built a foundation of solid performances and word of mouth an A&R man was dispatched to watch Bagatelle at their gig in Toners, hopes were high; however the band had no contact with him that night, hoping it might have been Woods himself who would have come and introduced himself. A day or two went by with no word.

Had they blown it?

Had he come, seen the band, and left unimpressed?

There was an air of disappointment for a day or two before the band changed tack. John remained convinced Woods would show interest in Bagatelle and set up a gig in Stella House in Stillorgan, a popular pub with a solid reputation for live bands. It was also a venue that John Woods would pass on his way back from work at Polydor.

This time Woods took the bait.

"The band played "Summer in Dublin", "Trump Card" and "Leeson Street Lady" – all songs already written, fresh and new. This was original music in a time nobody dare venture that path. On the strength of those three songs alone I knew he would sign the band."

Gerry Madigan

With the head of Polydor Records on the hook it was time to reel him in and reap the rewards. So off they went......to Burgerland!

It was among the everyday folk munching on quarter pounders and milkshakes that Liam, Ken, John and Wally, signed a three-album deal contract with Polydor, a bold move not heard of before for any Irish band. It showed how much faith Woods had on these budding novices.

"Some bands sign million-pound contracts in huge offices with marble tables and record producers who are smoking a fine Cuban cigar. We signed ours over seven cheeseburgers, five packets of chips and a couple of fish fillets in Burgerland" **Ken Doyle**

The group could dare to dream.

The hard work of the Boulder Band which transformed into Bagatelle had come off. They had, like many working bands at the time, given everything for this shot at glory and they felt they were owed some respect. A deal was negotiated, terms agreed for the band as well as an advance up front to cover current debts (the figure was around £4,000) and the band would go into studio to cut their first album under Polydor Records.

Polydor was a well-known and respected record label by this stage. Established in 1954 as a British subsidiary of German company Deutsche Grammophon, the label could boast the talent of The Who, Slade, The Jam, The Bee Gees, James Brown, The Moody Blues, Status Quo and Elton John in their company. A prestigious stable full of musical thoroughbreds. Bagatelle would have to prove they could run alongside such amazing talent.

It was agreed the Liam Reilly penned "Trump Card" would be the lead single that would be lifted from Bagatelle's first album despite the fact they would have Reilly's little known "Summer in Dublin" by this time in 1979. Gerry Madigan would help produce the original version which Polydor released in October 1979. The group's profile had been raised enough to secure some column inches in the national tabloids as the snowball began its descent down the hill, gathering pace as it went.

"Bagatelle are one of the most promising young bands on the Irish circuit. Their first single "Trump Card" (Polydor) may prove to be aptly named and it already earns consistent plays on the radio and even impressed superstar Leo Sayer! It marks an important contract with Polydor which will result in a debut album in the new year."
Sunday Independent 21.10.79

There would be one change in personnel with Marian Byrne having since departed. A decision was made to replace her with 20-year-old Maggie Cody, a Monkstown girl who sang as good as she looked who had fronted a local band called Freebird.

Her natural beauty even got Bagatelle their first picture in a national newspaper, The Sunday Independent, in October '79. However, it was Maggie alone holding up a winning hand of cards (for the launch of "Trump Card") with the boys nowhere to be seen in the photograph! See remembers her time in the group fondly.

"I had joined Bagatelle from a group called Freebird. We came from Monkstown, Dun Laoghaire and Sallynoggin. Southsiders I guess! We played heavy rock which I loved. I just wanted to be Janis Joplin. I only spent about a year with Bagatelle but enjoyed it very much. It was pretty cool that at a young age I was playing with an established band

who already had a lot of gigs, so I learned a tremendous amount. John O'Brien was a wonderful man to work with. Bagatelle was his baby and he guided and helped all of us. Being a little older than the rest of us he was everybody's dad or older brother. Ken Doyle was also a pleasure to work with. So easy going and cheerful all the time."
Maggie Cody-Ferguson

Despite the potential, the hype, and the label, "Trump Card" would almost sink without a trace. But the group were young, determined and despite this setback were having a lot of fun.

And there was always that untapped original material to fall back on. Sure, a safe bet would have been a well-known cover version to get them started but Woods and Polydor had signed them on their ability to write superb original content.

Despite this the group were plugged in all the right places. Polydor did some solid PR work and it seemed a television appearance may not have been too far away. When it did come it simply could not have been to a bigger audience.

The Late Late Show, the longest running chat show in the world, (astonishingly since 1962 and celebrating its 58th year in production in 2020) and commanded nearly one million viewers back in its heyday, came calling. They wanted the band.

It was decided that Liam Reilly's ode to the capital "Summer in Dublin", the piano man's autobiographical tune about a day in his life in Baile Atha Cliath would be the song they would introduce themselves to the Irish public with on the Late Late Show.

Little did the band know that appearance, that song, would become bigger than the show, bigger than the band, bigger than anything imaginable that year.

The show aired on February 15th, 1980 with a song that would reach iconic status.

On the night an unsuspecting Gay Byrne announced them as an 'interesting band' (in that they wrote their own material) as the group were introduced to the nation.

"Lads and gentleman, a treat for you now. A band made up of members from Bray and Dundalk making their first appearance on the Late, Late. An unusual band who write their own material and are playing one of them tonight. I think it's great to see our young musicians writing songs with relevance to our society and locality. So, ladies and gentlemen, Bagatelle" **Gay Byrne**

The Late Late Show. 15th February 1980.
Bagatelle's first ever TV appearance.

"That was a huge break. So many times, we tried to get a slot on television. Especially the Late, Late Show. Before then we sent in demo's, but they just weren't up to scratch. They had been recorded in small studios in our early days and I'll admit sounded a wee bit rough. RTE certainly thought so at the time. But we knew how big a deal it would be if we somehow got on the show and now, we had a label to back us. And obviously it was, and still is, the longest running entertainment show in the world". **Ken Doyle**

Put simply the band could not have chosen a better song to introduce themselves to the public than "Summer in Dublin". A classic written of course by Liam Reilly over 40 years ago but as fresh, original, and memorable that it is sung from the highest rafters of pubs in Ireland or wherever the foreign Irish diaspora congregate for a night out.

"I remember I went to see The Boomtown Rats in Moran's Hotel and I recall the opening act – a guy signing Bob Seger's "Rock & Roll Never Forgets". The next thing I'm walking up Grafton Street, that's when the buses could come down Grafton Street, with Seger's song embedded in my brain. I just couldn't stop signing it, so much so that I nearly got creamed by an oncoming bus – the driver abused me from the hilt from his window. At the time I was living in number 2 Leeson Street. Shortly after that I got a 46a with my guitar in hand. I remember sitting down, minding my own business when I saw this drunk guy in front of me. He was telling me in his infinite wisdom how I should get rich. I got home with all the thoughts of the day in my mind and wrote "Summer in Dublin" in about two hours. Every word of the song is autobiographical and completely true" **Liam Reilly**

The song was the mother of all game changers. Just a few months after Bagatelle made that TV bow a young quartet from Dublin named U2 and singing "Stories for Boys" also made their first appearance on Gay Byrne's show. They were in search of that elusive record deal and admittedly looking enviously at the lads from Bray and Dundalk. Bono and the boys had to be content with gigs at the Dandelion Market on Saturdays with 50p entry for a wee bit longer.

It would also be the night Gerry Madigan decided to part ways from the band.

"The night of the Late, Late Show I told them I would no longer manage them as I had to deal with a difficult divorce situation. What a stupid thing to do? After all the hard work, it was about to happen for the band. They were about to explode on the scene, and I felt it would be unfair of me to hold on and try to manage them if I could not give them 100% of my attention. A stupid decision I regret to this day, as I had some great plans to break the band in the States and use a strategic management approach – something like what Paul McGuinness did with U2." **Gerry Madigan**

Madigan's replacement would be swift as Bagatelle turned to a born entrepreneur in Oliver Barry, a man who would be responsible for bringing the King of Pop, Michael Jackson, to Ireland in the eighties. A man who brought Prince to these shores in the nineties. A visionary who made sure U2 were booked here to display the groups worldwide success and in one dazzling concert secured not only Frank Sinatra but also his Rat Pack cohort Sammy Davis Jr. and the superb soprano singing voice of multi-million selling artist and Oscar winning Liza Minnelli to play a sell-out concert at Lansdowne Road.

Born the youngest of seven children, he spent five years at St. Colman's College in Fermoy then another year with his brothers' fruit & veg wholesale firm.

He pawned the first motorbike he ever got to put on a Nurse's dance. The money covered it so much that by Monday morning he got this bike back from the pawn shop. It was an early lesson on how good an entrepreneur he would become. Even as a late teenager he managed to bankroll his first real business venture when he opened the Sound Cellar record store along with Pat Egan. Located at the end of Grafton Street it became a mecca for new music.

Barry became a powerhouse within the industry. In 1966 he saw great potential in The Wolfe Tones whom he would manage for well over 20 years and also spotted enough promise in Stockton's Wing and showband group The Champions.

His real rise to prominence as a promoter would come in 1988 when the Banteer born impresario managed to get Michael Jackson to play not one but two shows in Pairc Ui Chaoimh in Cork. This was a huge booking. Jackson was on the European leg of his Bad tour with an album that would go on to sell 30 million albums by the end of the decade. At the time Ireland was just about to come out of a recession with the 'Celtic Tiger' not far down the road so bookings of major artists in Ireland were not very frequent. Booking Prince at the height of his fame and indeed U2 as part of their Zoo TV tour, kept Barry in the limelight, something he confirmed by bringing Sinatra, Sammy Davis Jr. and Minnelli to Lansdowne Road in 1989.

For Oliver Barry, securing Jackson for 'the greatest show on earth' was possibly the crowning glory for his career.

"Having made the contact through Jackson's agents in LA, I was able to convince his management that Pairc Ui Chaoimh was the ideal venue for the Bad tour. I'd already had U2 and Siamsa Cois Laoi there so I knew it would be perfect for him and the fans. It is hard to believe it's over 30 years ago. I remember presenting Michael Jackson with a copy of the Book of Kells. He came across to me as a very pleasant man." **Oliver Barry**

Bagatelle soon knew the asset Barry would become to them and coming with such a prestigious background the lads were a wee bit dizzy with excitement. Oliver's drive and enthusiasm for the job made it a whole new ballgame.

Suddenly all those dates of cramming into the corner of a pub you couldn't swing a cat in, playing to small crowds with even smaller pay outside of Bray went out the door. The group had better promotion, better stage management and more professional all around. Girls in Bagatelle t-shirts, a growing fan base. This was unheard of for a fledgling band. But Barry knew the direction they were going.

"The plan was to tour the band to support that first album. Both Polydor and I were fully committed to these boys. We knew their potential and they worked so hard on every aspect of their music. I knew they could be one of the biggest acts in Ireland within a year".
Oliver Barry

"Oliver had changed everything. Before he came, we were playing gigs in literally the middle of nowhere. At the end of the night when the money was divided up and after petrol expenses, we got around £30 each. We were codding ourselves really. We certainly wouldn't be retiring early going this route. Thankfully, Oliver had bigger dreams and designs on Bagatelle. I remember him telling us no more pubs in Bray or be seen in pubs in Dublin. He wanted bigger and better." **Ken Doyle**

John Woods also looked at what the lads wore. Their appearance was, shall we say, a little rough around the edges – like something the proverbial cat had dragged in to be exact. And secretly the band knew it. They had rocked up to gigs all over the country sometimes looking like they'd been plastering the neighbours wall earlier that day. This was especially true when it came to Ken Doyle whose fashion sense was along the lines of a guy painting a house and playing in his overalls the same night plastered in white paint!

They also needed some solid form of transport. Woods gave the likely lads £3,000 to do something about it. When they got the cash in hand, they overdosed on denim but also purchased a cheap, slightly battered Ford Transit van so they could travel to gigs together.

John Woods was also the politest man the group could ever meet. The epitome of a gentleman, he never, ever swore. The closest of any resemblance of a curse would be *"If you lads don't make it big that will leave me in the muck!"*

On one occasion he shared his predicament as head of a major label with Liam and Ken during a chit chat at Polydor.

"I remember John telling us *"Do you know how many bands I have looking for record deals? Seriously? There are so many unsigned groups out there all looking for that break. I just met four young guys from a new and upcoming unsigned band yesterday who went as far as saying "If you sign us, we could be as big as Bagatelle!" The band members were from a group called U2."* **Ken Doyle**

Early band picture taken to promote a gig in
The Anchor Bar, Waterford for St. Patrick's Weekend 1980.
Picture courtesy of www.irishshowbands.com & the Reynolds family.

The group also got accustomed with Oliver Barry's style of management which brought them much amusement.

"Oliver was a class act with a great sense of humour. A Cork humour you could say. When we got a few bob and felt the money was coming in at a handy pace we went out and bought a Mercedes. He would frown on it immediately. "Just remember lads that 40p a mile. That's what you'll be paying for that lads!" His conversations rarely amounted to more than two or three words. It was normally "Yes", "No", "Fine" or the occasional two words "Good Luck" so he was very to the point, but he could also take a slagging and I secretly think he enjoyed the ribbing! But above all we knew what he had done for us. At the start of 1980 we played a gig in Galway for about £80. Soon we were getting something near £1,000. Wow! We actually have notes left over after gigs instead of coppers!" **Ken Doyle**

By the Spring of 1980 Bagatelle were on a new level now and tabloid exposure and regional newspapers had sat up and paid interesting attention. John Woods had wasted no time in getting the band into the studio to record their debut album. For this the group travelled to Hastings in East Sussex to a recording plant called Battle Studios (very clever) to lay down their first album.

The job of doing that fell to Chris Harding. The producer had been responsible for Bing Crosby's last album before he died so Bagatelle knew the calibre of man they were working with. He quickly got familiar with the band's work, so much so that six of the album tracks were actually recorded in less than a week at a cost of just £3,000 in total. A producer's dream.

"On the strength of their original material alone they compare favourably with the best in the international market. They perform with such verve and excitement, pumping out such sheer musical aggression, that I think with this, their debut album, the industry is about to be exposed to the most exciting band since Status Quo!" **Chris Harding**

From there it was off to the more esteemed surroundings of Abbey Road where strings were laid down for several tracks on the album. In all, Bagatelle's debut album was knocked out in just four weeks.

Although "Summer in Dublin" had created a buzz since that Late Late Show ice-breaking appearance, it hadn't been released officially as a single. In fact, the only cut had been "Trump Card" which had failed completely in making a dent in the Irish charts. However, with the new record deal, better production, and studio management along with accompanying strings "Trump Card" was completely reworked. It was a song which Ken stated *"Took 4 attempts to get it right. The first was awful, the second, slightly less woeful, the third was average and the fourth was perfect!"*

"First time round I think "Trump Card" sold about 300 copies! And most of our families bought those! But we were relatively unknown to that point. The album changed things and I think it cost around £3,000 to produce. A lot of people think the meaning behind that song had to do with a girl, or some revenge but basically it was written about every promoter or hotel owner who books you for a fee but ends up paying you half of it. Being promised £500 and getting £50. The lyrics came naturally. "Cause you took my soul and you broke my heart but now I'm gonna start and put you right!". It was about being taken for granted. And of course, then when you've made it big you get the same shower of bastards come back ready to lick your arse. I enjoyed writing it!" **Liam Reilly**

After recording the album, the band hung around in England for a while. It was there they met Lou Rodgers, a dancehall tour promoter and father of Clodagh Rogers who represented the UK in the 1971 Eurovision Song Contest with "Jack in The Box" which led to another breakthrough. Lou was impressed with the band as was Clodagh – she had received death threats from the IRA as a Northern Ireland girl from Ballymena representing the UK at that years Eurovision – and agreed to book some gigs for the band at NATO Airforce bases all over Europe! This would be huge exposure and the band could not contain their excitement.
But by God did they work for it.
They left from Harwitch bound for the Hook of Holland for their first gig and took in venues in Belgium, Italy and Northern France, giving it socks for four hours each night with a small ten-minute break each hour.
However, a bigger conquest came when the ambitious group got to play Stateside. This was truly beginning to look like the bigtime!

"America was unreal. We were fed and watered like Kings. The steaks I used to get would feed a family of six and it's also where I first tasted Gin & Tonic which became a favourite tipple. We were booked to play a base called S.H.A.P.E. It looked like something out of a James Bond movie. It was massive. All over the entrances in huge lettering was SOUTHERN HEADQUARTERS of ALLIED POWERS EUROPE (as we were informed) and it was full of nationalities and uniforms. On one break four British soldiers came up, bought us some drinks and we had great craic with them. One of them was a helicopter pilot who had been stationed in Northern Ireland and assigned to Air Sea Rescue. One day there was a knock on the door where he was staying with pals and when he opened it, he was greeted with three men in balaclavas. He stood there frozen in

fear before hearing one of the masked men say "You're all right. We're not going to harm you. We have great respect for the rescue work you're doing. We just wanted you to know we are here". **Ken Doyle**

A nervous excitement coursed through the four men's veins. A sharp intake of breath was needed all round. An iconic tune was about to be unleashed on an unsuspecting Irish public. Things would never be the same again. Ever.

THREE

LIVING LIKE THERE WAS NO TOMORROW

"Playing a sunny Dalymount Park with Bob Marley and 30,000 people singing "Summer in Dublin" back to us. I've had worse days."

LIAM REILLY

It was June 1980. Johnny Logan had just won the Eurovision Song Contest, bridging a gap of ten years since Dana in 1970 with Shay Healy's "What's Another Year". Indeed, Dana had topped the Irish charts a month earlier with "Totus Tuus" for a couple of weeks. Across the water Blondie struck gold with "Call Me" and "Atomic" both topping the charts while Stateside Michael Jackson had stepped out of the shadow of his siblings and started to clock up 20 million sales of 'Off the Wall.'

In keeping with that year's strikes in the Bank's, Post Offices and trains, amazingly the Irish music charts, compiled by IRMA went on strike as well. A completely unheard-of scenario. For a hefty 34 weeks not one single weekly chart was produced. From the Pretenders "Brass in Pocket" reaching Number 1 on February 2nd to "Don't Stand So Close to Me" by The Police on October 4th there wasn't a single chart put in print.

That strange situation would have a huge impact on Bagatelle as they got ready to release "Summer in Dublin". On their return from recording the album in England, Bagatelle prepared to launch it upon the Irish public.

John Woods was quietly confident.

Oliver Barry wore an impish grin.

They knew "Trump Card" had failed to make a real impact but now sounded a lot better after being reworked. Polydor resisted the re-release of it, instead choosing "Summer in Dublin" as a single. With the album and promotion in place now Bagatelle needed the music buying public to come onboard.

On the first day of June 1980 "Summer in Dublin" a song written in less than two hours by Liam Reilly was released.

By the end of that summer it had changed the lives of Reilly, Doyle, O'Brien and McConville.

Forever.

That 4 minutes and 49 seconds of inspiration would catch the public's imagination right from the get-go. Maybe it was the use of Dublin in its title. Maybe the mention of Grafton Street, the Liffey and a 46A to Dun

Laoghaire which many could identify with. Or maybe it was because it was such a damn good tune. After just one week of release "Summer in Dublin" went straight into number 4 (that was the number eventually attributed to the song) but with the strike the group couldn't see an official chart. Just when they had made it big, nobody could see the fruits of their labour!

The success of the song surprised the band as they were amazed how quickly it took off. After a second week of release Bagatelle were dealing with a juggernaut and really began to rack up serious sales. Queen's "Another One Bites the Dust", Don McClean's "Crying", The Jam's "Going Underground" and even Pink Floyd's 'Another Brick in The Wall' were all massive hits that June but were still being outsold by Bagatelle. By the end of that month 'Summer in Dublin' was selling over 10,000 copies a week and became the biggest selling song in Ireland. Had the charts been produced, Liam Reilly's tune would have racked up nearly five weeks in the Number 1 spot.

"I think it's gone down in legend that the song was never actually Number 1 on paper because of the strike. I'm not sure of the reasons (I heard different versions of alleged fixing of the charts) but in the end we knew how big it had become. I mean at one point we are selling over 10,000 copies a week and struggling to keep up with the demand. Each week the single kept being reprinted. I mean it was so surreal, but just a pity that it wasn't acknowledged officially on the Irish charts. If you listen to the lyrics, it's actually about a guy not so much in love with the place he's in – rather a place he wants to get away from.

"Take me away from the city and lead me to where I can be on my own. I wanted to see you and now that I have, I just want to be left alone."

It's a song that says, "Look lads, I'm getting out of here more than anything else!" People read a lot into the lyrics of the song and I suppose they can identify with a 46a bus or walking on Grafton Street. I'm not sure if they met any drunks on a bus though!" **Liam Reilly**

"It was an amazing time to be alive and to have that hit in our back pocket. I had many a band before Bagatelle that were good but never reached the level of success that I did with Bagatelle in the eighties and never since. I remember walking down the street one day and Ken asking me 'How long do you think the band will last?' I remember smiling at him and saying "Ken, some bands break up after a couple of months and if you're really lucky you'll get two years out of it, so that will probably be us old friend! Naturally, I was happy to be wrong". **John O'Brien**

By the time the Irish chart strike was fixed in October "Summer in Dublin" was still placed in the Irish Top 20, though everyone knew the single should have been number one for at least a month with the massive amount of records sold. Officially the highest chart position was number 4, which it came into in June. History will show that Barbara Streisand's 'Woman in Love' which spent four weeks at Number 1 in November, was officially the best-selling single of 1980 in Ireland. But the nation knew better.

If ever people doubted the popularity of "Summer in Dublin" from the sweltering heat of the summer of 1980 to present day, a 2014 poll by a national newspaper for 'Best Ever Irish Song' and voted on by the public, placed Liam Reilly's song at Number 3. Only 'Fairytale of New York' by The Pogues and 'One' by U2 were ranked higher.

To date it is estimated that there are over 100 official cover versions of the song in Ireland, Canada, America, Australia and the UK. An astonishing achievement for an afternoon of daydreaming by Liam Reilly. Liam and Ken will tell you over the years there have been around 50 people who have proudly informed them that they were that "drunk on the bus." Claims to fame must be getting harder to find.

And with the song came the plaudits.

"Whether you're from the Big Smoke or not, and regardless of whether you grew up listening to pub bands play this tune incessantly once the long evenings began rolling in, there's something about "Summer in Dublin" that evokes nostalgia like few other songs do. Technically it's all about leaving the city because of painful lovelorn memories, but when Liam Reilly sings about how the Liffey "stank like hell", and "young people walking down Grafton Street, everyone looking so well", you can't help but feel a pang or two of homesickness no matter where you are in the world." **Irish Post**

'It has been a long time since I've caught the 46A bus. These days it's all computers, texts, e-mails and confusing technology. Yet, despite all the changes, some things remain the same – like this classic. And to this day I still get as many requests for 'Summer in Dublin' as, say, "Hey Jude" or "Yesterday." **Ernie Gallagher, Dublin's Q102**

"A drunk on a bus to Dun Laoghaire told me how to get rich, I was glad we weren't going too far" must be some of the classiest lyrics of any song ever. It's a tune that captured the hearts of a nation. Well done Bagatelle, one of my all-time favourite bands."
Paddy Cole, Jazz Musician

"Bagatelle's "Summer in Dublin" is, without a doubt, one of the most iconic records in the history of popular music in Ireland. Having produced one of their albums, I have great affection for the lads and great respect for their contribution to the business. Their records are a testament to their talent, hard work and their unrivalled staying power." **Phil Coulter**

"This is a sizable breakthrough for Bagatelle, and they appear to be on the verge of greater achievements. This can be attributed to the phenomenal success of "Summer in Dublin" and the boys are rehearsing for an extensive concert tour – a remarkable venture for an Irish group of this size." **Sunday Independent 7.9.1980**

"As good as a song "Summer in Dublin" was, and how important it was to have John at Polydor and Oliver as our manager, the success of the song stunned us. Well certainly me anyway! I mean we had been playing it for nearly two years without much reaction at all. Nobody could have predicted what "Summer in Dublin" would go on to become. I often wonder when Pete St. John wrote "The Fields of Athenry" or when Phil Coulter wrote "The Town I Love So Well" did they realise the power and emotional cultural infection it had on the people of Ireland and way beyond. I remember playing Minnie's in Dungarvan in Waterford back then and for the first time we got a standing ovation. We all looked at each other that night and thought this could be the start of something special." **Ken Doyle**

Bagatelle's debut album and the record sleeve for "Summer in Dublin."

The song was everywhere. Every radio station cranked it up and played it incessantly. Record shops couldn't keep it in stock. You couldn't go to the local supermarket without hearing it on the speakers in between someone advertising two chicken breasts and a packet of rashers for a pound. It became an anthem for every Irishman or woman abroad. It brought an emotional outpouring from them and just for the five minutes of 'Summer in Dublin' they are back home. Over 40 years later that has not changed

Now came the fun task of trying to follow it up!

By September, the band would get ready to re-release "Trump Card" to coincide with Bagatelle's debut album (simply entitled Bagatelle) hitting the record stores. Oliver Barry ramped up the hype, Polydor gave the band huge promotion and the album went out of stock almost as quickly as it came in.

The group's radio friendly sound made sure plenty of tracks from the album found their way onto local, national and pirate radio stations. This was an era long before You Tube, Spotify and iTunes. The record store was king. Vinyl was final and the airwaves were just as important. Instead of iPhones we had the pocket transistor radio. Instead of CD players we had the Walkman.

The band's profile was further boosted by some television appearances. Now people could see the faces behind the music on a regular basis.

Gloria Hunniford's Good Evening programme which pulled in six figure viewing audiences featured the group. On RTE Dave Heffernan's popular Anything Goes show featured Bagatelle singing "Rock & Roll Fantasy" and several more television slots before the end of the year meant Bagatelle were one of the most exposed and talked about bands of 1980.

Despite all the publicity it was something that didn't sit well with the group's lead singer. Liam tried to detach himself from the hoopla but unfortunately it went with the territory. Even now he would admit it is something he feels uncomfortable with. There are times of grinning and bearing it for the Dundalk native in a nice way. He created a monster, one that many songwriters would have loved to have in their back catalogue.

With the joy came judgement. It was fine having a single of the magnitude as 'Summer in Dublin' but the album had to hit the heights as well. A nervous excitement gripped the group as the papers began to dissect their work.

"Bagatelle are about the most talented band to arrive on the rock scene in the last decade. A bold daring statement you might think but there are few bands that I can remember with such talent, originality, and drive. From what I've heard I would rate the band as being as talented as Thin Lizzy and the Boomtown Rats. They'll face a few tests with big support gigs coming up and they're a brave bunch to hope they can survive on original material. However, the band is producing a fine quality of music." **Evening Herald 2.7.1980**

"The group has been welcomed by the Irish public with a solid selling first album. John O'Brien contributes lead guitar, blues, harp and vocals. Liam Reilly on keyboards, guitar and vocals, Ken Doyle bass and vocals and Wally McConville on drums and vocals. "Summer in Dublin" and "Trump Card" are the standout tracks. "City Lights" along with "Leeson Street Lady" and "Say Goodbye" all continue in the same kind of vein with 'Truck Driving Man" and its "Convoy' intro the odd song out. While lyrically the band seem somewhat naïve and contrived at times, musically they sound great." **Irish Press 4.7.1980**

"The release of their debut album which features ten self-composed numbers will have the effect of catapulting the four musicians in this unique group to stardom. Their original release "Trump Card" has been smartly re-recorded and will be released after the hugely successful 'Summer in Dublin'. Bagatelle certainly have international potential as musicians." **Donegal News 11.10.1980**

"Bagatelle is a four-piece band that have progressed from a pub act to one of Ireland's main attractions. A band of many talents, all four of them write songs and are top class musicians all with a single goal – international recognition. And they are getting there. Their debut album could have around five or six hit singles with "Summer in Dublin", "Leeson Street Lady', "Rock & Roll Fantasy" and "Say Goodbye"' coming to mind." **Longford Leader 26.9.1980**

"Six months ago, Bagatelle were unknown and struggling to make a living on the pub rock scene, however along came "Summer in Dublin" and caught the imagination in a way that 'Limerick You're a Lady' did for Dennis Allen. The song by Bagatelle's piano player Liam Reilly exhibits the lyrical strength which hallmarks the group's material"
Southern Star 18.10.1980

However, the group did have their detractors. Some a bit dismissive. Some a bit snobbish. And some down-right brutal in their assessment of the group's first album. Where one Evening Herald critic had been kind, another was rather cutting.

"I have to get this out of the way from the start. The sleeve for Bagatelle's debut album is one of the worst I have ever seen. And that's a poor performance from the record company on the band's behalf. The sleeve with its glossy colour picture of the boys on a Liffey ferry resembles a cheap compilation album particularly with the titles listed across the front. The album features two very pretty and popular tracks in "Summer in Dublin" and "Trump Card" which is why it's selling well. Liam Reilly sings like Elton John/Leo Sayer and on "Dublin" and comes across like Van Morrison and some of the lyrics are uninspiring. Numbers like "City Lights" and "Leeson Street Lady" are weak-kneed ballads while "Say Goodbye" is the closest I've ever heard to the early Beatles "The Night Before" It's sad to say this about the product of a hard working ambitious Irish band" **Evening Herald 18.7.1980**

Bagatelle on the Polydor label would go straight into number 8 on the Irish album charts, rising to Number 3 a short week later. And they were in good company. Former Beatle Paul McCartney had his 'McCartney II'

45

album at number 4 and Eric Clapton's 'Just One Night' album one back at 5. In fact, it was a young Motown artist called Michael Jackson that kept Bagatelle off the top of the Irish charts with 'Off the Wall' an album that went on to go 8 times platinum in the US alone. But that would change.

Bagatelle's debut album lands at Number 1 in the Irish Album Charts. The group support the legendary Bob Marley & The Wailers in front of 30,000 in Dalymount Park. Copyright: Eddie Mallin.

The debut album went gold, with sales in excess of 25,000 albums by the end of the year making them bona fide stars in their own country and the group received the obligatory gold discs to match their smiling faces that December. Even sales of cassette tapes (remember them, dodgy sounding things that the recorder chewed up and you used a pencil to rewind the tape to the start) were extremely healthy. It wasn't a surprise. The record shop was the social media hub for teenagers back in the day. A place not to buy just your favourite LP or 45, it was an institution where people gathered to exchange views on the latest Pink Floyd album or why Shakin' Stevens was at Number 1 for the 45th week running.

All those hours of endless practice and copious amounts of coffee and the hard stuff at Sugarloaf Crescent was finally paying off. The band's drive coupled with the record label and management was working a treat. Above all their original music was sailing majestically through an ocean of cover versions.

A nationwide tour was arranged that summer. It started with a gig in the Downtown Club, a favourite haunt in Liam Reilly's Dundalk and climaxed with a sold-out show in the National Stadium to rave reviews.

With the success came the excess. Mainly drink.

"Sure, we lived it up after our gigs. It went with the territory. I remember drinking spirits out of pint glasses. Ken always used to drink Guinness, maybe sometimes Pernod and white or Gin & Tonic which I used to drink before moving onto red wine. We were really putting it away. One drink would become two, then three. We just didn't stop. Pint glasses of Gin or Pernod should have been a wakeup call. We used to go to O'Brien's in Leeson Street or Neary's and got tanked up, just so we could ask a girl to dance. We passed it off as part of the lifestyle." **Liam Reilly**

Another breakthrough came when the group finally moved to the Number 1 slot and topped the album charts which were compiled by *Hot Press*. To this day Bagatelle, even 42 years on, have never graced the front cover of what is considered the bible of Irish music and music journalism that is Hot Press. Predating Bagatelle by a year in 1977, *Hot Press* was always seen as *"a bit hip and cool for a band like Bagatelle"* as Ken remarked. *"We could sell a million and still get passed off as old hat."*

"It was the first and best album we ever made. The tracks on that album we'd been playing for a good while in venues, so many people knew the songs when the album came out. And those tunes stood up. I wrote around five songs for the album, something I'm very proud of. I would have felt that way even if the album didn't sell. Personally, I didn't feel any pressure when it came out. People backed us and the album." **John O'Brien**

By now setting up drums, bass and keyboards in tiny corners of pubs in the middle of nowhere were a thing of the past. Spare change after a gig was replaced by four figured paid concerts and sold out shows. Money wasn't the main goal for the boys, but it certainly helped!

"I remember one of our first £1,000 gigs was in Pontoon, County Mayo. It was this big ballroom practically in the middle of nowhere. We got caught in a huge traffic jam which was six straight hours of absolute chaos. It got so bad we actually abandoned the van and had to walk to the venue in the pelting rain. We arrived at the venue soaked to the skin to a packed hall of adoring fans. We got up on stage "1,2,3,4" and the four drowned rats started to play. But hey, that's Rock & Roll! When I was told by Oliver Barry what we were getting for the gig I was like "Jesus Christ! Seriously?" The promoter was a guy called Pat Jennings, who also owned the Traveller's Friend in Castlebar which he has turned into a beautiful theatre and hotel" **Ken Doyle**

"Oh, I remember that first £1,000 gig very well. It's stuck in my memory as I drove into a river on the way to the gig! We had the van, but I made

my way up in our new Mercedes. It was raining constantly when I came to a sharp 90-degree right turn and ended up going straight through a ditch and into the river! The front wheels were in the water, so I put it in reverse, and tried dragging it up the bank. Thankfully, a guy came along in his tractor and pulled the car onto the road. I couldn't thank him enough! I was destroyed in mud and made the gig with minutes to spare!" **Liam Reilly**

Big outdoor venues would become more evident with the backing of Oliver Barry. Suddenly support gigs to established artists were lined up. David Gates who fronted the melancholic group Bread with million selling singles like "Baby I'm a Want You" and 'Make It with You' in their back catalogue would come first.
Oliver Barry continued in the same vain.
Don McClean who hit big-time with "American Pie" in 1970 and hadn't looked back had sold a cool 20 million albums by the time Bagatelle supported the New Yorker. Glen Campbell the once fresh-faced boy from Billstown, Arkansas who crossed over from Country to mainstream Billboard success with songs like "Rhinestone Cowboy" and "Wichita Lineman" was another feather in the groups hat as they supported him at the RDS.
Rita Coolridge and Ronnie Laine would follow but it was Bagatelle's supporting slot to Robert Nesta Marley at Dalymount Park that was the highlight gig of 1980 and remains so in the band's memory 42 years later. The Jamaican was a bona fide superstar the world over. His 1977 album 'Exodus' had elevated him to that iconic status. In 1984 'Legend' had sold a staggering 25 million copies and remains one of the biggest compilation albums of all time, even though he had passed away three years earlier in 1981.
On Sunday the 6th of July 1980, Bob Marley played the now historic concert at Dalymount Park on Dublin's northside, the home of Bohemian FC. Marley relaxed by having a kickabout before the gig with his crew. Playing to sold out stadiums worldwide was second nature to the icon, not so Bagatelle. Despite the main support act The Average White Band present, the four lads took to the stage in front of nearly 30,000 fans who paid £7 to see the gig. Immediately any nerves were calmed by breaking into "Summer in Dublin" to the delight of the receptive crowd who sang it back with as much gusto as Bagatelle belted it out.

"Those support slots really put us on the map, especially the Bob Marley gig. We never got to meet him, he had a sea of security guys around him, which was a pity. Glen Campbell came across as a warm sincere person. Very genuine. We got a step further with Don McClean, knocking back a few beers with him after the show. He was great fun and very down to

earth considering what he had achieved by that stage. Carly Simon was there, and I got her autograph!" **Ken Doyle**

"Oliver Barry had us play at large outdoor events like Siamsa Cois Laoi which was well known for bringing in big international acts. Playing under Bob Marley on that sunny Sunday in Dalymount I think we blew a few people out of the water! It was such a prestigious gig and here we have 30,000 people singing 'Summer in Dublin' back to us. It was a marvellous feeling. Before the gigs you were chauffeur driven down a tunnel into the venue. At Siamsa Cois Laoi we were sandwiched between the Furey Brothers and Glen Campbell. There is a line I wrote in 'Second Violin' that goes "We used to live like there was going to be no tomorrow". That's what our life was all about at that time" **Liam Reilly**

Such was the relationship Bagatelle had with Oliver Barry, even long after he had moved on from the group, at a 2018 Carlow gig he turned up to see the band he had moulded for stardom all those years ago . After having a stroll down memory lane, he left two bottles of champagne back in their dressing room. *"That was a classy thing to do, but he was always a class act. Mind you, Ken and our guitarist Kurt nabbed the champagne!"* recalls Liam.
The first nationwide tour had been a success. Mind you there was the odd exception.

"I recall a gig in Fermoy down in Cork that almost proved disastrous! I remember it because the place was called The Twilight Zone and we seemed to be stuck in one because our van broke down (again!) a number of times on the road to Fermoy. The promoter was going absolutely nuts. Every time we got the van working it would break down about 100 meters up the road. It was a recurring nightmare for about four hours, and we thought about going home but we somehow made it to the gig before the van literally fell apart!" **Ken Doyle**

The revamped "Trump Card" was released on the 9th of September 1980 entering the Irish charts at number 17 and breaking the Top Ten a week later. It stalled at number 7 before leaving the charts after a healthy eight week run. Solid album sales along with 'Summer in Dublin' still inside the Top 40 boosted "Trump Card" which was Reilly's ode to those tight-fisted promoters who had screwed him over. This was no lovers revenge tune. This was Liam having a satisfied sneer at those who had fucked him and the band over.
There would be a brief flirtation with the song in the UK singles chart as well. Unexpectedly "Trump Card" made number 74 in a brief stay in the UK Top 100.

An icebreaker across the water?

There was always hope.

With all the success, the hype, the future looking red rosy, the band managed to keep their feet firmly on the ground. In Ireland there tends to be a bit of begrudgery when someone makes it big and is then constantly reminded by all and sundry not to forget where they came from, something that one Gilbert O'Sullivan had experienced.

As a young Ray O'Sullivan from the Cork Road in Waterford he carved out a wildly successful career with songs like "Nothing Rhymed", "Clair" and 'Get Down' as a fresh faced youngster but then saw his support dwindling when he sold less towards the end of the seventies. By that time "our boy" from Waterford City was old news, so much so his last Waterford gig attracted around 150 people.

He has not played in his hometown since.

Part of the reason Bagatelle never fell into that trap was the drive of Ken Doyle to make sure the group never lost their roots and remained true to them.

"Ken is the salt of the earth and kept us grounded. Two things about the guy. If you were stuck with two flat tyres in the middle of nowhere, he would immediately drive to wherever you were and fix the flats no questions asked. Just don't ever ask him to buy a pint...he'll go missing! Oh, and he eats to much garlic." **Liam Reilly**

Or as John O'Brien would say *"He could be the proverbial pain in the arse and I've had to bite my tongue on occasions with him but in truth his intentions for us in the band were true, and we never did forget where we came from."*

Before the year was out Bagatelle clinched another accolade – the Entertainment News Band of the Year, not bad for a group who were virtual unknowns to the music critics by June that year.

Some critics sighted Bagatelle's sound, almost American Orientated Rock (or AOR for short) as the reason behind their initial success. You could have been listening to a group fresh out of L.A. or New York and probably not have batted an eyelid. The relentless touring kept them in the public eye. Tough going – Yes. Fun – absolutely!

Along with adulation came female attention. Inevitable. When you're in a band every girl wants a piece of you whether you look like Brad Pitt or the Hunchback of Notre Dame.

RTE would be generous in their coverage of the group, regularly featuring them in concert, mainly on a weekend – prime-time viewing. By now the group carried some clout. Oliver Barry didn't have to pick up the phone and sell the band to record or TV producers. It was quite the opposite.

For "Leeson Street Lady" a Reilly/McConville collaboration, the band produced a video that aired on Vincent Hanley's television show on RTE, just before he hit it bigtime and brought us the pure utter joy that was MT USA.

It was also the first time the group produced a video for a song. In it our 'Lady of the Night' hangs around Appian Way, picks up a few clients, does the business and is found dead on the shoreline (which featured a girl actually on the beach being pelted by oncoming waves on a cold March morning in Dublin Bay as she almost certainly must froze her tits off) before the Gardai come to recover the body.

Polydor resisted the temptation to release "Leeson Street Lady" knowing full well that the groups fanbase would buy an album that had 'Summer in Dublin' and 'Trump Card' on it anyway but the tune became a real favourite, as it is today. No set list for Bagatelle was ever going to discard the ode to 'Ladies of the night' everywhere.

"The song came about after one night in 1978 when we were loading our equipment into our van (no roadies back in those days) after a gig in The Baggot Inn into what was the most battered Ford transit on the island of Ireland. It was awful! I remember driving home to Bray one night and being stopped by the guards. He walked around it with a torch checking everything. I mean the van was barely legal! He lifted his cap, scratched his head and said, "You know this thing is a disgrace to the road, don't you?" but let me go. Anyway, back to the Baggot and it was Rag Week at Trinity College, so all the students were out on the town with one to many beers. Then we witnessed, what Lugs Branigan a well-known Garda used to refer to as "Street Hostesses" surrounded by four merry young male students who were looking for a group rate for all four to which one of the ladies very cleverly replied in her best Dublin accent "Go way outta that would yew students. We know ya – all balls and no money!" What a great line. I guess inspiration comes in many forms!" **Ken Doyle**

By now the growing fanbase knew the lyrics and the songs, regardless if they were released as a single or not. This certainly became the case for "Rock & Roll Fantasy" the Reilly/McConville cut that proved instantly popular.

"Wally came up with the riff for it and asked me if I could contribute to it. Lyrically I put the song together and John O'Brien worked out the music. It was a fun collaboration. At the time you think "hmm that's catchy" and wonder how it would go over to the crowd. I don't know if we had high hopes for it, maybe quietly confident, but it became one of our most popular songs. The fans loved it. That's what mattered most." **Liam Reilly**

Bagatelle rock Siamsa Cois Laoi in Cork where they played support to a host of well-known recording artists including Glen Campbell and Don McClean. Manager Oliver Barry would be instrumental in setting up this event.

The song-writing duties were shared between Reilly, O'Brien and McConville (who also penned "Rock & Roll Drummer") whereas bass player Doyle would add backing vocals on most tracks. Every song a sheer labour of love except for the penultimate track on the album, "Truck Drivin' Man", a song that in Liam Reilly's words he absolutely hated!

"I love writing songs and am proud of what myself and the band have done. However, I can safely say the only time I was ever pissed off writing a tune would be 'Truck Driving Man' the second last song on side two of the debut album. Its purpose was just to fill out the album. Christ, I hated that song. I knew nothing about trucks and put in all this CB lingo the drivers used, you know '10-4 good buddy'. It done my head in!" **Liam Reilly**

Ironically the Bagatelle front man had written the song for "Make a noise at Clonmacnoise" the first ever rally organised by the National C.B. Association. At the time CB radios were all the rage, with over 100,000 users in Ireland. The rally itself was attended by over 20,000 people.
The attention Bagatelle had received over such a short period dwarfed a lot of talent in the country. By the end of that surreally successful 1980 a fresh faced U2 had been around four years and under the wing of Paul McGuinness had released songs like "Another Day" and "11 O'clock Tick Tock" as singles, having finally got the record deal they hadn't when Bagatelle had. Island Records would take U2 onto their label, releasing the album 'Boy' in November of 1980 which would chart at number 52 in the UK but more impressively crack the Top 50 in the United States.
Famously, Larry Mullen who had asked John Woods of Polydor to sign U2

and said they would be bigger than Bagatelle, would follow up that quote by calling the lads "Bag-a-Money" in reference to the growing fame and fortune of Bagatelle.

U2 would go onto worldwide stardom and received critical acclaim. At home *Hot Press* featured the band on its front cover at least half a dozen times in the following years. It was one area Bagatelle would fail. Where punk, rock & reggae would always feature between their pages, Bagatelle were strictly middle-of-the-road in critics' eyes and ears.

"In the early years we got a fair bit of coverage from Hot Press. Look at who was recording original material at the time. Very few. It was us, U2, the Boomtown Rats, Horslips, Paul Brady and Clannad. I have an early copy of Hot Press with the late great Phil Lynott on the front cover and Bagatelle in big letters alongside it while down in the right-hand corner in small print was U2, Halcyon Days and Horslips. This would change. You see, these bands were always "hip" in the eyes of the critics. We were told they had an edge. Maybe in their look, style or music. Horslips pre-dated us and had the Celtic Rock/Folk scene covered. The 'Rats' had a charismatic Bob Geldof and would have success in the UK as would U2. We just didn't fit the profile over time, yet we went on to top the Album charts which Hot Press compiled!" **Ken Doyle**

To many in the music industry Bagatelle were an 'overnight success', when in truth the four-piece band had been plying their trade for well over two years now. If you counted the Boulder Band, it would be a longer period of time.

There seemed to be no limit as to what the band could achieve in Ireland. Money was rolling in, extra dates added. No more sleeping in vans. This was the big time for Bagatelle. However, by 1981 the focus would turn on potential success in the overseas market, particularly the United Kingdom. "Trump Card" had charted in the UK, if even just for a couple of weeks, but to continue their upward trajectory Bagatelle would really need to crack that lucrative market.

If the low chart position of "Trump Card" was deemed a small setback, as time would pass it would become a real source of frustration. One step forward in Ireland, two steps back in England.

Top Left; Gus Dungeon and the crew working in the studio on Bagatelle's second album. Top Right; An early Boulder Band gig in the Mississippi Rooms. Middle: Liam, Ken and John receive platinum discs for sales of Gold: The Best of Bagatelle. Above, The group in serious 80's pose.

Above: The ever-shy Ken Doyle, always making
the most of a photo opportunity!

Above: Bagatelle made a video for "Lesson Street Lady" which entailed some
poor actress almost freezing to death in Dublin Bay in the video before being
taken away by the police! Bottom; Bagatelle sign for Polydor Records. An
envious U2 would have to wait their turn!

Above: A retro Boulder Band snap from 1976. Next: Second Violin vinyl record. Middle: Knocking them dead in Long Island. The band would regularly play to sold out shows Stateside. Above: Soundcheck for Blind Aid gig in far off Macau. These boys sure did get around!

A very early snap of a young Ken Doyle (left) with sister Rosemary in the middle and brother Martin with Ger popping his head up in the middle. Right, Doyle in the FCA circa 1968.

Below: Liam belts out "Love Is the Reason" at Siamsa Cois Laoi where the band always went down a storm. Bottom: On the bill with Bob Marley in Dalymount 1980, Bagatelle's first big outdoor gig which opened them up to a much bigger audience.

Above; A leather clad Bagatelle snap taken in 1984. Picture courtesy of the Reynolds family and www.irish-showbands.com. Middle; Spreading the joy across the water in America. Below: Liam belts out "Somewhere in Europe" at the 1990 National Song Contest. Right: Bagatelle on the Number 11 Liffey Boat for the cover of their first album in 1980.

Saturday October 3rd Music at 11:00 pm

LIAM RIELLY and **188**

BAGATELLE LIVE AT

Tickets **$20.00**

JOHN MULLIGANS FIRESIDE PUB
4272 Katonah Avenue • Bronx New York 10470 • 718-655-3201

Bagatelle

Bagatelle playing to a packed crowd at Siamsa Cois Laoi in Cork, June 1983.
The picture includes Tommy Mangan who would play with the group during
the early eighties before having success with another Irish Group – Allies.
Picture courtesy of Tommy Mangan

FOUR

THEY LOVE US IN URUGUAY

"I remember my last year in work I made about £1,200 for the entire year. In 1980 I made about 5 Grand!"

LIAM REILLY

By the Spring of 1981 and still touring and selling out venues Polydor felt it was time to quickly cash in and release a follow-up Bagatelle album.
There was obvious pressure to produce an album somewhere along the lines of their quality debut album. Even at this point the group knew a song like 'Summer in Dublin' which was such a mammoth success would be almost impossible to recreate, though the personnel hadn't changed, and the same strong song-writing credentials were intact. For many groups in the annals of music history, a second album would prove extremely hard to recreate the success of a debut album. Bagatelle's debut effort made it to number 1 in the Irish charts and went gold selling 37,000 copies. Was it fair to ask them to create a follow up album with similar success?
The group went back into the studio to test the water.
John O'Brien took it all in his stride.

"If our first album had tanked and we were coming back into the studio to record a follow up, yes then there would have been pressure. I certainly didn't feel any. Not after the huge success we had with our debut. Pressure? No, we just relaxed and got drunk. I can even remember what we were drinking every night! We accepted the first album would possibly be our best and hard to top. Would we get another 'Summer in Dublin' again? To me it didn't matter. We had a head start. Maybe it was because I was a bit older than the rest of the group and had seen acts come and go. At point had the group finished I would have accepted that." **John O'Brien**

"Going back into the studio so quickly kept us fresh and relevant I felt. Look, it was always hard if not impossible to match that first album. It was such a benchmark that we knew there was no way we would surpass that. We had toured the country and when you have thousands singing 'Summer in Dublin' back to you each night we were like, Jesus Christ we're never going to top this are we? But thankfully, due to the brilliant song writing of Liam Reilly and John O'Brien they created songs like "I

60

Need You", "Love Is the Reason" and "Second Violin" for the new album. There was one for everyone in the audience!" **Ken Doyle**

As much as the group would have their detractors among the media when they went to record the new album, Bagatelle scored some brownie points with the printed press by securing a multi-million selling producer at the helm for that second album.

The album would be produced by Gus Dudgeon, a man who had the distinction of producing over a dozen multi-platinum selling Elton John albums to his name. He had first teamed up with Elton John on "Your Song" which broke the humble Reg Dwight into the UK Singles Chart (peaking at No.7 in October 1970) and eventually catapulted him to unprecedented success in America and Gus would have a long successful spell with Elton during his heyday. He could also count Joan Armatrading, Gilbert O' Sullivan, Fairport Convention, Elkie Brooks, Chris Rea, The Dubliners (Gus called his dog "Barney" after Barney McKenna) and Ralph McTell as artists he produced.

"Having Gus on board was a major boost for us. We all admired him and what he brought to the table. I mean this was a guy who had produced multi-million selling albums for Elton John. And here he was, working with an Irish band he wouldn't have heard of a few months ago. If we weren't to crack the UK market now, we could at least say we had a producer who had and could. We were hopeful." **Ken Doyle**

Polydor sent the group to London for several weeks to work with Gus and record the album. It also meant a bigger budget to make sure the group would have the clout needed to succeed. The band listened attentively to everything Gus Dudgeon said and done, still star struck at his presence on the album.

"A lot of my style actually came from Elton John and I was completely in awe of the partnership he had with Bernie Taupin. Although I was a classically trained pianist it was his music that moulded me and having part of that in Gus Dudgeon producing us was a nice connection for me. Of course, he made a comparison on the way I looked compared to Elton. He used to say, "You know what Liam it's amazing how much you look like Reg" (Reg Dwight being Elton's real name.) **Liam Reilly**

"Gus was the first real high-end producer we had worked with. I remember the first day we met him. We were in the studio recording and this guy just strolls in wearing a big brown American style bomber jacket and a white scarf like Biggles. So, in he comes and says "Well guys. For a start you're going to have to lose two thirds of that song you're recording." And we said, "Oh really now?" But in fairness, who were we to be arguing with a guy who produced multi-platinum albums for the likes of Elton John. And of course, in the long run he made our second album sound superb and although we couldn't match the first album, the production on this new one definitely sounded better. He was a great producer and a lovely guy to work with. The engineer was Gerry Boys and the Tape op was Dave Lord who went on to produce Tears for Fears. Ian Anderson of Jethro Tull owned Maison Rouge Studios where we recorded the album. What a great bunch to hang around with." **Ken Doyle**

Sadly, on the 21st of July 2002, Gus Dudgeon would lose his life in a car accident when the car he was driving veered off the M4 between Reading and Maidenhead. His wife Sheila was also killed in the accident. The inquest had found it was an accidental death. Both had suffered severe head injuries and were trapped in the car, which landed in a storm drain, and may have died by drowning. Elton John's 2004 album Peachtree Road was dedicated to the memory of Gus and Sheila Dudgeon.

One of the greatest compliments Gus would bestow upon the group was when he proclaimed *"You know what? Tony Bennett could effortlessly sing your songs."*

Of course, for the new album meant new songs. The lead single from the album was crucial to kick things off. Although there was nervous excitement about this, inspiration would come from Dundalk's favourite son as Reilly emphatically delivered another big Bagatelle number.

"You can get all types of inspiration for different songs. Mine came from a flat I had in Monkstown which had this beautiful view of the sea. For some reason I was looking at sheets of music which read "first violin, cello, viola, second violin, second fiddle, and so on". That was around 3pm in the afternoon. The boys were due to pick me up for a gig we had in Kyteler's in Kilkenny. By the time they had collected me I had written 'Second Violin' in full and played it for the lads that very night. It became a huge hit for us. Not bad for a song I actually wrote in about 8 minutes!"
Liam Reilly

Again, the simplicity and genius of Reilly made sure the group would have a very strong single to lift from the album. It also helped that the group could now appear on primetime shows around the country. If Bagatelle had a single or an album to plug, then just phone Larry Gogan.

"The late great Larry Gogan paid us the ultimate compliment when we were with him one day in RTE. He said – I love the music of Bagatelle. Great lyrics. Great melodies. The bell-tone clarity of Liam Reilly's voice. Your band are writing modern day standards. Tony Bennett could easily sing the songs of Bagatelle. We were like, "Wow!" **Ken Doyle**

By now Gay Byrne, who had announced the band to the world on their Late Late Show debut a year ago , was a firm fan of the group and brought the group to the Montrose studios were the band featured "Second Violin" for the first time to the Irish public.

By now getting recognised in the street was a given, much to the slight annoyance of bass player and dumpster hopping Ken Doyle!

"By the time "Second Violin" was released I couldn't go anywhere without being recognised and being a suburban archaeologist (which is a posh term for someone who relives skips of its contents) I am a bit of a hoarder but that went out the window for a while when we became so well known in the public eye. After that came out, I couldn't even haggle with people for what was in the skip! I remember I was loading a Belfast sink into the car when I spotted a skip and a guy who recognised me pulled up and said "Jesus Christ Doyler I thought you were supposed to be doing well for yourself." Old habits die hard I guess!" **Ken Doyle**

"Second Violin" was released on the 7th of April 1981 with the album coming out a week later.

The public backed the band and sales in record stores were healthy. The song immediately broke the Irish Top 10, coming in at number 7 before rising to number 4. The group sensed another Number 1. This time they would come up against Shakin' Stevens who topped the charts with 'This Ole' House' that April for three weeks, quickly followed by Buzz Fizz's Eurovision Song Contest hit 'Making Your Mind Up'. However, the single was still selling and would eventually top the Irish charts in May for one week.

It was a superb start to the follow-up album. And it felt good.

John O'Brien. Where would Bagatelle have been without him?

"You often find artists that owe almost everything to one song and get completely pissed off playing it each night or having the crowd request it. You know. They go "For Christ sake not that song again. Do you know how many times I play that a week? Though we were never that way about "Summer in Dublin." At the same time, it was nice to have new material to showcase when we hit the road. So, we played as much of the second album as we could." **John O'Brien**

Strangely like their first album Bagatelle never titled their follow up album release. The first had simply been called *Bagatelle* with a picture of the group on a boat. The second was also titled *Bagatelle* but would become known as the '*Waterfall* album' after the picture depicting a waterfall on the front cover. The lack of a real title would confuse many however the album sold extremely well and made the Top 5 in the album charts.

The 'Waterfall' album began to sell in big numbers, eventually going gold with sales of 25,000, a superb achievement and a solid follow up to the original album which had now gone on to sell almost 40,000 copies.

For an original Irish band this was the stuff of dreams.

Again, the group had esteemed company in the Irish album charts. Adam & the Ants had just released their 'Prince Charming' album which included two UK number 1's whilst Australian act Men at Work garnered huge international success with 'Business as Usual' which would top the Irish, English and Billboard charts in America, selling 15 million units in the process. Throw in John Lennon who had back to back number 1's with 'Starting Over' and 'Woman' from the multi-million selling 'Double Fantasy' album and you would allow the band a moment to pinch themselves rather hard to be sure they weren't dreaming.

On the back of the second album the group took to the road to promote it. This again meant an extremely hectic schedule with little time off and long nights on the road. When you are living out of each other's pockets however it was natural for the boys to have a fight or two.

"Any band that doesn't have an argument every other week are liars. It's part and parcel if you are with a successful band over whatever number of years. In our case after 40 years we have run out of arguments! Even to this day I can't travel with Ken, though that's because he scares the living Jesus out of me with his driving!" **Liam Reilly**

Again, the critics would be kind with generally favourable reviews, but with the group now having a solid fanbase, Bagatelle knew sales of the 'Waterfall' album would be good.

But it wasn't only "Second Violin" that had good airplay. Songs like radio friendly "I Need You" and the anthemic "Outrageous" became firm favourites. Yet again that original sound connected making Bagatelle one of the most listened to acts of the early eighties.

"Songs like "Love is the Reason" and "Second Violin" are among the best tracks on an excellently produced album by Gus Dudgeon of Elton John, Lindisfarne and Fairport Convention fame. It might fail to deliver the promise of their first album, but it won't deter fans of Bagatelle buying it" **Southern Star 31.10.1981**

"Bagatelle must have been the first major Irish rock band to break through the deathly showband monopoly of Irish dance halls and bring their message to every green field of this island. They are very much a sellable package with guaranteed appeal to the vast middle ground in the music business. The songs on this album are melodic, easily remembered and simple lyrics concerning things like lost love, going home again and such. This is light rock cleanly and very professionally presented" **Longford Leader 27.11.81**

Above:, Sorting things in the studio. Right: Sleeping on the job! A Bagatelle roadie gets some much-needed rest in-between recordings!

"The new album speaks for itself and one can't help but notice the high-quality song-writing standard and the beautiful harmonies. It is this formula that has made Bagatelle such a success since they broke onto the scene just a mere year ago. The fact they continue to trust in their own compositions, and rightly so, makes them just as much appealing and their bravery is rewarded again on this album. **Munster Express 20.12.81**

"Since their formation in 1978, Bagatelle has become one of the top Irish groups in the country. Their lyrics follow a storyline and their rhythm & blues style has wide-ranging appeal as witnessed by the great success of 'Summer in Dublin' and their first album. The boy's new album will doubtless give their fans what they want" **Meath Chronicle. 12.9.81**

Indeed, fans of the group did get a solid sequel to their first album but not everyone would be as forthcoming in praise for the bands new release, even when they were reviewing someone else!

Christopher Cross (album; Another Page)
"I was just thinking to myself, if Christopher Cross can get away with producing pretty, but rather bland, music and become a superstar on the back of it, why isn't Bagatelle's Liam Reilly worth millions? **Evening Herald**

"Yes, we didn't appeal to the cool crowd. That never mattered to us. We were producing original music which is why I got into this game in the first place. While others were going up and down the length and breadth of the country singing covers of well-known tunes we stuck to our guns and just smiled at the detractors. You will always get them if you're successful at something. You get used to the begrudgery." **John O'Brien**

Despite the success, the continuing limelight and lagers was beginning to take its toll on Liam Reilly. Selling out show after show and months on the road left little in the way of a private life for the group. Liam slowly began to hate it.

"To be honest when it was before the real hype that Oliver Barry had helped bring us to a bigger crowd, I was alright with it. You had a drink, done your gig and went home. But that changed. Bigger stadiums and crowds yes that was great but now everybody wanted a piece of you. They wanted to meet you the moment you arrive at the venue, or during soundcheck or immediately after the gig. If we do a 90-minute set, I'm absolutely knackered, and I just want to rest. I think these days that's amplified even more because of the whole Meet & Greet section. Most artists do their gig, go backstage and change their clothes and if lucky get a half hour to themselves but with Bagatelle it's straight from the gig to the desk where we sign cd's, pose for pictures, chat to the fans. I have a small problem with one of my eyes and I've gone through probably thousands of flashes from mobile phones in the last few years! I appreciate people coming out for us. Of course, I do. But Ken was always the crowd pleaser in that respect." **Liam Reilly**

The sold-out shows continued. Bagatelle made it to the four corners of Ireland and beyond (they would soon tour in America which became an annual pilgrimage to the Irish diaspora abroad), with little rest, but when the adrenaline is following you don't feel tired. You could not open the pages of an Irish newspaper on any weekend of 1981 and not see a picture of Bagatelle staring right back at you. Though venues were bigger, none would match the RDS where the band held court at least twice a year.

"As their fans packed the RDS to testify that they have become a very accomplished and entertaining outfit. There may have been doubt that they could master the venue as the main hall in Ballsbridge is an awesome task. It took some old favourites to set the place jumping. From there on however it was a total conquest." **The Irish Press 13.11.81**

"There are a number of very good reasons why you don't see many indoor fireworks displays and one of them was evident as Bagatelle came on stage for their first headline concert in the RDS. The show opened with a blaze of Roman candles which had the front section of the audience rubbing their eyes as smoke billowed from the stage, but when it cleared the band gave a packed RDS a show the likes of which is rarely produced by any Irish rock act.
Everything the band played was greeted with wild applause. It's hard to see why Bagatelle hasn't yet cracked the English charts, perhaps that will change. Their songs are of high quality and performed professionally by a band that would leave many currently in the charts standing" **Patrick Murray, Southern Star**

By now the band was making serious money. The normal PAYE worker would be stretched to earn in a month what the band were earning in a couple of nights. Cash was earned and spent just as quickly. One story of the group buying three cars from the same car dealer in Fermoy in the same afternoon becoming one of folklore.

It sounds bigtime but it's not true.

The group became renowned for their high octane, give-it-some-balls-concerts. Back in the day before the big time they had paid their dues with four hour shows in military bases so now that they had broken the Irish market, they were expected to do the same.

This meant England became the next port of call.

For the first time since Bagatelle formed in 1978 a real attempt at trying to crack the lucrative UK market was launched. Polydor put their money where their mouth was and backed the band.

Oliver Barry struck a deal with Capital Radio in London, who had five million listeners in the capital, to broadcast a Bagatelle concert which they performed in England together with an elaborate promotional campaign to push 'Second Violin' in hopes of a breakthrough. There was a substantial amount of Irish who, bewildered with rising unemployment and little job prospects at home, had emigrated to England and this was a section Bagatelle hoped would back them with the release of the song and album.

Though selling records to get into the Top 10 in the UK these days requires about 57 people to buy your record, back in the early eighties it was much different and a lot harder.

Singles like Nik Kershaw's superb debut "Wouldn't It Be Good" could sell 200,000 copies and not make it to Number 1, while Westlife would release

"Swear It Again" in the nineties and instantly take the Number 1 slot with half that amount of sales.

Again, this was a time before Napster, or Spotify, iTunes or downloadable music. It was a time we all recorded our favourite music on a blank cassette at home after the DJ's voice had faded out, and before he came back on at the end of the track. A time when we went out to buy vinyl. And we did it in our droves.

"Second Violin" would debut in the UK Charts in August 1981. After a couple of weeks, it had made it to Number 47 before falling out of the charts. In contrast, another Irish band, The Furey Brothers & Davy Arthur, scored big with 'Sweet Sixteen' which spent almost three months in the UK Top 40, making it as high as Number 14.

Scratching their heads in puzzlement, Bagatelle had fallen at the first hurdle. Liam Reilly had his own thoughts on why this was, with the bad luck being attributed to Wimbledon!

"It probably sounds a bit corny now but when the single got inside the Top 50 we cautiously thought we might be onto a winner here, however the people paid to promote our single in the UK decided to take a couple of weeks off to watch Wimbledon. Even Oliver Barry was annoyed!"
Liam Reilly

"We were disappointed with the chart placing of 'Second Violin' as we felt sure with the promotion it would make the Top 30. Sadly, I think one of the contributing factors was there was a section of Anti-Irish feeling in England because of the IRA, Bobby Sands, the hunger strikes and bombings at the time which I think didn't help. Attitudes have obviously changed now but there was a lot of unrest at the time." **Ken Doyle**

I am not sure the lads can blame Bjorn Borg, John McEnroe or Jimmy Connors for not having a hit single across the water, however there would still be a break in the international market, astonishingly coming not from America, Europe , Asia or Australia but Uruguay of all places!

That's right. You heard correctly. Uruguay.

It was a changing time in the music business.

Punk had given way to a more synth- based sound. Groups like Depeche Mode, the Human League and Kraftwerk were the order of the day and Bagatelle suffered because of this. The Ska and New Romantic movements also featured. Men were wearing make-up and women's clothing on Top of the Pops with a more sterile sound from bands that was miles away from the stories Bagatelle would weave in their songs.

Disappointed by not disillusioned, Bagatelle returned home as the scorching summer of '81 gave way to a mild, pleasant Autumn and with it another Irish tour.

However unknown to the group, Oliver Barry and John Woods at Polydor, "Second Violin" had found its way onto the playlist of Radio Independancia, one of Uruguay's main radio stations and began to get some solid airplay. Like wildfire the song caught on and most of the country's AM & FM stations quickly had Liam Reilly's classic on their set-list. This simply astonished the group. How could a South American country with a population slightly less than Ireland, and whose main language was Spanish, fell in love with an Irish group they never heard of before?

It resulted in "Second Violin" becoming a Top 20 hit (number 9 to be exact) and even today is still one of the most popular singles by an Irish band, 39 years later.

Take that U2!

Above; "Love Is the Reason" single. Band photo by Trevor Rogers. Design Martin Brown. Right: The Bagatelle "Waterfall" album which the group would earn a gold disc for.

That summer the band would suffer the tragedy of losing one of their sound engineers. English born Andrew Walton who was under contract with the band died when a truck in which he was a passenger struck an ESB pole in Monasterevin, Kildare. Andrew who was living in Regal Road in Dublin had been returning from Cork with his assistant when the incident happened around 5am in the morning.

Sadly, the sound engineer got trapped in the cabin of the truck which was loaded with his equipment and had been used the night before by the band as Bagatelle had been gigging at Siamsa Cois Laoi. Andy wanted to go back to Dublin as his wife and kids were flying in that day. The group got the phone call hours later. A tragic loss to one so talented.

Though the group returned from England disappointed (yet amazed at the news from Uruguay), a second single was released, this time relying on the song-writing capabilities of John O'Brien and Liam Reilly for the up-tempo feel good "Love is the Reason."

"I have so much respect for John O'Brien, both lyrically and musically. He was the founder of the band. He recruited and handpicked us and helped drive us on. He put himself in debt to buy a small PA system and microphones. There would never have been a Bagatelle without him. I remember one night before a gig we were doing he came into the dressing room and started strumming this tune which grabbed my interest. We took it from there and worked out what would become "Love is the Reason." **Liam Reilly**

"It was a tune I had played around with before Bagatelle struck it big, when I was in the Boulder Band. I brought it to Liam's attention one night and we worked it from there. He put his own stamp on it and brought it up a notch. He made it superb. It is a song I was extremely proud of. This came during a period of time when our song-writing capabilities really knew no limits." **John O'Brien**

It was a song to put a smile on your face. And you couldn't help but. Any tune that can be sung back to you after 39 years since it was released with an even younger generation embracing it is something special.

Polydor could not be happier. After all this was a music company giant who had a small Swedish 4-piece combo signed in the mid-seventies called ABBA before they took on the whole world. A record company who got on board with the Brothers Gibb before they sold over 34 million copies of the Saturday Night Fever Soundtrack when disco ruled the airwaves. Add people like Elton John who had by then sold over 100 million records and you see how prestigious it was for Bagatelle to be on the Polydor label.

In their own mindset, everything the band brought out needed to be close to the quality of their debut album. There seemed to be no room for filler here. They continued to tour and became extremely accessible, often playing the same venue twice a year.

"At this point I started to get a wee bit tired. It wasn't strictly down to Bagatelle. I had been gigging with various bands long before this. I had been doing this as early as the sixties and through the seventies, so I was a little road weary. I was sort of a slave to this big machine, this industry, that dictated I get on stage, smile, and play several times a week. You lose track of the towns and the mileage. Was it a privileged lifestyle? Yes. But one I founded harder to get out of." **John O'Brien**

"Even during the height of our success there were times John felt like leaving the band. We had been touring together constantly. Then again, show me a group that hasn't fought when they spend so much time on the road and I'll show you a liar! I think there was a Bray camp (me and John) and a Dundalk camp in Liam and Wally when we did argue. We

decided to make sure we all had separate rooms and not spend as much time with each other outside of the gigs we had to play. It was supposed to alleviate the pressure, but it proved to be the first small crack."
Ken Doyle

While touring, one of the problems that really concerned the group was that of playing gigs North of the border. This was a period when the Troubles were still very prevalent in Northern Ireland. Any touring Catholic band crossing the border and playing up North ran the gauntlet and the real danger of reprisal.

Under Oliver Barry's supervision we eventually went and when we nervously arrived at a gig in Knocknamoe Castle a wonderland of wonderful people opened up to us. This was not the battlefield scenes we witnessed on the news or read in the papers. The Ulster people are warm and friendly on all sides and we are so lucky to appeal to them. We owe them a lot. I remember one time a threat was issued from the UVF that they were going to shoot bands from the South who dared to cross the border into Northern Ireland. We unfortunately had to cancel some gigs to the disappointment of ourselves and our audience. Then the UDR promptly issued their own statement denying they ever issued that statement and they would – take care of whoever did – much to our relief. We were very relieved, especially after what happened to the Miami Showband." **Ken Doyle**

On the 31st of July 1975 near Buskhill, County Down members of the Ulster Volunteer Force (UVF) attacked a van carrying members of the Miami Showband at a bogus checkpoint. The group had been travelling home to Dublin from a concert in Banbridge in County Down. They were near to Newry when they were stopped. The van in which the group was travelling exploded (which killed two members of the gang) while three members of the Miami Showband, Brian McCoy, Tony Geraghty and lead singer Fran O'Toole were shot.
Bass player Stephen Travers, who survived life-threatening wounds, and saxophone player Des Lee. were able to identify two of their assailants – both of them UVF members also serving in the UDR, and subsequently given life sentences though they were released in 1998.
It was a senseless murder sadly of the times, one that hit close to Ken Doyle. Miami Showband lead singer Fran O'Toole was also a Bray native who lived close to the Doyle residence. He was just 29 with a young wife and two small daughters aged just three and four. A singer-songwriter who liked Elton John, listened intently to Gilbert O'Sullivan and had a head full of dreams to aspire to. He was taken from this world long before his time, another victim of a savage past this island bore the brunt of.

"I can remember my mother coming into my bedroom to tell me that he had heard on the news that Fran and his colleagues had been murdered. It was tragic. Fran was a lovely guy. He lived 500 yards away from me in Bray. His father Mick O'Toole owned a bingo hall called Mick's Pongo. As kids we would sit on the wall outside, watching them play and every now and again you could hear Mick shout "Wow, and who's going to get it?" He was a character.

Fran was a few years older than me which was a big gap at that age. His mum ran a vegetable shop and his sister was a hairdresser. We were like urchins back in the day, but Fran's hair was always stylish, and he wore the best of clothes. He had the very first pair of Levi's jeans. We had only just heard of their existence, yet he actually had them. He really had that X factor and could play six different instruments. A great singer-songwriter, he had it all. If someone had asked me at the time who I wanted to be I would have said Fran O'Toole.

We were just starting out as musicians in bars and I felt a real sense of anger over the killings which were totally senseless. I could not believe that anyone would want to murder a band of entertainers. **Ken Doyle**

40 years after his death, in 2015, Fran O'Toole was honoured along with his fellow Miami Showband members as the bridge connecting the Main Street to Castle Street in Bray was named in his honour. A lot of hard work had gone into this especially the tireless work of Peter Carroll, an M.S. sufferer who despite his painful life tirelessly badgered the local council into doing the right thing. Many see him as a mixture of St. Peter and Lieutenant Gerrard from The Fugitive!

"That was the time back then. Hunger strikes, the H Block and Maggie Thatcher. People knew of the tension and troubles in Northern Ireland, so a lot of bands ran the gauntlet when it came to be playing over the border." **Liam Reilly**

A short break from touring popped up at the start of 1982 and the four members got some time to recharge their batteries. *'I loved the guys but when you spend two years constantly touring you grow to get sick of the sight of each other- though I mean that in a nice way"* remarks Ken. It was also a time when more and more Irish artists were beginning to write their own original material. Horslips were one of those bands and the founders of Celtic Rock, successfully combining traditional Irish music with rock music and went on to inspire many local and international acts. Formed in 1970, the band pre-dated Bagatelle by 8 years but there was never a rivalry, more a mutual respect of what both bands had managed to do and succeed in an Irish market that was still stuck in the dancehall showband days.

"Horslips were a superb group and we learned a lot from them. They looked great, sounded great and put on a great show every time they played. It was great for us to have an Irish band of that calibre. Barry Devlin on bass, Charles O'Connor on electric fiddle (and that lovely cream and black electric mandolin), Johnny Fean as his Les Paul guitar, Eamon Carr on drums and Jim Lockhart who played keyboards and two tin whistles at the same time! I remember they used to play a lot in the Filmore West, a Bray venue (formerly the Arcadia Ballroom) and I recall seeking Planxty there and a group called Curved Air with Stewart Copeland on drums just before he founded a trio called The Police. Sometimes we would cross paths with Horslips when on the road. I remember one night there was a Garda checkpoint ahead of us on the road. We naturally had to stop, tell them who we were and where we had come from. The guard just smiled and said "Ah, Bagatelle. Good stuff. About 10 minutes ago we had Horslips here and we had a chat with them too." We sort of felt like the new kids on the block at that point. Horslips had been around since the early seventies, played all over Europe, had an album in the UK Charts and brought Celtic Rock to the masses. But we never felt in competition with groups like that. But I think by that stage in Ireland we were on an equal standing." **Ken Doyle**

With his song-writing credentials never in question with Bagatelle, by now Liam was experimenting with the idea of writing for others. Having a writing credit with Bagatelle was one thing but writing for someone else opened new avenues, as well as revenue. His first attempt at this struck gold, and with it a song for the ages that surpassed a lot of what he had done with Bagatelle.

The Dundalk man was about to take it up a level.

FIVE

A LEGEND AT THE HELM

"We went from piling into a van eating leftover mouldy sandwiches and playing in the back arse of nowhere and now had this Irish icon looking after us in the studio. I was thinking "Hmmm, we've done alright here."

JOHN O'BRIEN

When Liam Reilly wasn't touring with Bagatelle, he was writing songs. Having penned Bagatelle's most iconic song on a piece of paper back in 1979, a piece of paper almost lost forever when he was moving to a new house, coming across the lyrics by pure chance in a box, he dabbled with the idea of writing songs for people outside of Bagatelle. A chance meeting with Tommy Byrne of Wolfe Tones fame would lead to writing one of the most recognisable songs of not only the decade but for the ages. A song as relevant as it was back then as it is now.

"I remember how "Streets of New York" came about. At the time there was no bar in RTE so me and Tommy Byrne used to pop down to Madigan's in Donnybrook for a drink. I remember being at the bar one night and asking Tommy "Why don't you sing a song that's not a Republican tune. Why not try something else." Tommy smiled and said, "Sure why don't you write a song for us then?" So, I sat down one day as this idea formed in my head which became "The Streets of New York". There is no chorus in the song as I didn't know how it was going to end. When it was finished, I brought it to Oliver Barry's office, played it and got rapturous applause. I knew this was going to be a hit." **Liam Reilly**

The song was naturally picked up by The Wolfe Tones, a song tailor made for them. Even by that stage the group were an Irish institution and had been plying their trade since 1963. Taking their name from Theobald Wolfe Tone one of the leaders of the Irish Rebellion of 1798, the daddies of rebel music had almost a dozen Irish Top 20 hits (let's face it they were never going to burn the charts up in England, not with albums called "Rifles of The I.R.A') and 10 albums, most of which went gold, to their name.
Songs like 'God Save Ireland', 'Come Out Ye Black & Tans' and 'A Nation Once Again' had been roared out by thousands of drunken Irish at the end of night in a pub yet despite all those accolades, Liam Reilly's tune would

actually surpass any single the group had produced up to then (and indeed since) as "The Streets Of New York" became the Wolfe Tones biggest Irish chart hit.

The song entered the Irish Charts on June 30th, 1981 (climbing past 'Second Violin') and going to Number 1 a week later. The song stayed in the charts for almost five months. In 1973 the group had their only other number 1 ('Up, Up & Away') but Reilly's hit remains the staple diet of the Irish diaspora around the world. By the time it became normal to walk into an Irish bar in Boston and hear "The Streets of New York" its songwriter should have had healthy royalties, but Reilly has not seen any from one of his most popular tunes.

Over time, Paddy Reilly and the Dublin City Ramblers would also have huge success with the song. Even back when it was released it had the hallmark of a Reilly classic. The Dundalk man was making a song for the ages by tapping into the subjects of Irish, unemployment and emigration which was Ireland back in the early eighties. It was something he would successfully harness again with tunes like "The Flight of Earls" and "Boston Rose."

The start of 1982 had been ushered in by one of the worst snowfalls in the Irish history. A full week of constant snow had brought the country to an absolute standstill. 400,000 homes and businesses lost power for days, roads were impassable and there were bread and milk riots at shops (something that hasn't changed given the fighting over milk and the last loaf of bread in the snow of 2018) for those that ventured out. Snow drifts of 10 feet high hit areas as temperatures dropped below freezing for more than a week - minus 19.6C in Glasnevin was the lowest recorded.

With nobody moving, Bagatelle cancelled all gigs for the month of January and February. Stuck indoors it also gave Liam Reilly a chance to relax. Though that meant putting together a few tunes for a third Bagatelle album.

No rest for the wicked.

Having two extremely well received albums behind them, Polydor again pushed for another release to capitalize on the band's popularity.

By 1982 no Irish group had toured Ireland as much as Bagatelle. It became the norm to do two, sometimes three separate tours in a twelve-month period. The travelling became utterly insane, but this was offset by the ever-increasing amount of money at the end of a gig for the foursome. If you wanted Bagatelle you were going to pay through the nose baby!

It was agreed that after the upcoming third album the boys would take a break. The schedule of playing everywhere from Down to Donegal and Westmeath to Waterford for Ken, John, Wally and Liam just had to stop. Having had Gus Dudgeon on the *Waterfall* second album it obviously brought his experience along with superior production and better sound. There was now a standard to keep.

For this Bagatelle turned to a bona fide Irish icon. A composer and singer of some of the most recognisable songs on these shores and beyond in the past 50 years. A Derry native whose presence on the album gave Bagatelle a real shot of prestige.

Phil Coulter would produce what was to become Bagatelle's third album *Are We Keeping You Up?*

The accolades and awards bestowed upon Phil Coulter in the last five decades are simply astonishing.

To date he has amassed 23 platinum discs, 39 gold discs, 52 silver discs, two Grand Prix Eurovision awards and five Ivor Novello Awards, which includes Songwriter of the Year. He's been honoured at home (Meteor Award) and been nominated for a Grammy, the one award which has so far has somehow escaped him. It is simply an astonishing testament to such a prolific singer-songwriter.

Some of those accolades are embedded in a generations mind. For the 1967 Eurovision Song Contest Phil, along with Bill Martin, composed "Puppet on a String" for Sandie Shaw, which would win the prestigious competition for the United Kingdom.

When Cliff Richard was announced as the Eurovision UK entry a year later in 1968, Coulter and Martin penned "Congratulations". Though it finished second it turned out to be a wise move, royalty wise. I mean, have you ever gone to a family or friend's wedding where you didn't hear "Congratulations" at the end of the night?

The correct answer is NEVER.

Phil would also write for a certain Elvis Aaron Presley. His song "My Boy" would reach the Billboard Adult Contemporary No.1 slot in 1975 and was also successfully covered by Richard Harris. His amazing song-writing partnership with Martin would also produce another US Billboard chart topper with "Saturday Night" for the Bay City Rollers at the height of their colossal fame in the early Seventies. It was this ability to have such success over a broad spectrum of styles that made Coulter such an in-demand composer.

Not bad for someone who came from a small two-up two-down terraced house in Derry.

To many it would be Coulter's "The Town I Loved So Well" a personal lament about his childhood in Derry that was the pianist's most personal composition. A heart-rending ballad about a once simple and happy lifestyle that had been replaced with barbed wire and bombs in a city caught in the height of "the Troubles" in the sixties. He paints a gritty picture of how hard life had been in Derry and yet despite the hardship the people of the city were generally a happy folk. It is an incredibly moving and emotional song that pulls on the heartstrings because of the subject and the content. A multitude of singers have covered the song, but it would be the vocal of Luke Kelly, founding member of The Dubliners, which is forever remembered most, a fact made more poignant because of his untimely passing in 1984 at the age of 43.

With both of their albums having gone gold it was a colour the band had got used to. Platinum would soon come before plywood (my own term for selling about 46 copies of an album) but hopes were high. Coulter himself was happy to take on the challenge. Maybe even bring Bagatelle to a different level.

"It was the bands record label who approached me first. I knew John (Woods) and he was a great believer in Bagatelle. I also knew Gus Dudgeon who had been involved in their last album. I have always had great regard for Bagatelle and that Liam Reilly was one of the best and most underrated songwriters of the time. I thought that was one of the problems as I saw it, being underrated. Of course, everyone knew "Summer in Dublin", but take a song like "Second Violin", what a great record. Add to that a tune like "Trump Card" and to me they were really on the money. A contemporary band with very well-made records."
Phil Coulter

Over the course of 1982/83 Bagatelle would make a host of television appearances to promote "Are We Keeping You Up"

Bagatelle went into the studio in the summer of '82, determined to keep the hot streak flowing.

For the album the group relocated to Chipping Norton Studios, set in the beautiful Cotswold town of the same name to fulfil the last of the three album deal they had signed with Polydor.

However, a very productive start in the studio would be interrupted by the passing of Ken Doyle's father George.

"We lay down tracks like "Is It Raining in Paris Tonight?", "Johnny Set 'Em Up Tonight" "Jersey Girl", "Midnight Child" and "Don't Play a Sad Song" (a John Lennon tribute.) On Halloween Phil brought his family

down and we set off fireworks. We had a great first week there but by the turn of the second week my father George had become ill. It had been that way for a time, but he had got progressively worse. I was living in the beautiful village of Roundwood which was the highest village in Ireland where we also had the highest pub in Ireland – Kavanaghs, and in 1982 phones could be hard to come by so my wife would call from Kavanagh's pub to the studio in England to tell me how my dad was. My heart jumped every time the phone rang. One day Phil answered the phone and I could tell from the look on his face that was it. I had written "Midnight Child" for a friend of mine. Midnight Child is the title of people born at midnight between two astrological signs. I took a few hours off on my own, going over the past in my head. My journey took me to Oxford University, and I walked the hallowed grounds. I returned about 8 that night, recorded "Midnight Child" and flew home for my father's funeral the next day." **Ken Doyle**

"To be honest even though it was our third album in as many years I felt we were still inexperienced. Gus certainly took us under his wing with the second album and was there to hold our hands so to speak. And now here we were, working with someone with the stature of Phil Coulter. I had been writing like crazy, so we had a ton of new original material to fall back on." **Liam Reilly**

The title of the album would be attributed to drummer Wally McConville. Often Ken would be half asleep getting his gear together on stage and Wally would hit his drum and hi-hat instantly waking up Ken – Ah sorry are we keeping you up Ken?
With such lofty expectations set by the band it seemed Bagatelle needed to top or emulate the success of the first two albums. Polydor had invested and expected results.

"One thing I thought that worked against Bagatelle was an unrealistic expectation in the media that the band were the new Elton John or such which I thought was unfair. Liam's a terrific songwriter and I saw snippets like "Move over Elton John" in papers and I thought it set the bar too high for them. They were superb to work with. Never a dull moment. Ken Doyle belongs in a secure institution! I am delighted when I run into him, as we live close together in Bray, to find out he has even less sense these days then when I met him first! He is one of the great eccentrics of this world. Liam was intense yet a very talented writer, John was great and Wally was an absolute nut. The band didn't take themselves too seriously which I thought was great" **Phil Coulter**

Despite Coulter producing the album, many might have thought a collaboration was in order with Liam Reilly. It seemed the natural choice as both were so strong in that field, pianists and songwriters. Phil Coulter's credits as a writer, especially when it came to the Eurovision Song Contest, was superb and ironically Reilly would go desperately close to winning the 1990 Eurovision with 'Somewhere in Europe."

"I'm quite happy to stand on my track record in Eurovision. I don't think many people have got a better one, but I didn't want to build a career on it. I wanted to outgrow the competition and move on. I'm quite hard on myself as I think I'm not a great co-writer anyway. Through the years I had a lovely collaboration with Bill Martin, but we actually didn't co-write a lot. It was like I looked after the creative end and he looked after the business end. I could name my co-writers on one hand (Albert Hammond, Ralph McTell). It was just something I never considered doing with Liam." **Phil Coulter**

One thing the Derry native did do however was to suggest a cover version for the album, something that the group had never tried before. Sure, Bagatelle had included staple Rhythm & Blues numbers back in the day to fill out their set yet here they were almost 5 years in and no cover version, even as a filler on one of their albums.

"One of my contributions in broadening the band's repertoire was to suggest the Tom Waits song "Jersey Girl". I felt the song harnessed a lot of Bagatelle's abilities like Liam's voice, and that suited them. It also took them in a slightly different direction, but I was glad they covered it and then released it as a single" **Phil Coulter**

"I got on great with Phil. One day I was out playing the accordion, but Phil couldn't see me. He asked, "Who is on the accordion?" to which Ken said "Ah that's only Reilly. He won a few All-Ireland titles back in the day!". We were just about finished the album but needed another song. Phil had suggested the Tom Waits classic "Jersey Girl". "Do you know that tune guys?" My face lit up and you could probably have seen my smile from space – I absolutely adored Tom Waits. It was a superb choice by Phil. I couldn't wait to record it." **Liam Reilly**

In a rather odd move Polydor decided to release the Liam Reilly penned "Old Soldiers" as a forerunner to *Are We Keeping You Up?* That kept Bagatelle in the public eye as they awaited the release of the album, however the song only went as high as Number 22 – the first song by the quartet not to make the national Top 20. The song never made it onto the new album.

Are We Keeping You Up? was released the first week in December of 1982 just in time for the lucrative Christmas market, though these days it is normally the month many artists use to release a Greatest Hits of Best Of compilation.

The album landed at number 7 in the charts. Larry Gogan would feature it as his "Album of the Week" which practically guaranteed its success.

"Hats off to Bagatelle. This is an album of originality which should please fans and may add a few more. The group will certainly continue to keep a high profile while adding a back catalogue of solid material."
The Irish Press 10.11.82

"Bagatelle just cannot do anything wrong. They have been on top of their game ever since the spectacular "Summer in Dublin" was launched upon the Irish public. This new album is again original material, with a hat tip to Tom Waits on "Jersey Girl." This release again continues to keep the band firmly in the public eye with trademark original material to boot"
Munster Express

"The music is middle-of-the-road yet diverse in influences. John O'Brien is more strongly featured alongside Liam Reilly in the song-writing stakes. Bass player Ken Doyle gets his song on the vinyl while drummer Wally McConville cuts loose on the cowbell for his own track "I Need A Woman." A first ever cover "Jersey Girl" is certainly one of the better tracks as is "Farewell" and "I Know I Threw It Away."
Southern Star 12.11.82

Despite good reviews and solid airplay some papers focused on Bagatelle's battle to break the lucrative overseas market. It was something the group was well aware of and didn't need reminding.

"You have to ask just how long it will be before Bagatelle achieves international status. On the home front they have become superstars not alone in the recording studio but also on the concert circuit. For keyboard player and vocalist Liam Reilly, guitarist John O'Brien, bass player Ken Doyle and drummer Wally McConville the trip to the top here has been swift. But on the British circuit the task has been difficult and despite good airplay from their albums and singles they have yet to make a great impact. The hope is their third album will provide that elusive breakthrough" **Donegal Democrat 20.12.82**

"Working with Phil Coulter, Are We Keeping You Up? has some excellent new tracks from the ever-original Bagatelle. Songs like "Johnny Set 'Em Up Tonight" and "Midnight Child" with a vocal from bass player Ken Doyle stand out. The album should have several potentially big singles.

Phil Coulter being on board should give them the international fame they urgently require as they are now at a musical crossroads."
Donegal News 22.01.83

And remember the Evening Herald critic who lambasted the group for their uninspiring debut album cover? Well he (or she) came back with a bee in their bonnet – again!"

"It may be a small but not insignificant point that from a commercial viewpoint Bagatelle have been ill-served in the past when it comes to album sleeves, (their first being the worst ever.) And it's happened again with their third album, "Are We Keeping You Up?" which uses on the back cover a picture of the band which has been in circulation for at least a year. Surely the fans (and band members) deserve better than this? Their third album has now hit the shops in time for Christmas. Worth a listen, provided you don't take them as seriously as others have in the past." **Evening Herald 21.12.82**

Not that album covers mattered to the band at this point.
"Don't pay any attention to what they write about you. Just measure it in inches" as Andy Warhol once remarked.

By that time "Jersey Girl", the Tom Waits classic that Phil Coulter had thought would make an excellent single, was released. Taken from his 1980 "Heart Attack & Vine" album as a tribute to his future wife Kathleen Brennan, it remains one of Waits most tender ballads. When fans heard a chorus of "Sha La La" several times they might have been wondering was it a Bay City Rollers cast-off, but the chorus was catchy. *"Sha-La-La's always go down well if you can't remember the words of the song or are too drunk to know any better"* remarked one paper. Bruce Springsteen would cover "Jersey Girl" in 1984 making it a stadium pleaser on subsequent tours, but Bagatelle would get their first.

Bagatelle played to a packed Siamsa Cois Laoi in 1983.
Picture courtesy of Olive Daly.

"Jersey Girl" entered the charts at number 17 on the 6th of February 1983 but climbed to Number 10 a week later on Valentine's Day which made sure the song got heavy airplay and Bagatelle complemented this with a Late, Late Show appearance.

37 years later it remains one of Bagatelle's biggest crowd pleasers.

Some know all the words. Some are just happy to roar out "Sha-La-La" back to the band.

There was no rest for the slightly wicked as Bagatelle continued to tour relentlessly.

Somehow the band managed THREE Irish tours in a 12-month period, packing them to the rafters wherever they went. Their hard-working ethic made sure thousands around the country didn't have to wait too long to see the boys in action.

Old favourite haunts included places like The Lilac in Donegal, Strandhill in Sligo, Hillgrove in Co. Monaghan, The Majestic in Mallow, The Beaten Path in Co. Mayo and the National Stadium in Dublin which they would sell out no matter how many times the group played there.

By now Tommy Mangan had become a welcome addition to the group, playing with Bagatelle for three years before achieving success with Irish group Allies – themselves signing for Polydor Records.

By the start of 1983 another break was needed.

"It had gone a bit stale. Everyone in the group knew that. We were constantly touring which meant we were constantly tired at the end of each gig. Nobody wanted a clean break from Bagatelle, but we felt like doing our own thing for a period of time was best so that we could come back rejuvenated. It was a subject we all agreed on." **Liam Reilly**

In between this Liam had decided to experiment with synthesisers at the expense of his trusty piano which gave the band a new sound, something which he experimented with in a recorded session with the RTE concert orchestra that Autumn. After all, it was a time when synth-pop ruled the waves.

Even when the group took a rest from bright lights and sound bites Polydor were quick to capitalize on the band's name, releasing a special four track EP, containing three old favourites along with "Is It Raining in Paris Tonight?", a very popular Liam Reilly cut that he wrote about a fleeting romance with an air hostess he had met.

"Are We Keeping You Up?" managed to sell around 10,000 copies. Not as much as their first two albums but not a disgrace by any means.

Polydor decided against releasing another single from "Are We Keeping You Up?", despite the band favouring "Johnny Set 'Em Up Tonight" which is now a regular on the set list and a nod to a local Dundalk bartender that

Liam used to know, that has become a firm favourite of fans.

By now the fans who followed the group were hopelessly devoted. Going to Bagatelle would be the perfect "Girls Night Out" or a night for cuddling couples to get lost in Bagatelle's big ballads. Often the men would be dragged along (against their will but secretly loving the gigs) even if they sounded begrudging to the wife that brought them there in the first place. It was a hedonistic time for the four young men. I would like to say they took full advantage and give the juicy details but I'm a poor man going through a divorce and I can't afford to be sued at this point!

The break helped the band recharge their batteries and seven months later they came back fresh ready to rock & roll.

A hot, sweaty summer of 1984 (where temperatures hit 35 degrees) didn't help with an exhausting schedule, packing them in from Clonmel to Claremorris and all points in-between with over 45,000 coming out to see Bagatelle play over a three-month period. They would end 1983 with a New Year's Eve gig at The Olympic in Newcastlewest that was sold out eight weeks previously.

To keep a presence in the charts "Can't Get You Out of My Mind" was released, just breaking the Top 30.

Then, from out of the blue, a crack appeared.

SIX

GOLD IS GOOD, PLATINUM IS PERFECTION

"The stage manager for Self-Aid was extremely strict. I remember him saying somewhat ironically "When your time is up, get off the stage quickly and don't panic because there's a crowd of 30,000 out there." I smiled and replied, "It's grand. We've just come back from playing to 60,000 at Siamsa Cois Laoi so I think we'll be fine."

KEN DOYLE

Life on the road was second nature. Bagatelle knew any amount of success home or abroad would mean a period of constant touring until the bands split or got tired of it. Days of playing gigs to no-one and losing money were well behind Bagatelle.

It was a head start many aspiring bands of the day would not have the luxury of.

No manager. No funding. No record label to fall back on.

Many dreams of stardom have fallen flat for many a band, tired of playing smoky venues for a pittance. Gazing out through that mist hoping for a full venue yet playing to 12 people. The motivation and drive that had been many a foundation lost in a lifestyle that dictated mileage over marriage.

Indeed, Bagatelle was a marriage of sorts. Four strong opinions not always seeing eye to eye, living out of each other's pockets yet united in one common goal.

By this stage Bagatelle had covered every one of the 32 counties and played to record crowds. However, seeing each other more than they saw their families, tiredness (and tempers) had flared often on tour. More often than not Ken Doyle had acted as peacekeeper. A negotiator that kept band members happy whilst reminding them of the lifestyle they craved and now had. Another band meeting was called.

Another break was needed.

Though not formally splitting up, the group temporarily went their ways to do their own things. To John O'Brien the success of the group had already been achieved and it mattered little. Along with him Wally McConville wanted a break away from all things Bagatelle. With that in mind they set their focus, albeit temporarily, on a new musical project.

The result would be Ground Zero.

In October of 1984, and with three new members Neil Whiffen, former bass player for The Radiators along with ex-Gentry guitarist Eric Sharpe. and former Boulder Band member Bree Harris, Ground Zero started gigging around the country.

Bree had been at the forefront of The Boulder Band when they split and owed it to herself to take a second bite at the cherry.

They would soon build up a strong following, but their ambition didn't stop at just gigging. O'Brien got the band into the recording studio at the earliest moment possible. The result would be "Till the Dawn Comes" written and sung by Harris. Uniquely all band members were songwriters. O' Brien could count on tracks like "Love Is The Reason" , "Nowhere" and "The Heat Is On", while Wally McConville had helped pen Bagatelle tunes like "Leeson Street Lady", "Rock & Roll Fantasy" and "Rock & Roll Drummer" so all songs where used in Ground Zero's set wherever they travelled.

"Till The Morning Comes" and its commercial sound should have been strong enough to chart in Ireland's Top 30 however it didn't, but a major slot supporting The Moody Blues in the RDS that November was the proverbial feather in the cap as Ground Zero aimed to keep themselves in such a prestigious spotlight.

Ken Doyle stayed at home while Liam Reilly went to America where he wrote, produced and travelled the States in a move that saw him as productive as ever without the glare of an all too familiar spotlight at home.

"One of the main reasons Bagatelle is still together I think is that like a good torque wrench we knew when it was time to break. There was nothing wrong with a break. We had an extended one in 1983 before we got back touring, so maybe we expected to try and fit those breaks in on a more regular basis after five years of the same thing. We had done well to hold it together at this point given the fact we had nearly 100 gigs a year." **Ken Doyle**

Though Bagatelle had over a dozen charting singles by now, other Irish artists began to struggle for success. From March 1981 Joe Dolan's "More & More" to U2's "Unforgettable Fire" in May 1985 there hadn't been a single Irish artist or band at the number 1 slot in Ireland.

A few months later Ground Zero called it a day.

John O'Brien seemed to have enough of it. Enough of the music. Enough of the endless touring, sleeping under the stars or in an unwelcoming B&B or hotel room. Though he would remain a member of Bagatelle and return to the fold.

"Forming Ground Zero, though still in the music business, gave me a boost. I felt we could have gone places, but I had been used to things

falling away on me before. Yes, we got things back on track after Ground Zero folded, and we had a successful reunion (if you want to call it that) but by now Bagatelle should have stopped maybe four or five years after we started. I'm serious when I say that. Even by 1984 I felt Bagatelle had run its course. We had been at our zenith and produced great songs but now I didn't like the material. It seemed we were churning out anything. I just kept hoping after every tour we would take another long break to keep us fresh. After all, we were still relevant. What would it matter if we took a year away? But it never happened. We keep touring constantly. From being immensely proud of the band and our beginnings I was getting annoyed at what I was doing." **John O'Brien**

Despite things being initially frosty when the group got back together again, there was still a huge demand for Bagatelle and the group undertook a major 28 date concert tour.

The ballroom scene, part and parcel of Bagatelle when they broke out, was now dilapidated and dead. Showbands acts like the Royal, Capitol and Carlton had long disappeared along with the long lines of people emigrating. Some cynics even classed Bagatelle as a showband.

Ground Zero. A short-lived breakaway group formed by John O'Brien and Wally McConville. Also, in picture Neil Whiffin, Bree Harris and Eric Sharp. Munster Express Feb 8th, 1985

The one man who had successfully broken away from that scene would be Rory Gallagher. A God given talent that would go on to sell 30 million albums worldwide, Gallagher got his start playing after school with Irish showbands, joining Fontana in 1963, before shedding that to form rock band Taste in 1969.

He would go on to play the Isle of Wight Festival, have several albums well received all across Europe and was Melody Maker's Guitarist of the Year in 1971, a year Eric Clapton had left Blind Faith to record his first solo album. It was also a time when Country & Western came to the fore. At the time Bagatelle where at their peak, we had our own little Country & Irish niche that packed venues from Derry to Dundalk. Irish performers like Big Tom, T.R. Dallas and Johnny McEvoy were the big winners.

While Brendan Shine, Ray Lynam also coined it in, acts like Joe Dolan,

Gina Dale Haze & The Champions and Freddy White were also very successful.

On the Traditional Folk scene Christy Moore, The Fureys, The Dubliners and the Wolfe Tones all commanded respect, while Mary Black had emerged from De Dannan and would go on to create *"By The Time It Gets Dark"* now a seminal Irish album which was re- released in 2017 on its 30th anniversary.

A smart move by Polydor came with the release of a *Greatest Hits* package in 1985. After all it had now been seven years since the likely lads from Bray and Dundalk had formed from the ashes of The Boulder Band, to eventually hit it big. Though Bagatelle's back catalogue would easily fill a *Greatest Hits* it was decided the new album would be fresher if a couple of new tracks were written.

Wally McConville would contribute "Hurting Inside" a song which would eventually be released as a single as was Liam Reilly's "All Fall Down Philadelphia" a song he wrote whilst taking that crucial break Stateside.

"I enjoyed my time in America, getting away from Ireland, the band and the pressure. It was while there I wrote "All Fall Down Philadelphia". Me and a few guys in a band called Terra Nova, who hailed from Drogheda, had great craic there, most of the nights we were in the horrors! A friend of mine in Philadelphia called John Wicks owned a recording studio called TSR. So, I decided to write a song based on my time there, those drunken nights out with the lads, and what I thought of Philadelphia. It was a new track that fitted nicely in our Greatest Hits package" **Liam Reilly**

To kick the *Gold: The Best of Bagatelle* album off, Polydor released the infuriatingly catchy "Can't Get You Out of my Mind" on St Patrick's weekend 1985 when it debuted in the Irish Top 30. That weekend Bagatelle joined in the festivities by playing a first ever gig in Cookstown – the Glenavon Court Hotel to be exact.

There would be no let up on the promotion, gigs or indeed the singles. "Hurting Inside" would make number 25 in the Irish Charts while "All Fall Down Philadelphia" hit No.11 and hung around for another month.

It was around here that the group really began to spread their wings. Over the course of 40 odd years Bagatelle have played in almost every corner of the globe. America above all would be toured on an almost annual basis. That elusive break into international waters had not materialized with an overseas hit yet but there was a demand for the foursome anywhere there was an extended Irish community.

Back home the album was an instant success upon release, outselling almost anything that year by any Irish artist at home and became one of the biggest *Greatest Hits* albums ever seen on this Emerald Isle.

It kept pace with other *"Greatest Hits"* packages from the likes of Billy Joel, James Last, Mike Oldfield, Aretha Franklin and Depeche Mode. At one point it even gave Dire Straits seminal album "Brothers in Arms" a run for its money.

Not bad for an album that eventually went on to sell more than 30 million copies.

By 1988 *Gold- The Best of Bagatelle* had gone platinum. That year the album was re-released as part of the bands 20th anniversary. To this day it remains the groups most successful *Greatest Hits* Cd.

Seven years on from their start in 1978 the band's popularity was at an all-time high. Polydor could not have been happier. Once again, the band received a few more column inches.

"When Bagatelle temporarily split last year, I thought it may be the end of an era. The Bagatelle years will always bring back memories, their sounds beating out in every disco in the country. We had a top-class band and we knew it.

Thankfully, Bagatelle are back with new singles and a new album, the best of the band since their formation in 1978. Bagatelle Gold – The Best of Bagatelle kicks off with "Summer in Dublin", quickly followed by "Love Is the Reason" and "Is It Raining in Paris Tonight?" both showing a definite country influence. All of their other hits like "Trump Card" and "Second Violin" are obviously included along with some of their better album tracks. Their single "Hurting Inside" is probably the best song on the new album and shows the band heading in a new direction, moving away from a very raw acoustic sound to an Americanised synthesizer sounding band. Liam Reilly's spell in America seems to have paid off on "All Fall Down Philadelphia" along with the experience of other new projects by Bagatelle's members." **Tuam Herald 28.8.1985**

"We know Bagatelle are an exciting four-piece group who write their own material. They have already been hailed as one of the most promising Irish groups to develop from being a foot tapping Rhythm & Blues band playing pop, country and ballads to being international entertainers. They have been on every major television show in this country. They are back with a new album and a new single in "Hurting Inside" which sees the band head off in a new direction in the hope of finding their feet again after a year in the doldrums.
Leitrim Observer 13.7.1985

"An apt title, this album forms a precious collection of the groups best material. Listening to the album I renewed old friendships with "Summer in Dublin" and "Trump Card". The tragedy of "Leeson Street Lady" which has gained force with age and still stands tall with "Second Violin" – two

of the band's more sedate pieces. They change pace with "Rock & Roll Fantasy", a louder foot stomper, and is maintained with "Outrageous". If Bagatelle repeat their set to the same effect in Britain and America, they will achieve the success that has so far eluded them. Like a fine wine the band has matured with age and are just as focused and ambitious."
Connaught Telegraph 16.10.85

The band promoted *"Bagatelle Gold"* right through 1985 into the first half of 1986 but there was no resting on any laurels. Success is not final; failure is not fatal. The boys were still loved. From housewife's humming along to the latest Bagatelle hit while doing the laundry, men bopping along in the car to a Bagatelle tune or your boss at work howling one of the groups numbers, Bagatelle remained a firm favourite. It had been a quick eight years.

Above, Bagatelle would play Self Aid in the RDS which took place on the 17th May 1986 and included Van Morrison, U2, Clannad, The Pogues and Rory Gallagher among the line-up.

One thing that had surrounded the group everywhere they played would be the continuing problem of unemployment and immigration that was sadly part of life in Ireland in the late seventies, early eighties. The Emerald Isle was basically living a third world existence. By 1985 unemployment had hit a record high of 20%. Comically there had been a shortage of petrol in 1981 and 1984. The fuel shortage saw huge lines of cars queuing up for the last of the petrol and diesel. Some petrol stations had completely run out of fuel or had introduced a rationing system. It was certainly one of the state's bleakest times since possibly the depression of the 1930's.

An extremely irresponsible budget by the majority Fianna Fáil government in 1977, which included the abolition of car tax and borrowing to fund current spending, combined with some global economic problems would end up ruining the Irish economy for most of the 1980s. The Fine Gael-Labour government of 1982-87 made this bad situation much worse with more massive borrowing and tax rates as high as 60%.

At this point the 'Celtic Tiger' was so far off the horizon that nobody could have envisaged or seen what would happen.

A group of concerned Irish musicians tried to do something about this. To many it might have felt like a thumb holding back the water in the dam at the time, but this would be a progressive step forward, however brief. Thus, Self- Aid was born.

Self-Aid was a benefit concert for unemployment held in Dublin on 17 May 1986. The concert performances were primarily by Irish musicians, who wanted to stop the revolving door at Aer Lingus to the USA and help our own disillusioned unemployed. Though primarily Irish artists, Elvis Costello and Chris Rea were designated "honorary Irishmen" for the day and the event was promoted by Jim Aiken.

Self- Aid came in the wake of the Geldof inspired Live Aid which raised millions for Ethiopia after the opinionated Irishman was moved to take action after seeing Michael Burke's bleak BBC report from Ethiopia which looked like a biblical famine.

Live Aid focused on two mammoth concerts in Wembley and Philadelphia (but also included the Soviet Union, Japan, Austria, Australia and West Germany) and was one of the largest-scale satellite links and television broadcasts of all time; an estimated global audience of 1.9 billion, across 150 nations, watched the live broadcast.

Ireland had done its bit, sending more money per person than anywhere in the world, and also contributed a charity song "Show Some Concern" featuring the likes of Paul Cleary, Christy Moore, Twink and Red Hurley.

At the time Self-Aid was the biggest ever live concert to be attempted on these shores. The message was simple – getting as many Irish musicians of note to converge on the RDS in Dublin to highlight and help the unemployed.

With RTE tagging along to do a telethon the idea was certainty well meaning.

The belief was that acts like U2, Thin Lizzy, Chris Rea, Christy Moore and company would encourage people to stand up, grab the phone and find jobs for the many that needed them.

And the idea did work with just over 1000 jobs being created. Some were critical of the concept, but the event served its purpose.

The 14-hour concert produced almost 1 million viewers when it aired. All the musicians that took part donated their time free of charge. All profits from the concert and subsequent album, "Live for Ireland", went to the Self Aid Trust. The telethon raised a couple of million of pounds for a job creation trust fund as well as those 1000 job pledges.

The song chosen for the finale was "Let's Make it Work", written by Christy Moore and Dublin songwriter Paul Doran. Tributes were paid to

Phil Lynott who had died just 4 months earlier, including a performance by a reformed Thin Lizzy with Gary Moore on lead vocals.

It was also broadcast on RTE Radio One while over 30,000 attended the RDS in Dublin's Ballsbridge to watch the 27 acts.

Brush Shiels opened the show with a tribute to Phil Lynott playing "Whiskey in a Jar" and there would be further star turns by Irish acts like Those Nervous Animals, Auto De Fe, In Tua Nua and Freddy White , all holding their own among more established international Irish acts like Clannad and Chris De Burgh. When Geldof takes to the stage, he's almost an iconic figure for what he had helped produce a year earlier. Pleading to the audience and those at home to donate money or job opportunities while announcing the Boomtown Rats would call it a day.

Stay away from the pub and ring in with the price of a pint of Guinness we were asked.

And most responded.

Bagatelle confirmed their interest the moment the idea was formed and were quickly added to the bill. Still riding high on *Bagatelle Gold*, now with platinum status, the group had penned a new song "Just Say No" at the time they had been approached to do Self Aid.

And what good company they kept during the concert. Elvis Costello, Chris Rea, Paul Brady, Rory Gallagher, The Chieftain's, Moving Hearts, Van Morrison and of course U2 to name but a very few.

Back in the RTÉ Studios in Donnybrook presenters and celebrities manned the phones at the Telethon taking pledges for jobs and financial donations for the cause.

On the day Bagatelle lined up after Brush Shiels and before Blue in Heaven. Almost old-timers at this point, they took to the stage as confident as any of their peers. As comfortable as an old pair of slippers.

The late Frank Kelly (the loveable Father Jack from Father Ted) would announce their arrival.

"Ladies and gentlemen, Self-Aid, a great day for Ireland. Here's a wonderful band whose album 'Gold' has gone platinum and have a new single out that's called "Don't Say No". Sure, who else on a day like this could bring you a summer in Dublin.... Bagatelle!

Messrs – Reilly, McConville, O'Brien and Doyle took to the stage just before 1.45pm, belting out a medley of hits, all lip-synced by the fans.

Every single word.

With just 15 minutes to impress, the foursome opened with "Rock & Roll Fantasy" whipping the crowd up into a storm. It was followed with "If It Gets in My Way" a new number, before tearing into a medley of "Second Violin", "Summer in Dublin" and "Trump Card."

If there was a roof on the RDS it would have been blown off.

In short, they killed it.

"For the concert we decided to do a medley on the day which worked really well and bang on the 15-minute curfew. We were named the "Queen of Self-Aid", a lovely compliment as they had stolen the show at Live Aid. The stage manager was both big and brash. Oh, and condescending! I remember him saying to us right before we went out on stage, as if we were school kids, "Alright you guys, I don't want you to get nervous but there are 30,000 people out there" to which I replied " That's Ok. We played to 60,000 at Siamsa Cois Laoi last week so we'll be fine!" He said, "Ok so you know what you're doing then?" "Yeah we think so" came my reply from all four of us." **Ken Doyle**

"It was a revolving stage which was new to RTE at the time. With so many acts our time was limited so we had these lights to guide us. Green, Amber and Red. Green you're on stage, red you are off. In total fifteen minutes. We thought it best to do a medley of our hits which went down a storm. The cream of the crop was at that gig. I remember at the end we did a rousing rendition of "Whiskey in the Jar" in memory of Phil Lynott who had just passed away. Bono came over to me and said – Liam, Van Morrison is singing the first verse, I'll do the second and you and Chris De Burgh do the third. Good times." **Liam Reilly**

On the back of that performance "Don't Say No" entered the Irish charts 3 weeks later, charting at Number 20. Though never the critics' choice Bagatelle were nominated in the Best Group Category at the 1986 IRMA Awards.
A forerunner for the rather more well-known Meteor Awards, the IRMA's was the chance for the industry to give back to Irish bands on an annual scale. The group were nominated along with Cactus World News, U2, In Tua Nua and Stockton's Wing but lost out inevitably to U2 as they would again a year later in 1987.
At that point, the Irish music industry was healthy as some new stars began to shine bright.
Paul Brady, though already well known, released *Back to The Centre* to critical acclaim, with an album that produced the heart-breaking "The Island" a song with its roots firmly planted in "the Troubles" up North. Donegal's finest Clannad, would tour the world on the back of hits like "Harry's Game" and "In A Lifetime". There was the mammoth "Lady In Red" from Chris De Burgh which also broke the adopted Wexford man in the UK (where it topped the charts for two weeks) along with the Number 1 slot in Belgium , Norway, South Africa, Canada and breaking the lucrative American market , going all the way to Number 3 in the Billboard Charts. Former Undertones front man Fergal Sharkey went to Number 1 with "A

Good Heart" and even the relatively unknown Cork band Microdisney would score an unlikely UK Top 40 hit with the infectious "Town to Town" in early 1987.

And there was U2.

Of course, there was U2.

Back home in 1986 the only Irish singer to reach number 1 on the charts came from a pre-Father Ted Dermot Morgan singing "Thank You Very Much Mr. Eastwood" an ode to Barney Eastwood, then trainer of the Clones Cyclone, Barry McGuigan.

It had proved the most productive period of Bagatelle in their history. Buoyed by success and in one of his most creative spells, Liam Reilly would write another emigration song, not knowing what a holy row it would cause between two of Ireland's best-known and much-loved traditional bands.

"Flight of the Earls" was written in November 1986 and pitched by Reilly to The Dublin City Ramblers, The Wolfe Tones, Foster & Allen and Paddy Reilly for any of the four to use as a single. It was a smart move by the Dundalk native. "Streets of New York" had topped the Irish charts in the summer of 1981 for the Wolfe Tones, so naturally the group were keen to record the song.

Trouble was so were Patsy Watchorn and his Dublin City Ramblers.

With both group's intent on outdoing each other "Flight of The Earls" was released by both groups within a week of each other.

The first real sign of any public argument came when the Dublin City Ramblers got a court injunction to prevent the Wolfe Tones from performing it on Sunday night at the Gaiety.

The Ramblers had claimed the sole rights to the song had been acquired by them however a few days later the injunction was lifted.

The next chapter in the saga was when the Wolfe Tones launched their version of "Flight of the Earls" on the Late Late Show, thus given them maximum coverage as Gay Byrne's chat show would have almost 1 million viewers of a Friday night. Along with that the Wolfe Tones headed off on an extensive US tour where the song would get exposure Stateside much to the annoyance of the Dublin City Ramblers. However, they would respond to that by featuring themselves on the "Sunday night at the Gaiety" and introduced Liam Reilly on stage.

The Wolfe Tones weren't pleased with the original injunction stopping them playing Sunday Night at the Gaiety claiming they would have responded with a defence against the injunction, but it was far too late as they found out literally a couple of hours before the show.

In the end both groups would use "Flight of the Earls" in their sets and proved extremely popular with their fan base.

After that, the only battle left was in the Irish charts.

With that, The Wolfe Tones released "Flight of the Earls" two days BEFORE St. Patrick's Day 1987 and debuted at number 6, going to a high of number 3 but spent an astonishing 22 weeks in the charts with sales close to 50,000. To counter that, The Dublin City Ramblers released their version five days AFTER St. Patrick's Day and debuted at number 6 in the Irish charts where it topped off, spending almost two months in the Top 10 with sales close to 20,000.

A highly successful song either way for Mr. Reilly.

"The Flight of the Earls was confusing, but in the long run successful for me. It got such attention in the media. You see I had made cassettes of the song and they went to the Wolfe Tones, Dublin City Ramblers and Foster & Allen. I went on stage one night with the Ramblers and played piano on the tune so that was kind of an endorsement. But then they had trouble with The Wolfe Tones. That said it proved extremely successful, for both groups, so there's sort of a happy ending!" **Liam Reilly**

Paddy Reilly later got in on the act and recorded the song, taking it to Number 1 in the Irish charts, thus becoming a hit with three different Irish acts.

The history of the song probably amounted to a storm in the proverbial teacup however Reilly's emigration tune was so relevant when released as the songwriter had tapped into that source in the same vein that had made "Streets of New York" such a big hit six years earlier.

Having tested the water rather successfully with Tom Waits "Jersey Girl", Bagatelle sprung a surprise by releasing another cover version in April 1987, this time with Amen Corner's "(If Paradise is) Have As Nice" which would be a forerunner for a new album the group were planning for 1987. The original was written by Italian Lucio Battisti but translated into English by the psychedelic rockers from Wales. It proved their biggest hit, going all the way to Number 1 in the UK and selling over 1 million copies in the process. The group would have four top 10 singles under the guidance of lead vocalists Andy Fairweather Low though would last a mere three years, breaking up by the end of 1969.

The Bagatelle cover made number 25 in the Irish charts for a couple of weeks.

As the band fast approached over a decade together, they took stock. It had been nearly 10 years of sustained success against the odds, plying their trade first through the corner of dark, smoke filled pubs and dance halls with 1950's flooring to outdoor stadiums, headline tours, and supporting a host of international acts.

By the time Bagatelle's fifth album *Cry Away the Night* was released in the summer of 1987, the boys were thankful of what had gone before.

The travelling was tough. The money however was compensation.

"Look it was good money. I remember us piling into the back of a van and playing places in Holland, Wales, England and Germany. Yes, we were playing abroad but getting £75 a night is not exactly glamourous! But you persevere. At that point getting your name out there and the thrill of playing in Europe drove us. If we were in it for the money, we would have quit in the first year." **Ken Doyle**

"Naturally the more reputable the band, the better the money. I'm not sure if everyone in the band found it that way but I appreciated where we had come from. I remember dating a girl named Karen who I knew through Oliver Barry who often came upon envelopes I had at home filled with money. That wasn't a boast. I'm just saying that was the type of money and situation we were in at that point. We were comfortable. Very comfortable." **Liam Reilly**

Over the course of time Reilly would blow a vast amount of the money yet had the comfort of making most of it back through touring. That was the cushion. Blow a grand in the afternoon, make it back with two hours on stage in the evening. *"Yes, I made it, lost it and had to start again from scratch – believe me"* as he admitted.

By this point Oliver Barry had left the band in good hands for new manager Peter Smith to take over the reins. Banteer people will tell you that Oliver was always quick to spot an opening or opportunity from an early age and he had been an extraordinarily successful addition to the Bagatelle family. His crowning glory was yet to come; getting the King of Pop to play Pairc Ui Chaoimh in 1988.
The ticket price was £18.
Taking over from Oliver Barry, Smith would keep the band firmly in the limelight, overseeing the release of their new upcoming album. If we were taking cars, Oliver had taken them as a battered Fiat 127 and turned them into a finely tuned Mercedes. All Peter had to do was take the keys and drive it onwards.
Though his time as manager of Bagatelle was short, each member appreciated the direction and effort from Smith.

"Peter Smith was an absolute gentleman and we were delighted to work with him. He always did his best for the band and had our best interests at heart. He had a music background as part of the Mighty Avons showband who had been on the scene since the early sixties so knew the business. He took us over after Oliver and kept the band relevant."
Liam Reilly

Self-Aid
R.D.S., Dublin
Saturday 17th May 1986

ARTISTS: RUNNING ORDER

12.00	– 12.15	Opening And Introduction
12.15	– 12.30	Brush Shiels
12.40	– 12.55	Bagatelle
1.05	– 1.20	Blue In Heaven
1.35	– 1.50	Stockton's Wing
2.05	– 2.20	In Tua Nua
2.35	– 2.50	Clannad
3.05	– 3.20	Big Self
3.35	– 3.45	Les Enfants
4.00	– 4.15	The Chieftains
4.30	– 4.45	Chris Rea
5.00	– 5.05	Freddie White
5.05	– 5.15	Those Nervous Animals
5.30	– 5.45	The Pogues
6.00	– 6.15	Cactus World News
6.30	– 6.45	Scullion
7.00	– 7.15	De Danann
7.30	– 7.45	The Fountainhead
8.00	– 8.15	Paul Brady
8.30	– 8.45	Bob Geldof & The Boomtown Rats
9.00	– 9.15	Auto Da Fe
9.30	– 9.45	Moving Hearts
10.00	– 10.15	Rory Gallagher
10.25	– 10.40	Christy Moore
10.50	– 11.05	Elvis Costello & The Attractions
11.15	– 11.30	Chris de Burgh
11.40	– 11.55	Van Morrison
12.10	– 12.45	U2/Finale

All times are approximate

SEVEN

THE START OF ANOTHER NIGHT

"When you're surrounded by all these people, the band, the public, it can be lonelier than when you're by yourself. You can be in a huge crowd yet feel you can't talk to anybody. I suppose the music had been a refuge. It filled the gaps when I wasn't feeling this way."

JOHN O'BRIEN

Though *the Gold- Best of Bagatelle* album had been a huge seller, Bagatelle, being Bagatelle, wanted a new album of almost completely original material. It had now been five years since *Are We Keeping You Up,* the last album of original cuts, so 1987 spawned a brand-new album in *Cry Away the Night.*

The title track would be a standout single, a classic Bagatelle ballad though this time written by Wally McConville and John O'Brien. It could easily have jumped off a Phil Collins album.

"John and Wally borrowed the money to record that album and lucky enough Harmac Records brought it out. John O'Brien would collaborate on most of the songs on the album. I had two offerings "Heartache Street" and "Kiss Away from Heaven" – the latter dedicated to the village of Roundwood in County Wicklow, the highest village in Ireland, where I lived at the time. I think this seemed to be highlighted on the front cover of the album which placed Wally and John to the front of the picture and me and Liam to the back. I could see which way the wind was blowing on that album! **Ken Doyle**

Along with "Cry Away the Night" which kept up Bagatelle's record of having every released single making the Irish Top 30, songs like "Kiss Away from Heaven" and "Only Love" from the album became firm favourites when played on the road. Sales for the album, though not as high as their heyday, were still promising. Everyone was fully aware it was the first album release since the platinum selling *Gold – The Best of Bagatelle* album and many groups never recreate the same type of success once a Greatest Hits package has been released.

"The album is vintage Bagatelle. Naturally, eight of the ten compositions are their own, the remaining two from producer Nicky Graham. Anyone who thought Bagatelle was a one-man band in Liam Reilly can forget it. All four members can write, and outstanding stuff at that! There are some super cuts. Title track "Cry Away the Night" has a piano and sax intro to what is a lovely lush and romantic ballad. "Only Love" is an instantly recognisable Bagatelle tune, though written by Nicky Graham & Bob Mitchell. My favourite track on the album is "Gone Too Far" written by guitar player John O'Brien and drummer Wally McConville. It's a light, happy, commercial pop tune, real chart material." Other solid tracks include "Thinking of You" and "Quiet Moments". All in all, another fine album from the highly talented and always underrated Bagatelle"
Anglo Celtic 22.10.87

Naturally, the hours were put in on the road, travelling the country. The four likely lads were well aware that hundreds of Irish bands would criss-cross the country every weekend, and some during the week, trying to earn their crust. For some the hardship could prove too much or the realization it just wasn't worth the few pound they were earning.

One of the things that made Bagatelle so popular was that they were so accessible.

Money can only do so much though.

By 1988 Liam Reilly's 11 years with the band looked like it was coming to an end.

The songwriter needed a change of scenery again.

"I needed a break. I had done that in 1984 when I went to Philadelphia and that was such a relief, getting away from constant touring with the band. Despite was some perceived it was never meant to be myself leaving Bagatelle. Far from it. In my time Stateside I produced nine albums for recording artists over there, so it was different producing others rather than writing and recording Bagatelle albums. I spent time in Savannah, Georgia doing the same.

I had kept myself busy within the industry and was happy to go back to Bagatelle after it. But after the new album it was different. It was more difficult. I needed to get away but frankly I needed time away from the group even though we were doing extremely well."
Liam Reilly

Liam would leave in January 1988. Though bassist Ken Doyle remained, it was only another couple of months down the road before he left as well.

"Liam was the first to leave and to be honest I wasn't far behind him. When he went, we obviously had to audition for a new singer. One guy came in after the other but the only person that seemed to suit was Derek Jordan. My mind was made up and I wanted out by that stage. I wasn't going to leave the group in the lurch and said I would stay and even help the group get a new bass player and then leave. But it was a sad and frustrating time to be with Bagatelle personally." **Ken Doyle**

Above, Cry Away the Night cover. Photo courtesy of Chuck Fishbein. Design by Mike Harper

The duo's departure should have meant an uncertain future for Bagatelle. However, O'Brien and McConville were quick to fill in their spaces and keep the group going.

On vocals in came Derek Jordan. Fellow Dubliner Paul Finlay came in on piano to directly replace Liam Reilly while Arklow native Martin Byrne came in on bass as a replacement for Ken Doyle, making the group a quintet for the first time.

Naturally, it meant going out on the road again, and though half of the band had essentially left, reviews for the band's new look proved positive. That new look Bagatelle would have their first gig at the Carraig Springs Hotel in Crosskeys, County Cavan. They would go on a nine-week annual summer tour as always, playing a lot of their old haunts and some new ones to boot.

"The new Bagatelle line up seems to have a raunchier sound than the original band and is now more rock orientated then pop now. They have recently played dates in Britain and America and that market looks like expanding further as so many of their fans have been forced to emigrate in recent years. They still sound good" **Southern Star 18.3.89**

One of the first things this version of Bagatelle did was to promote "Only Love" a song taken from the *Cry Away the Night* album, with Derek Jordan now taking over the duties on vocals.

"Only Love" is a strong hook filled pop/rock song, complete with a brilliant vocal from Derek Jordan and a polished, top-of-the-line production. It sounds like Starship or Reo Speedwagon, but this is Bagatelle, a hit band waiting to explode in Europe or even North America. "Only Love" should be the song to do it." **The Music Brokers**

That expectation was a bit lofty. Yes Jordan's vocals differed slightly from Liam Reilly's but if the group hadn't crossed over to the British and American record buying public with songs like "Summer In Dublin," "Second Violin" and "Trump Card" then it was unlikely the first single to feature a new vocalist and line up would be the one that broke Bagatelle in those lucrative markets.

In the end *Cry Away the Night* sold modestly. Enough to keep the guys touring and in the public gaze, but nowhere near sales of Bagatelle's first four albums. Perhaps it was unfair to match that album with a new line-up against anything that had gone before. When touring it became obvious that founder members Reilly & Doyle, were not on stage which would lead to the obvious questions by fans of where are they gone? Why are they gone? Are they staying gone?".

"It was naturally a question we had to answer. You couldn't just take Liam and Ken out of the band and not expect people to say, "Hey, I think you're missing a couple of people!" I had taken the time to look at the situation and at that point, anyway, felt myself and Wally should continue but needed to recruit new members quickly to try and make the transition as quick and comfortable as possible." **John O'Brien**

Unlike other Bagatelle albums, *Cry Away The Night* hadn't produced any major hits, though some songs on the album remained fan favourites but in August 1988 the group released a single "Just Another Lover" which became the group's first Top 20 hit with Jordan on vocals. Indeed, the single would do well, reaching Number 15 and spending a couple of weeks there.

By this stage however the group were no longer recording with Polydor. The record company who had backed them from the beginning had gone their separate ways after that *Gold* album as *Cry Away the Night* and "Just Another Lover" had been released on different labels.

The obvious punishing tour schedule was second nature to the group by now, so they dug deep to keep their fans nationwide happy by touring almost constantly during 1988 and 1989.

But again, this would lead to an unhappy period for senior member John O'Brien, something he would express himself through the lyrical content in some of his songs.

"The Start of Another Night" for instance.

Having been part of showbands and original bands since he first got the bug in the sixties and having travelled to Britain and started half a dozen bands before he even joined Bagatelle, O'Brien was becoming more disillusioned with his life as a travelling musician. Most people within the band's circle could tell you he was going to quit, they just did not know the year, time or place. "The Start of Another Night" was a superb tune in its own right, however the subject of the song had a different meaning for the then forty something.

"I remember going back to my room after doing a gig in Cork. I was looking out my hotel bedroom at people hurrying around town, most of them lining up to get into a disco. Though the band has sold out the gig and I was making good money, I never felt as alone as I did staring out that window. Suitcase on bed. Just wishing I wasn't here. I believed in every lyric I wrote and penned "The Start of Another Night", a song about how I had lost my identity and felt I had nothing more in common with the rest of the band. There were times I would rarely even speak with the lads other than a gig. It had become a tiring routine by that stage." **John O'Brien**

The opening lyrics of the song would echo this.
"Well I'm sitting on a bed looking around at the hotel room.
And I'm writing a card looking forward to seeing you soon
And I'm feeling so lonely but there's not a lot that I can do
But read the sign on the wall that says guests must vacate by noon
On a chair by the wall the suitcase holds all that I own
Just some easy-clean clothes and some memories that I call home
But it's not what you have that makes you whatever you are
It's just the price that you pay when you find that you're on your own
TV in the corner is turned down low, just some pictures of famous people that I don't know
And the phone on the table is staying quiet
It's just the end of the day and the start of another night"

Though Ken Doyle had taken time away from Bagatelle he hadn't taken a break from the music industry. Soon after Doyle, with his brother started a group called It's A Secret. It was a band that Doyle in his own words *"Sounded like Horslips on steroids"*. A Celtic rock group that had it come out after Riverdance, would probably have made a fortune. By his own admission when It's A Secret had called it a day Ken was absolutely knackered. Enjoyable but tiring, an early retirement looked on the cards.

Above, A new look Bagatelle (without Reilly and soon to lose Doyle but still with McConville & O'Brien) would emerge between 1988-91 and toured Ireland. The original four members of Bagatelle would successfully reunite in 1992.

1990 and the start of a new decade saw Irish groups like the Saw Doctors, The Frames and The Hothouse Flowers take up the mantle of original Irish acts for a new era and generation.

The sickly-sweet manufactured sound of Stock, Aitken & Waterman which dominated the charts in the latter half of the eighties had given way to the emergence of dance music. Big hair, shoulder pads and heavy make-up (I'm only talking about the men here) of groups like Europe, Motley Crue and Van Halen had given way to Guns & Roses, Green Day and The Red Hot Chilli Peppers.

Grunge was a couple of years away and Rap and Hip-Hop began to dominate the music scene both at home in the UK and Stateside.

At home between 1990-1992 Irish acts to top the Irish charts included "The Fly" by U2, Sinead O' Connor's haunting rendition of Prince's "Nothing

Compares to You" and the Saw Doctors "I Useta Lover Her". However there was room for novelty hits like "Put 'Em Under Pressure" from the Republic of Ireland Football Squad, "The Christmas No.1" from Zig & Zag and Mick Lally's "The By-Road to Glenroe" , which spent five weeks at No.1, were proved to be annoyingly but extremely successful.

By 1992 Bagatelle, in one form or another, had clocked up 14 years as a band. No-one had toured harder and criss-crossed the country like the group, often playing the same venue twice in as many months.

However, by this point the success of former frontman Liam Reilly was about to eclipse the five-piece band by entering the most successful music competition that Europe, and arguably the world had ever seen. The Dundalk native was about to do something he could not achieve with Bagatelle. If the band had led a close but no cigar existence on the continent, Liam was about to experience both Heaven and Hell on the one night.

EIGHT

OH, CYPRUS WHAT HAVE YOU DONE?

"The Italian jury came on air, announced themselves as the Spanish jury and proceeded to give not a single point to Ireland, France or Iceland, who just so happened to be their closest rivals in the contest."

THE EUROVISION SONG CONTEST; 50 YEARS OFFICIAL HISTORY

Relaxing in Savannah, Georgia, Liam Reilly seemed a contented man. A break from Bagatelle. A chance to recharge the batteries. A period of time alone, far away from years of hectic travel and a chance to contemplate life, detached from what had gone before him – over a decade on the Rock & Roll roundabout.

At that point coming back into the Bagatelle fold seemed far off. Indeed, when Reilly did make his way back to these shores it was not to join or jam with Bagatelle, but to enter the 1990 National Song Contest as a solo artist with a view to going forward to the Eurovision.

The Eurovision Song Contest. Back in the day a serious singing competition that could lead to European if not worldwide success. A platform for a singer, songwriter, or group to perform at a competition that regularly gains a television audience of 600 million each May.

These days. It's a joke.

Though it seems far removed from the block voting, back scratching, mutual masturbation sessions of neighbouring countries voting for each other, there was a time when the Eurovision Song Contest was one of the most important, prestigious song contests on the face of the planet since its inception in 1956.

With the winner practically guaranteed fame and the fact Bagatelle had been overlooked on mainland Europe, Reilly set about trying to remedy that. Falling back on a trademark ballad Reilly entered the 1990 National Song Contest, hoping to take first place and represent Ireland in Zagreb that May.

His first bite of the cherry came in 1988 when he was a finalist in the National Contest. Ireland had returned from obscurity after Johnny Logan won the 1987 Eurovision in Brussels with "Hold Me Now" so with Ireland hosting the 1988 event it gave those competing in the National Contest that extra incentive to perform on home soil whilst a global audience watched on.

104

By then, despite leaving Bagatelle, Reilly's creative juices were still flowing. It would lead to writing yet another major hit for The Wolfe Tones in "Boston Rose."

"That came about when I was in the Mount Brandon playing at the Rose of Tralee festival. It just so happened the escort of the Boston rose came from Dublin and he was, let's say, very attentive to her! So, I was with Ken relaxing in the hotel and decided to go upstairs, took out my pen and basically wrote the song in just over an hour. I remember recording it on an old cassette tape recorder and always had the Wolfe Tones in mind. So, the next day me, Val and Dierdre (who owned Lombard Studios in Dublin) travelled to Tommy Byrne's pub in Rathcoole to see what he thought of it. It only took him 3 minutes to agree. "Yep, we'll definitely have that one Liam" came his very grateful reply!" **Liam Reilly**

So with the successful song-writing capabilities of Bagatelle's front man it was surely only a matter of time before the likely lad from the council estate in Fatima in Dundalk would chance his hand at the Eurovision where a decent tune (at the time) could win you the contest.

His 1988 entry was a tune called "Lifeline" but lost out to Jump the Gun's ballad "Take Him Home". As unlucky Reilly would have felt, the winning tune was superb from a group that would sadly vanish as quickly as their stardom came.

Disappointed but undeterred, Reilly would skip 1989 but come back with "Somewhere in Europe" and uplifting and clever ballad for the 1990 Nationals. Little did he know exactly where this would all lead. A period of heaven & hell about to be bestowed upon the Dundalk man's shoulders.

Ireland had a solid track record in the Eurovision which would go into overdrive with three back-to-back victories between 1992 and 1994. Linda Martin's "Why Me?", Niamh Kavanagh "In Your Eyes" and Paul Harrington & Charlie McGettigan singing Brendan Graham's composed "Rock & Roll Kids" had made Ireland the envy of Europe. We still hold the record number of wins – seven in total.

In a strange twist of fate Liam Reilly had actually been offered "Rock & Roll Kids", by Brendan Graham as a possible Eurovision entry but both parties couldn't reach an agreement regarding royalties. And so, went the chance of performing a song that utterly destroyed all the opposition in Dublin in 1994, amassing a record score of 226 and practically sealing victory at the halfway mark of all 25 countries!

These days it's ridiculed and practically a death-knell for any respectable singer or group to win. Case in point, established Brit/American group Katrina & The Waves, who won it for the UK in 1997 with "Love Shine A Light", didn't release a follow up single and broke up a year later.

The contest was due to take place in Zagreb in the former country of Yugoslavia. The year before in 1989 five-piece band Riva had just edged out English group Weather Report with their tune "Rock Me" – a decision that severely pissed off our friends across the water who had been overwhelming favourites coming into the competition.

Mind you the winners suffered that Eurovision hex – Riva broke up almost directly after the competition as the song failed to light up even the European Top 40.

The first step for Reilly was to win the National Song Contest.

That year he faced opposition from Linda Martin who went on to win the 1992 Eurovision with Johnny Logan's penned "Why Me?" in Sweden.

However, inspiration would come from a lost love and with that "Somewhere in Europe" was born.

"When I lived in Savannah, Georgia for a while I remember travelling from there to a friend of mine in Philadelphia who happened to own a recording studio and it was there, I met this German girl called Sylvia. She'd been married to an American GI but was now divorced. We spent some time together but alas it didn't work out. I spent a lot of time in America but after a while decided to come home. I remember being in Tommy Mangan's house, a good friend of mine and a fine musician, and had started this song about Sylvia. I had a few lyrics that went....

"Meet me in Paris on a Champs Élysées night
We could be in Rome again, 'neath the Trevi fountain light
We should be together, and maybe we just might
If you could only meet me somewhere in Europe tonight"

And Tommy was like *"Hold it one fucking minute there!"* He went out of the room then came back with one of those old reel to reel recorders, stuck it on top of the piano and said *"Now sing exactly like you did just there."* I did not see what the fuss was about at the time, but Tommy was persistent. A few weeks later I was told my song, which I called "Somewhere in Europe" had made the final of the National Song Contest. Little did I know it was Tommy who had sent off the recording." **Liam Reilly**

"Around the time of that Eurovision I was playing in a group called Allies and we had just won an Eastern Europe Song Contest that went out to around 500 million people. We had become very successful and toured that region, so I knew Liam's song had a fabulous chance of winning it. I just couldn't see it being beaten on the night." **Tommy Mangan**

The Eurovision Song Contest has been an ongoing part of history, for good or for bad (and it's certainly been bad over the last decade) since 1956 when the competition was held in Lugano, Switzerland with 14 countries taking part and the Netherlands winning that first competition.

Ireland had a love affair with the Eurovision ever since former Capital Showband crooner Butch Moore brought "Walking the Streets in The Rain" to sixth place in Naples when Italy staged the competition.

We had to wait until pretty little Dana Rosemary Scallon secured our first win in Amsterdam in 1970 with "All Kinds of Everything" – fending off our near neighbours across the water in the shape of Mary Hopkin and "Knock, Knock."

Ten years later, Sean Patrick Michael Sherrard masquerading under his stage name, Johnny Logan, brought us all to tears (at first) then elation with Shay Healy's beautiful winning ballad "What's Another Year". It should have set Johnny up for a long and fruitful career (it topped the charts in the UK, Sweden, Belgium, Norway and Ireland) but the machine broke down and it looked as if his fleeting fame would ultimately prove fickle. Redemption came along seven years later in the last chance saloon when Logan threw everything that he had into an unlikely second Eurovision win.

His second bite at the cherry proved just as sweet as "Hold Me Now" – with that brilliant lyric "What do you say when words are not enough" won handsomely that night in Belgium.

Eight songs lined up in the Gaiety in April 1990 for the National Song Contest. Linda Martin was the early favourite but The Memories entry "If It Means Losing You" was hotly tipped as well. When the time came for Liam Reilly, he approached his piano and produced a calm assured performance which saw him win out on the night.

Liam Reilly performs "Somewhere in Europe" which won the 1990 National Song Contest and the Bagatelle songwriter went forward to represent Ireland at that years Eurovision in Yugoslavia.

Another feather in the cap already full of so many feathers he could have a swan on his head. More importantly it brought the Bagatelle singer back into focus after several years of blurred vision after his hiatus from the group.

It also proved his knack for writing hit singles hadn't left him. Everyone knew Liam Reilly & Bagatelle coming into the competition and many were rooting for him to have a successful solo song in Europe, something he could not seem to achieve in his Bagatelle days.

With the Eurovision Song Contest came the inevitable pressure.

Ireland may have the record number of wins but there were also a lot of close calls to boot.

In 1984 Linda Martin took the Johnny Logan penned "Terminal 3" to second place, just edged out by 8 points by eventual winners' Swedish group Herrey's with a bland Buzz Fizz castoff. Acts like The Swarbrigg's, Colin T. Wilkinson and Luv Bug had all finished Top Five through the years. You could even go as far back as 1967 when Sean Dunphy finished second with "If I Could Choose". Ironically, he lost out to Sandie Shaw who Phil Coulter wrote "Puppet on a String" for. The Derry native had also written Ireland's 1965 entry "Walking the Streets in the Rain" for Butch Moore. It's still astonishing that "Congratulations" which Coulter penned with Bill Martin for Cliff Richard's 1968 UK Eurovision entry lost out to Spanish singer Massiel and her "La, La, La" song and its 457 "La, La La's" in the middle.

Devote Christian or not I'm sure Cliff let out a few expletives on the night over that one!

The Eurovision Song Contest was in the first week in May so there was a couple of weeks to ramp up the hype so that Liam could go there with a fighting chance.

There was no need.

Irish songs tended to be among the favourites each May when the contest took place, and this wouldn't be any different.

Paddy Power had immediately put Reilly's ode to a lost love at even money to finish first. Some foreign bookmakers followed suit. The Bagatelle singer's clever use of European cities in the song (Paris, London, Rome, Seville, Amsterdam) gave the song a real European flavour.

A wise move.

Over 600 million people would tune in on Saturday May 5th, 1990. Though rubbished and ridiculed by many it was still a ratings winner across the board.

"The Eurovision is a brilliant platform. If people want to criticise it, they should come up with a better alternative. I know the contest is bound to open lots of doors for me in Europe. If the song does half as well as "Summer in Dublin" we will certainly be in with a chance."
Liam Reilly in Evening Herald 20.4.1990

However, things nearly finished off the Irish entry before he even got to a piano.

A delayed flight in Dublin held up Reilly and the entire RTE delegation who were on route to Zagreb. They arrived to find themselves in hot water with the Yugoslav organisers who weren't in the least bit impressed.

The group's late arrival had won them few friends among the other competing countries, especially those who had to have their rehearsal timetable changed to fill the gap left by Liam's absence. They just about managed to do that, but the Yugoslav officials gave it both barrels when the Irish delegation finally arrived.

The fierce criticism the home officials had to endure upset everyone yet there was really nothing anyone from the Irish group could have done about it. On arrival the guys made for Nenad Puhovski the contest director to ask what time Liam Reilly's slot was only to see a line drawn over Reilly's name. *"We've only been here 12 hours and now I suppose we'll have to put Ireland on after the others"* sighed the director.

It was just past 10pm when Liam Reilly finally walked onto stage for his first rehearsal. There had been a series of technical hitches and orchestra problems which had added to the already tense situation. Liam just done his bit and walked away a tired man.

Rehearsals on the Thursday night, two days before the competition, went much better. Ireland filled their slot. Under the guidance of the conductor. the late Noel Kelehan, the song was performed without any last-minute hitches or fuss.

In his lifetime as a conductor the Dubliner (himself an accomplished jazz pianist) took charge of Irish Eurovision entries no less than 24 occasions. He had started way back in 1966 when Dickie Rock had represented Ireland with "Come Back To Stay" which finished fourth and would go on to conduct five of Ireland's Eurovision winners from 1970 , 1980, 1987, 1992, 1993 and 1996 (he missed 1994 as "Rock & Roll Kids" did not need an orchestra to accompany Paul Harrington & Charlie McGettigan.)

He retired from RTÉ as staff conductor in 2000, although he continued for some years after arranging and conducting. In 1984 he had even written the string arrangements for U2's album *The Unforgettable Fire*.

Sadly, Noel passed away in 2012 after a long illness aged 76.

22 countries were under starters orders on Saturday May 5th, 1990. All chomping at the bit to get going. It would also be the year of a change to the rules. The Eurovision Song Contest in 1990 was the first to implement an age rule.

The European Broadcasting Union (EBU) were forced to bring in a restriction rule after criticism arose over the ages of two performers at the 1989 contest, being just 11 and 12 years old. From 1990 no artist under the age of 16 could perform on stage. This rule meant that the record for the youngest ever winner at Eurovision could never be broken, as Sandra Kim, who won for Belgium at the 1986 competition, was just 13 years old. The 1990 contest was the first to feature an official mascot, Eurocat, created by Joško Marušić. This mischievous purple cat popped up during the 'postcards' of each of the 22 entries much to the annoyance of everyone. "I wish that fucking cat was put down" my father remarked.

I covered the ears of our black kitten Choo Choo so she didn't hear those horrific words.

A notorious mishap occurred at the start of the very first song, when the backing track used by Spain's Azucar Moreno failed to start. When it eventually started up the music was out of synch with his words. He then walked off the stage much to the rage of the audience who were totally confused. They restarted the song and despite such a complete balls-up he still finished fifth!

Not a way to start a long night in Zagreb.

Ireland were drawn out to perform 17th of the 22 songs. A slight advantage as the tune would be fresh in people's minds, or maybe performed too late after a string of solid songs depending which way you look at it.

Of the performers that night in Yugoslavia, Liam Reilly was one of the most experienced. The real competition was expected to come from the French entry "White and Black Blues" a song performed by black dancer, model and actress Joelle Ursull and penned by the legendary Serge Gainsbourg of "Je t'aime" notorious fame. This track was not as filthy as Serge's 1969 classic and despite the English title the song was sung in French. Had she won Ursull would have been the first black singer to win the competition. Others expected to do well included Israel, Cyprus and last but not least Portugal who made an impression of the wrong kind.

"The Portuguese effort was 'Ha Sempre Alguem' (There's Always Someone) sung by the sultry Nucha. It wasn't a ground-breaking effort and Nucha had made a poor choice in costume, wearing black cycling shorts under a short black velvet dress. She walked back and forth on the stage giving the impression that something was preventing her from standing still"
The Eurovision Song Contest: 50 years Official History

Above: Toto Cutugno who represented Italy. Despite being a rank outsider at 33/1 (and an awful song to boot) the Italian won the 1990 Eurovision Song Contest, along with some very questionable voting on the night.

After all the 22 acts had been seen and re-capped on Television we got down to the serious stuff – the voting. Liam, whose parents, and Sylvia whom "Somewhere in Europe" was written about, were in the audience bedded in for a night of nerves.

Ireland started with a bang, collecting 10 points from the Spanish jury – the first country to announce their results. Only one nation could gain the maximum 12 points and that went to Italy's Toto Cutugno.

Toto was a major star in his own country and his song 'Insieme 1992' (All Together 1992) was dedicated to the EU. It was an average song that did not impress much in the previews or rehearsals but took maximum points from that first jury.

Ireland scored well with the next five jury's (Greece, Belgium, Turkey, the Netherlands, and Luxembourg) and we got all giddy as we led at the halfway point.

So far so good.

One of the battles we always liked was finishing ahead of the old enemy across the water. 500 years of fighting with each other still extended to besting the UK in a song contest, much to the annoyance of Terry Wogan who gleefully called Ireland "them" while having a near orgasm when the United Kingdom picked up maximum points.

Fair play to them though. They gave us 10 points.

We gave them six.

As the voting from every other country came through, "Somewhere in Europe" consistently picked up points: a minimum of 5, a maximum of

12. By now the nation (though most wouldn't like to admit) was glued to RTE. Could we win it?

Would Liam Reilly join Dana and Johnny Logan as the only other Irish winners of this event?

Coming into the last five jury's Italy were a mere six points ahead of France with Ireland back a further two points. Iceland and the UK were a distant 4th and 5th (stop crying Terry – your country lost) and it was tighter than Rod Stewart's wallet as we headed into the final furlong.

The temperature backstage rose considerably when Sweden gave Ireland the maximum 12 points and France only 5.

Then something extraordinary and controversial happened.

The Italian jury came on air, announced themselves as the SPANISH jury, and proceeded to give NULL POINTS to Ireland, France and Iceland, who just so happened to be their closest rivals in the race. The maximum 12 points went incredibly to Austria who were back in tenth place.

Smell a rat? I smell a whole bag of them that stunk so bad it's like they had been eating garlic and suffering from halitosis!

Only three countries remained after that. Italy's backstabbing job had done the damage keeping Toto on top.

The third last jury was Austria.

Italy gathered 7 points from the Austrians, but Adolf Hilter's native country gave us the full 12. Now it was Italy 129 points. Ireland 128.

One single point separated the two of us with Iceland making a late run on 117 though France were just four points back on 113.

And then came Cyprus.

And with it a vote by a country I have vowed never to talk about (except here), learn about or even visit. Cyprus, with their entry on 30 points well out of contention , a country who have produced not a single artist on a single week on a singles chart in the UK or USA and probably every other member of the EU somehow became only the third country, along with Yugoslavia and of course Italy, that gave Ireland the dreaded "NULL POINTS".

Italy in contrast got the full 12 points.

It put the Italians 13 points ahead of Ireland.

Even if Liam Reilly had received 12 points and Toto Cutugno zero, from Finland, the last jury to vote, Italy still had it in the bag. As it turned out, Finland gave the Bagatelle man 4 points and Italy 8. France came with a late run and would tie with Ireland for second place.

If my blood was boiling, how did Liam Reilly, Noel Kelehan, the Irish contingent and the other three million people in the Emerald Isle feel?

The final scoreboard made for heart-breaking viewing.

Italy 149 points.
Ireland & France 132 points.
So close but yet so far.
Fuck you from a height Cyprus.

"It was a controversial night for sure. At the time each jury was only allowed to announce their votes in English or Spanish, yet the Italian jury spoke in Italian and there were some very strange voting patterns. However, it was RTE that cost me the victory in the end. They would give Toto the maximum 12 points which in the end gave Italy the victory. I thought I had it in the bag. When it was over, I sought out Toto and congratulated him, he was delighted despite a heap of Grecian 2000 running out of his hair!" **Liam Reilly**

It had been a major surprise for the 33/1 rank outsider to win the 1990 Eurovision Song Contest. A real rarity.

But the story didn't end there. The French delegation made a formal protest about that strange Italian voting and the fact their jury introduced themselves as the Spanish jury.

Toto himself had arrived with five backing singers who didn't even know the words to the song! So much so during the first rehearsal the backing singers arrived on stage and read the lyrics from a few sheets of paper.

Unknown to Liam and his entourage there was probably a huge sigh of relief breathed back in Dublin. Rumours had been rife before the competition that the powers that be were absolutely terrified "Somewhere in Europe" would win the Eurovision then Ireland would have to host a competition they had no money for!

When asked about the contest coming to Ireland Executive Producer of the show Liam Miller said "RTE will first have to consider if it's going to stage the contest."

It was a half-truth in fairness as in reality, as much as it would have set the organisers back, plans had been made just in case Liam Reilly came out on top of the 22-country pack. One of the ideas put forward was hosting the contest at Pairc Ui Chaoimh in Cork, making it the first open air Eurovision Song Contest ever. Thankfully, the organisers remembered we get around two hours of sunshine in May and almost four weeks of rain so that idea was squashed. It may have meant a few thousand more people could fit inside the venue but also the risk of electrocution on a stage from the monsoon that would have poured relentlessly from the sky.

Cork would finally come into contention when Millstreet hosted the 1993 contest, an event that had an even closer finish than Zagreb 1990 with Niamh Kavanagh winning on the very last vote to pip United Kingdom's entry, Sonia with "Better the Devil You Know."

That made it a wee bit sweeter!

Despite the defeat Liam Reilly and gang arrived home to a tumultuous reception from family fans and friends at Dublin Airport. Disappointed but not downhearted the 35-year-old knew "Somewhere in Europe" could well chart in Europe and was already planning a return to the continent to cash in on his newly acquired international status.

There would be a private reception in Billingham Castle in Dundalk where Liam and the entourage partied into the early hours.

If they were disappointed, they sure did not show it.

By that stage the single was on heavy turntable rotation from RTE Radio One to 2FM and a multitude of local radio stations in between as "Somewhere in Europe" had just been released. It came into the Irish charts in late May, peaking at No.6 and staying in the Top Ten for another month or so.

Ironically, the song was stopped from getting any further up the charts by two homegrown songs in "Give It a Lash Jack" by Liam Harrison and "The Game" by The Memories.

The Eurovision bug caught hold of Reilly again just a year after his close call in Zagreb.

This time the Dundalk man would just compose the song and left the singing duties to Kim Jackson for the 1991 Irish National Song Contest.

"Could It Be That I'm In Love", performed by Jackson, was another trademark Reilly ballad that had entered the song contest as favourite in the 1991 search for an Irish star to compete in that year's Eurovision which was of course taking place in Rome.

Jackson had started her early career as backing vocalist with some of Ireland's most successful cabaret groups and was a backing vocalist on "Somewhere in Europe" in 1990.

On the night "Could It Be That I'm In Love" took the honours, finishing first. It would pip another singer named Reilly (Brian Reilly to be exact) and his effort "Too Many Questions" which came a close second.

So off on his travels went Liam, Kim, backing singers and the whole entourage to Rome to try go one better than their 1990 controversial heartbreak.

Despite a lot of hype, the song was never a frontrunner for the top prize on the night, finishing eleventh of 22 songs on 47 points with good old Luxembourg giving us 8 points on the night – the biggest score from a European country. The 1991 contest was eventually won by Yugoslavian Bebi Dol and her song "Brazil."

The show was also notable for an absolutely awful attempt at hosting the event by none other than Toto Cutugno, winner in 1990. The Italian made headlines for all the wrong reasons and as I watched that night on television, I couldn't help but smile.

"Toto was joined by Italy's only other ever Eurovision winner, Gigliola Cinquetti, and let's just say none of them were best equipped for the task in hand. One of the many problems was that Toto seemed unable to speak any other language than Italian, nor did any of the duo appear to have any concept of the contest, it's rules or format!"
The Eurovision Song Contest – 50 years Official History

However, this would give the Dundalk man a new lease of creative freedom. Not that he was shackled down in lead weights when performing with Bagatelle. A new album of fresh material followed as Liam went back into the studio. The newfound solo success saw Reilly pen *Throwing Caution to The Wind* , a first ever solo collection of his material.

The album contained a couple of old Bagatelle classics along with "Somewhere in Europe" but also new original tracks like "She Doesn't Live Here Anymore", "Savannah Serenade" and the Gerry Ryan favourite "Bainbridge Avenue".

"What a truly great song Bainbridge Avenue is. Let's be honest. If that had been written by someone like Bruce Springsteen it would have been a worldwide hit. **"Gerry Ryan**

The song would again tap into the story of emigration, so relevant to the Republic at the time. Songs like "The Streets of New York" and "The Flight of Earls" had been the first two tunes by Liam to sing about the masses that left Ireland for work in America in a decade of eighties depression, unemployment and rising dole queues. "Banbridge Avenue" became as popular as it's two predecessors in bars in Boston, New York and San Francisco. It remains so to this day. By penning these hits, it gave the hard-working Irish stateside a reminder of their identity at home everywhere from Cork to Cavan, or Dublin to Donegal.

A second single, the title track "Throwing Caution to the Wind" charted in the Irish Top 20 and kept O'Reilly firmly in the spotlight. The decision to cut away from Bagatelle, possibly for

the future had now looked to be a wise choice. In the end the album would sell around 10,000 copies – a decent return for the Dundalk crooner.

The album had got some serious airtime. Phil Hadaway would produce the album which saw the experience of Robbie Brennan, Davy Spillane, Paul Ashford and Robbie Overson also in the studio.

The inevitable tour followed. It would kick off the first day of June in 1990 and Reilly was backed by an experienced set of musicians. The cream of the Irish crop. They included Noel Bridgeman on drums (he had worked with Mary Black and Christy Moore). Tony Davis on vocals and acoustic guitar (Freddie White, Paul Brady and Moving Hearts.) Backing vocalist Mandy Murphy (Mary Coughlan), Eoghan O' Neill on bass (Chris Rea,

Van Morrison) and Liverpudlian Graham Kin on keyboards who backed the legendary Gary Moore and American music director and lead guitarist John Banks who Liam had met in Savannah, Georgia.

"Liam Reilly has written many fine songs and his new album is no exception. It's an album recorded in Dublin and the USA with some of the finest musicians who could be collected from both places. It's also something of a Greatest Hits collection with songs like "Trump Card", "Second Violin" and "Flight of the Earls" included and his Eurovision effort "Somewhere in Europe" which was so unlucky to have won. It includes a nice couple of old standards in "Moon River" and aptly the old Hoagy Carmichael track "Georgia on my Mind". **Eamon Holmes Meath Chronicle 15.12.1990**

"A new album and a new beginning for the former Bagatelle man. And it's an accomplished affair. Already reports from the live circuit suggests that Liam's band is creating a stir, similar to the one that greeted Bagatelle over a decade ago." **Evening Herald 29.11.90**

This would lead to some confusion with promoters around the country wanting to book Reilly. For those not up on the recent history of Bagatelle most still thought the Dundalk man was still part of the group. The fact that he had achieved this newfound success whilst not sharing the stage with Messrs O'Brien, McConville and Doyle should have been indication enough.

People began to wonder was this Liam O'Reilly charging down the road alone against the rest of the world and would Bagatelle ever again feature their main man?

It would be another two years before we got that answer.

Above, A whole host of tickets through the years. Bagatelle would often play three tours in the same year during the early eighties. If there was a town you lived in, chances are the group have probably played there.
Middle photograph on ticket copyright of Dave Keegan photography.

Top: Bagatelle receive an Irish World Award for their services to music.
Middle left; Ken Doyle relaxing in his home studio in Bray. Middle Right:
"All Fall Down Philadelphia" which the band released in 1984. Below, Group
portrait from 1983; photography by Peter Ashworth.

Above, Bagatelle at JFK Airport as Ken shows off his extremely relaxed attire complete with pink vest. Middle; Bagatelle with Dr. Hook lead vocalist Dennis Locorriere. Below, Number One with a bullet. *Bagatelle Gold* keeps Springsteen, Dire Straits and Madonna off the top of the Irish album charts. Take that U2 and Bryan Adams!

1. Gold .... Bagatelle
2. Born in the USA............................ Bruce Springsteen
3. Brothers in Arms...................................... Dire Straits
4. The Kenny Rogers Story
5. Like a Virgin .... Madonna
6. Piece and Tranquility .... Phil Coulter
7. After All These Years..................... Foster and Allen
8. The Best of the Eagles
9. The Unforgetable Fire U2

10. Reckless.. Brian Adems

Bagatelle triumph at Ballsbridge

SOUNDS

"Bagatelle's" Album For International Release

DUBLIN-based band, "Bagatelle", have just returned from a month in England, where they were recording their first album for Polygram Records. They went to England in late January, played a few gigs in London and then moved into Parkgate Studios in Hastings and actually lived in the studio while they laid down twelve original most played discs on radio during the last three months of 1979. Although it received no chart success it was rated by many of the prominent disc jockeys as the best quality single release by an Irish band in that year. Their next single will be released within the next six weeks in the U.K. with concurrent releases in Canada, Scandinavia, Germany, and

Bagatelle Will Remember This Summer In The West!

Bagatelle and U2 aim for tops with top promotion

BOTH Polygra
spend a vast a
Bagatelle and
So over the ne
pushed with t
BBC network h

Bagatelle for Caesar's Palace Friday

BAGATELLE SELLOUT

BAGATELLE ARE BACK

Bagatelle (remember them) are back again with a new single and a new album. And to coincide with these new releases, the band are going on a nationwide tour and will play Glentarne on Saturday, July 27th.

and you should hear a lot more of the group in the coming months.

In early '79 John O'Brien, Liam Reilly, Ken Doyle and Wally Mc Conville joined forces to form a band called Bagatelle.

Within days of the announcement, all venues were completely sold out. Producer Gus Dudgeon, who became renowned for producing hits for David Bowie and Elton John, got involved with the Band and produced

Above; Bagatelle with TV presenter Gerry Kelly receiving another platinum disc award backstage before the Gerry Kelly Show.

Above; Liam Reilly and Ken Doyle being presented with an Outstanding Achievement to Irish Music award by Emer Costello, then Lord mayor of Dublin in August 2009. Picture copyright of Dave Keegan Photography. Bottom; Bagatelle manager Jim McQullian and a sold-out Bagatelle show in The Irish Times Pub, Los Angeles.

POP SCENE

BAGATELLE IRELAND'S NUMBER ONE

In a period of just under two year emerged from obscurity, and h leading attraction, with sell-out co selling records. Now the four-pie major international promotion Records, in a bid to win their nev Violin' a place in the coveted alongside Thin Lizzy, Undertones, Fingers.

BAGATELLE MAKE IT BIG

IN LESS than 2 years Bagatelle have established ~~themselves~~ as the country's top attraction. Their ...... ~~D~~ublin," has now sold over ...... p Card," "Second Violin" ...... ove Is The Reason" have ...... ost familiar, most popular ...... t band in Ireland.

Big break for Bagatelle

A STU week. F most pr the Ir moment Atlantic have br fashions vear's o

BAGATELLE PLAY THEIR TRUMP CARD

THE RELEASE of their debut album "Bagatelle," featuring ten of their self-composed numbers, had the effect of catapulting the four musicians in this unique group, Bagaelle, to stardom. Formed in mid-~~1070~~ ....

BAGATELLE TO SPREAD THEIR WINGS ...

BAGATELLE must have been the first major Irish rock band to break through the deathly showband monopoly of Irish dance halls and bring their message to almost every green filed of this island.

NINE

AND THEN THERE WERE THREE

"I think we are a bit like Corn Flakes. We are in nearly every Irish household. Everyone knows us but nobody raves about us. A bit like flared trousers. If you hang around long enough you will come back in fashion."

KEN DOYLE

1990 had proved an extremely productive year for Liam Reilly. It had started with his European Odyssey, a solo album and in December 1990 he was presented with one of the Bank of Ireland/Rehab People of the Year Awards for his success the past 12 months.

Over in the Bagatelle camp things were to change.

By 1991 Derek Jordan, who had taken over vocal duties, had left and there was a period of inactivity for the group with others leaving. It had been a number of years since Bagatelle had bothered the Irish Singles Chart but there was always the "reunion" word floating about the Irish music scene. With nobody within the Bagatelle or Liam Reilly camp making a move, it was down to someone else to take the proverbial bull by the horns and set things in motion.

This came in the shape of Mr. Brian Finley.

Brian, who had been part of the successful Mighty Avons Showband felt it was time to see all four of the original members of Bagatelle get back together again. Finley was the drummer with the showband who had been a huge draw on the showband circuit of the sixties and seventies when they made their name along with bands like the Royal Showband, Clipper Carlton, Butch Moore & the Capitol Showband, Joe Dolan & the Drifters and The Blue Aces to name but a few.

The Avons original line up was Larry Cunningham (vocals), Ronnie Griffiths (keyboards & guitar), Gerry Walsh (bass), Mick Brady (guitar) and Finley on drums. Finley would contact Bagatelle's manager Peter Smith to set the wheels in motion.

"Brian had the vision of the original Bagatelle back together again. At the time he was in Blackrock Clinic after a triple by-pass operation! That's how determined he was to get us back on stage! I knew him from The Mighty Avons of course. At that point I had the Eurovision and an album under my belt but was practically doing nothing by 1992 and neither

were the original members of the band, so Brian saw an opportunity I suppose. It took a while to get us to all sit down and decide where we would go from here.

Would we do an album? Could we put out a new single? Would people turn up to see us? Strangely at that point I had written a lot of songs if needed. We went back to the original Bagatelle formula if you like, which was writing from an Irish perspective for Irish people abroad and anyone willing to listen to our original material." **Liam Reilly**

"Brian came up with this concept of getting "the boys back on stage" in his own words. It took a bit of bargaining and a few arguments but basically it ended up working. Maybe on some level we were always going to have the original four members back, but Brian is the one you must credit, along with Peter Smith who managed the band at that point." **Ken Doyle**

John O'Brien felt he was between a rock and a hard place. He had felt very isolated but was willing to give the reunion a go as was Wally McConville. The plan worked. Bagatelle agreed to reform with the original four members, 14 years after coming together in tiny 100 Sugarloaf Crescent in Bray way back in 1978.

Sadly, Brian Finley, one of the last surviving members of the Mighty Avons, passed away in December 2002.

"You know we are all very different to each other and we have only really one thing in common and that's Bagatelle. It's a big thing to have in common. Huge. It's like we're married to each other, indeed it's like a four-way marriage. I'm sure there's a French word for what we are doing! We don't always get on well about everything, but we do regarding Bagatelle. I mean we don't like the same things, eat the same food, love the same music, don't have the same hobbies, so when we are not Bagatelle, we are completely different. Somehow it works." **John O'Brien**

Getting the fab four back together wasn't exactly smooth sailing. They had come off the road as a successful unit in 1988, tired of touring in Doyle's and Reilly's case, while the three replacements for them (Derek Jordan, Martin Byrne and Paul Finlay) were no longer part of the plan. However, the enthusiasm that Brian Finley had projected to the proposal meant that the original Bagatelle of Liam Reilly, Ken Doyle, John O'Brien and Wally McConville, agreed to reunite again for the first time in over 4 years.

Despite being seasoned professionals, there was still a healthy dose of pre-gig nerves in the dressing room before their sold-out reunion gig in the Spa Hotel in Lucan.

Would the crowd come?
Would they remember the songs?
Would they be happy with the old line up?
They went on stage and came off it more than two hours later after a standing ovation and three encores. Bagatelle was back.

"Yes, I was a bit apprehensive about us getting back together but when we did the band were playing better than ever. Of course, then we wondered would anybody know or remember us and our songs? So, we went out on stage in the Spa Hotel in Lucan. The place was absolutely jammed with people who knew the songs better than we did! And that was fine because we were rusty and struggled to remember half of them ourselves!" **Ken Doyle**

The group had an extremely successful reunion and kept touring in 1993. Brian Finley also coaxed the guys back into the studio, feeling new material should be recorded to go in tandem with the old classics. The result would be a new compilation album, this time under the Universal label who backed the band when needed and an inevitable new tour.
The result was *The Best of Bagatelle & Liam Reilly*, released late 1993 and sold well.
Among the new tracks was "If You Ever Come Back from England", a lush Liam Reilly ballad which could easily have represented Ireland in the Eurovision. The song tells of a heartbroken man in the West of Ireland whose love went to England for a week but never came back.
In truth the story had been told to Liam over a few drinks in a Dublin pub. The story of leaving Ireland, emigration and losing a loved one which obviously struck a chord with the Bagatelle ballad-master. After all wasn't that what Ireland in the eighties and nineties was all about?
By now Bagatelle would be guided by the hand of Jim McQuillan, who took up the job of managing the group after Peter Smith had left.

"I got a call out of the blue from Liam Reilly to see if I would be interested in looking after the band. We met for a coffee at the Rosnaree Hotel in Drogheda and basically that was it. I've been hooked ever since! Obviously, I was well aware of Bagatelle and their great music, how successful they were and what they had achieved so to get the offer to get involved in their management at this point something that really interested me" **Jim McQuillan**

Jim saw it as quite an honour to be asked on board but also a huge challenge. Though the group wasn't charting as regularly as they did in their 1980's heyday, Bagatelle were still one of Ireland's most popular touring bands. The back catalogue was enough at this point for the group

to fall back on but that didn't mean people were tired of hearing their hits. The phrase "For One Night Only" or "Coming to a place by you this weekend" seemed to have been made for Bagatelle.
The band became accessible on a global scale.

"Since I came on board (26 years ago this year) I've been involved with six of the group's albums, five of their anniversaries (20,25,30,35 & 40ᵗʰ) plus their "Final Year" Tour and multiple tours to places like Dubai, Riyadh, Abu Dhabi, Macau, England, Scotland, Wales, Isle of Man and all parts of the United States. There have been a lot of awards for the group which included ones from The Irish Post, Sunday World, Irish World, Irish Voice, UTV, IMRO, the Late Late Show and even the NYPD (which was for "The Streets of New York") But awards-wise IMRO was probably the most momentous – in that they organised a special event at the IMRO Headquarters in Dublin to celebrate Bagatelle's "40 years of original music." It was a very special occasion.

I have seen so many unreal changes in the business – marketing, social media, downloads, "All You Can Eat", €9 per month, and "Look if it's a group rate you want how about €15 per month and you can bring as many as you want! And so, royalties have virtually disappeared for songwriters, to the point where some bands or artists have given up writing altogether or have given their albums away online for free! That's how bad its got from a writers point of view. In that respect the music biz has turned on its head. Bands used to tour (sometimes at a loss) to promote sales of their albums. Now it's gone in reverse. Bands are releasing albums to promote tours. That said, it's still a great and interesting business. Mad, crazy but always great and interesting. But don't go into it unless you love music. Don't go into it for the money only."
Jim McQuillan

"We were delighted when Jim came in. One thing he had done was to "clean us up" when we went on stage. I'll admit I can be a scruffy bastard and didn't put too much thought into what I would wear at the time, offstage or on it for that matter! And to be honest to an extent I couldn't give a toss but when Jim came onboard, he recommended change. I listened to him, got where he was coming from, despite the years of touring and wearing what we wanted.
The way we look and perform, our presentation on stage now is all down to Jim. When I am not with Bagatelle I can on occasion revert to comfortably scruffy! **Ken Doyle**

Reunion or not, 14 years put back together, Bagatelle would still have their critics. Some saw the reunion as simply a money maker in the way that some bands regroup, go on tour, make a million then go back into relative obscurity safe in the knowledge their finances are looked after for the future. For the Sex Pistols see The Police, The Eagles etc.

"The crowds were amazing, but we always had the odd hiccup! I remember we did a gig in Borris, County Offaly and I don't think we even got 100 people in the place. It was in the arse end of nowhere and to make it worse, it was an awful night out. The owner sort of had a whip around and came up to us with a few bags of coins!" **Ken Doyle**

Liam Reilly & The Best of Bagatelle brought the group back into the Irish Album Charts (number 9 to be exact) and sold well. Ken took a while to come around to dressing properly.

"You Know I remember a time when I was working on the house up to a few minutes before a local gig and arrived at the venue and hopped up on stage looking like something the cat dragged in. I remember we played one night in Lurgan. I had been working solid at home all that Saturday and hopped in the van half full of cement and coffee, hair going in 50 different directions and I arrived at the venue having completely forgotten to pack a fresh set of clothes! There was a girl called Miriam who was manager of the hotel and she was mortified at the way I looked. "Come up to my room and we'll try to sort you out" she said and somehow, she managed to come across a pair of jeans two sizes too small for me and a t-shirt for me to wear. It was only when I got out on stage and saw the spotlight beaming on me that the jeans, well let's say it showed off my package in full glare! I had to use the bass constantly to try hide it from the crowd. Talk about embarrassing! Miriam was later to become one of the management team at the Carrickdale Hotel in Dundalk and became a great friend of Bagatelle before she passed away. RIP Miriam Callan." **Ken Doyle**

One thing that had a profound effect on the group around this time had been the murder of a young two-year-old child called James Bolger from Kirby in Merseyside. He had been abducted from the New Strand Shopping Centre on the 12th of February 1993 by Robert Thompson and Jon Venables and brutally murdered on a railway line 4 kilometres away in nearby Walton where his body was found two days later.
Thompson and Venables were charged on February 20th with Bulger's abduction. They were found guilty on 24 November 1993, making them the youngest convicted murderers in modern English history.
The case struck a chord with the band , so much so, the group put forward

their single "Cry Away The Night", a song written in 1987 but actually about the passing of one of the band members nephews, as a single that any proceeds and royalties from it would go towards the James Bolger Memorial Appeal. A press conference was set up with the Mayor of Liverpool at the time to announce this.

"James Bolger's death had such an effect on the whole of the United Kingdom that the only way they could identify with the grief of the Bolger family was to send money which they did to the Merseyside police and the Mayor's office in Knowsley. It was because of this that the James Bolger Memorial Appeal was founded.
I understand that the song "Cry Away the Night" by the Irish rock ballad band Bagatelle was written and composed when one of the band members was mourning the death of his young nephew. I want to thank the band for their generosity in donating the record because originally it wasn't their intention as I understand to release the song, but the sentiment and the tragic death of James Bolger had an influence on the band, so they eventually did. I trust that not only the people on Merseyside but of the whole country will support this venture so that the children of Northwood Kirby in Knowsley will be the ultimate beneficiaries."
Mayor of Liverpool Francis McWilliams

With the reunion long behind them at this point, old habits began to creep in and soon there would be arguments and an air of tension, particularly when it came to Liam and Wally. Those long hours on the road, tired eyes and weary bodies were par for the course for any band that wanted to make it. If you didn't put the hours in, you could go back to practicing in your mum's garage. It just wouldn't work. There were also egos to keep in check. Bagatelle proved no different to those who had come before or after them.
There had been a few differences of opinion when Bagatelle decided to reform in 1992 with their original four members and by 1994, they would come to the surface. All the success in the world means nothing if you can't perform as a group on stage. The dynamic shifts from what you're performing to who you are performing with. A quarter of the original Bagatelle was about to leave.
It had been obvious to the band Liam and Wally just were not seeing eye to eye and tensions were right at the surface when they played on stage. Eventually the clash of personalities between Reilly and McConville would lead to the latter leaving the band after a gig in The Everyman Theatre in Cork where a heated argument meant the point of no return.

Wally had been such an integral part of Bagatelle, not only through his drumming but his song-writing credentials. It would be the last time the original four members would ever play together. Sadly, it remains that way.

"It became obvious to me that Liam was getting less and less happy with Wally. I think we could all see that. I mean you spend so much time on stage, gigging maybe 3 or 4 times a week during our most commercial times. Despite their differences we had gigs to play, obligations to the venues, promoters, and the fans. We knew life had to go on unfortunately." **Ken Doyle**

Drink had also become an issue. In a world of songs, sound-checks and success it proved inevitable the demon would at some point rear its ugly head.

"Drink? Yes. Let's be honest. That was always there. Always in the background. This wasn't your regular 9-5 job. Drink doesn't come into the equation when you're clocking in and clocking out. But this was the lifestyle. We weren't any different to any other successful band who'd been on the road touring almost constantly. It can cost you a lot. I've learned that harsh lesson over time." **Liam Reilly**

"I was very selective about drink. I liked a glass of red wine which is and has been my staple for quite a few years now. I often think had Napoleon won instead of Arthur Wellesley (the Duke of Edinburgh) we would have been drinking red wine, eating garlic and had a Mediterranean diet. No World War One or Two and our greeting would have been "Bonjour" instead of "Hello." Twists of fate. I also loved gin & tonic. I'd put five gin & tonics into a pint glass and save the bother of going back up to the bar! Add a few slices of orange and you might as well be in the tropics with that concoction. The roadies would join us after the gigs to unwind and we had some wild memorable unwinding nights with them. **Ken Doyle**

"We gigged but there wasn't much pressure on us. Not after the success we had. So, after gigs we'd just relax and get drunk. I can even remember what we were drinking after every gig (which is sort of sad.) And we used to put our spirits in pint glasses. Ken drank gin, but also loved Pernod and white, while I always liked Gin & Tonic. We were really putting it away. One drink would become two, then three. We just didn't stop. Pint glasses of Gin or Pernod should have been a wakeup call, but we just did not care. It was easy to pass it off as part of the lifestyle." **John O'Brien**

Despite this, in Ken Doyle the group had the glue who would have to keep the band together. Doyle became the bands spokesman, a job he does so brilliantly to this day (If there's a better PR guy that also plays bass in a band, I've yet to meet him) and the job of piecing everything together was supposed to fall to him.

That didn't mean that the road wasn't taking a toll on the band's bass player of 16 years. Living a Rock & Roll lifestyle was something his wife Ann had to adapt to and there were many heart to heart talks down the end of a phone line after a gig in Newbridge or Newry between Ken and Ann. Many "I Miss You Honey" but no time together between the couple proved hard on the heart.

Despite the departure of Wally McConville, Bagatelle made a surprise return to the Irish charts with an old well-loved number – the first time they had a hit with the same song twice. That was because "Summer in Dublin" was re-released, going back into the Irish charts in the summer of 1994, 14 years after its original release. It climbed as far as number 18 and stayed in the top 20 for 5 weeks. Astonishingly it would chart again in 2013 but more on that later.

The fact it had been voted the third most popular song in this country's rich musical history is testament to the band. "Summer in Dublin" may have been their first big hit but even back then it seemed to have cemented its place in Ireland's musical folklore.

"Yes, it's lovely to be remembered in such a nice way. The first time I was ever in a studio is when we recorded the song and our first album. In fact, we did the album in just five days on a budget that wouldn't bring us to the pub for a couple of drinks now! The version of "Summer in Dublin" that you heard in 1994 was not the original recording as we re-recorded it eight years ago around 1986. We done it because it was an experiment to record the same song in a better production atmosphere. We still felt better than ever before and have a wee bit more energy than a new band because of it. I say that because we've worked so hard at our craft and whatever we have now is very valuable." **Liam Reilly**

With Wally McConville departed Bagatelle didn't immediately recruit a full-time drummer and buoyed by the success of "Summer in Dublin" they released "The Beer & The Bible" another Celtic themed song in the mould of "The Streets of New York" and "Flight of the Earls."

This would also get the attention of *Hot Press*.

"The title may have indicated an alcohol-sudden-death-and-redemption ballad, but this is anything but. Despite a lilting melody and dextrous backing, this occupies an uneasy halfway point between Shane McGowan and Daniel O'Donnell" **Hot Press**

"I remember Hot Press not so long ago featuring Boyzone on their front cover. Now there's commercialism for you. They had been good to us in the early years, and we were grateful but somewhere along the line we seemed to fall out of favour. Maybe because we had a large audience base, they felt we didn't need them. Who knows?" **Ken Doyle**

Myles Drennan was placed with the responsibility of taking over from Wally McConville. It would be a role he would play for a number of years with the band as Bagatelle tried to make the progression from McConville's 14 years as seamless as possible.

Having extensively toured Ireland every year with trips to the UK and Europe thrown in, Bagatelle began to tour America with great success. In the early days the group had played naval bases abroad long before the height of their fame. Now the group were a household name and loved on the other side of the Atlantic as well. Their gigs in America were extremely popular. At one point the lads spent seven months solid touring from the east to west coast. In 1994 their tour coincided with Jack Charlton's Republic of Ireland side who had qualified for the World Cup tournament which was being held Stateside. And boy did they pack them in!

"America was fun. We would tour from Seattle to San Francisco, St Louis to Sacramento and always draw a good crowd. Our Irish connection meant we always got a great turn out from the Irish diaspora in America. We could tour there for months and make a small fortune. I remember one morning I went out to get some milk but realised I had about 75 cent in my pocket when I got to the store. So, I saw a nearby pub that had a piano. In I went, sang "The Cliffs of Dooneen" and "The Fields of Athenry" half a dozen times and made 375 dollars! It was so far removed from the first time we had played America in the eighties. We stayed at this horrible hotel on West 46th Street. We were trying to make a name for ourselves. This was long before "The Streets of New York" and success like that. John Woods, God bless him, had an emergency cash fund of 100 dollars. That's how threadbare it was for us at the time." **Liam Reilly**

"We got used to staying over in lovely hotels during our time in America. We were always very well looked after. It makes you grateful as you remember those days of travelling six hours from Dublin to Cork cross country in our battered little Ford Transit van and getting paid very little – in some cases the owners of the pubs we played having a whip round for us. I can laugh at it now but at the time I think we were like - Jesus, this isn't exactly the glamorous life of a rock & roll band is it? Success changed that and paid for us spending half a year in America, selling out venues to people who knew our music and even those that didn't who came along to see what all the fuss was about. You're humbled by that,

the same way we are humbled to have played all over the world and still together 42 years later."
Ken Doyle

"We would play places like the Irish Embassy in Saudi Arabia. In fact, we played there twice! We would get invited to play in many an Irish Embassy around the world. Most of our summers included at least one trip abroad. America became almost an annual pilgrimage. No matter where we went, Bagatelle would always draw a crowd. And I really enjoyed playing Stateside. The crowd was so receptive to the band and our music. If you were to see our itinerary you would have thought we were a world-famous band full of millionaires, not these four guys who struggled to make a living back in the late seventies and once had 15 people at a gig in Bunclody. And that included the bar staff!"
John O'Brien

"You know what, there are people who think we have only ever recorded one song , even though we've had seven or eight albums and I've wrote several Number 1 records, but there are times when I get on a plane to fly to the USA and I get half way down the aisle to my seat and passengers will start singing "Summer in Dublin." And yep it leads to me standing there with red faced embarrassment. But in truth it's great. As my father once said, "It would be worse if they weren't singing it!" **Liam Reilly, Evening Herald June 1994**

The band continued gaining more column inches, some praising the group for their longevity and stance of playing original music that still stood up while others were typically dismissive. The Irish Independent also charted the group's return to the singles chart.

"Cynics may suggest that what Ireland, or the world needs now in the middle of 1994 is a Bagatelle reunion (though they have since 1992.) Asked what the best thing Bagatelle has ever done over their long career the same sneering cynics may reply; Break Up.
That is unfair. You see Bagatelle are one of those bands who have always brought mutual feelings of either absolute devotion or intense loathing. Not that it bothers the members of the band that much. Despite what seemed a long demise and recent resurrection, Bagatelle appear as popular as ever with the people who really matter: the paying public. The band broke onto the scene at a time when young Irish bands were just beginning to make an impact. There was U2, of course, the Lookalikes, The Atrix, The Bogey Boys and Sacre Blue among others. But while most young bands followed the post-punk path, Bagatelle played to their strengths, relying on the melodic harmonies that have stood so well to them." **Irish Independent 10. 5. 1994**

1998 would mark the 20th Anniversary of Bagatelle. Would they or could they have imagined they'd last that long? If you had asked them, maybe not. They had lasted their second decade together despite the break that Reilly and Doyle would take from the group. The O'Brien/McConville revamp between 1988-90, a surprise reunion then the departure of a key group member.

There had been an element of luck. Many bands before and after would not survive a split in their respective groups, only to come back just as strong with the original line up.

Don't take my word for it!

The Beatles never came back from their 1970 split, having lasted a mere decade (by then half of Bagatelle's lifespan.) Abba sold over 250 million records but couldn't last more than ten years. The Smiths shocked the Indie world by imploding in 1987, a mere five years after Morrissey and Marr became the darlings of the alternative scene. Andy Summers, Stewart Copeland and Gordon Matthew Thomas Sumner (or Sting) wanted to kill each other by the time they departed the music scene in 1986 after nine years together as The Police (even more so after their 2008 reunion tour) and every hormonal teenage girl cried a river when Take That called it a day in 1996 after just six years together, though it has to be said the lads did make a somewhat successful comeback ten years later and are still going strong!

There had even been talk of a Top of The Pops appearance as the programme had begun to feature some artists who hadn't graced "the holy grail" so to speak. Paul Brady for instance, would have a set on TOTP, well deserved given his contribution to Irish music and indeed music in general. Here was a guy from Strabane who first tasted success with Irish folk group Planxty before launching a stellar solo career with seminal albums like *Back to the Centre* and *Trick or Treat* as well as writing for Bonnie Raitt and Tina Turner.

Alas Bagatelle missed out on that platform, something Ken Doyle laments but still remained philosophical about.

"That was the only downside. Missing out on that iconic show. But you know if we had done it and became famous, I'm convinced the group would have split up years ago. Because the pressure would have been amplified. I guarantee you there would have been many legal battles citing the old favourite "irreconcilable differences" and a nasty split. We would never have lasted over 40 years. I mean look at a lot of the English groups who split then tried getting back together. The Police did, but all you heard about were alleged arguments backstage. Some do it solely for money and bring out a Greatest Hits album and tour and cash in. I remember seeing Tears for Fears a while back in Dublin. Back in the day I think the group broke up backstage in New York. Here they

were playing 30 odd years later and I thought the chemistry between them was awful. I try to look at things as they are now with a positive attitude." **Ken Doyle**

"Look, we were very grateful for what we had. Everybody knows that U2 stated they eventually got the start in the business that Bagatelle had at a time when they were playing the Dandelion Market in Dublin for 50p on a Saturday afternoon! And yes, it was Larry Mullen Jr who famously said to our record company -If we got a chance we could be as big as Bagatelle. He christened us "Bagamoney". That seems to have gone down in history!" **Liam Reilly**

A tour kicked off on St. Patrick's Day in the Readypenny Inn on the Ardee Road in Liam's home turf of Dundalk. The prodigal son always got a rapturous reception any time he came home to play. The gig was part of a St. Patrick's Day Festival which saw them hanging from the rafters (literally in the case of one man I interviewed) at the venue.

All the hits were played, including three renditions of "Summer in Dublin." The song meant a lot to many but had taken on an extra special meaning that Valentine's Day.

On the Gerry Ryan Morning Show one Cork man absolutely hellbent on proposing to his French girlfriend for the day that was naturally in it , phoned Gerry's show looking for someone to sing "Summer in Dublin" on Dublin's Ha'penny Bridge while he got down on one knee to propose to her.

It just so happened that music publicist Johnny Lappin had been listening at home over a cup of coffee. Seeing a nice spot of publicity, he got in touch with Bagatelle's manager Jim McQuillan who got Liam on board and set the wheels in motion.

The Corkonian got his wish. Not only would he propose to his French soulmate to the sound of someone crooning "Summer in Dublin", but got the song's composer to sing it!

"It was great. Really funny I must admit. There we were, busking on the bridge, and he went down on one knee and proposed. Much to his delight the girlfriend accepted. Little things like that stand out and make you thankful. I've had a great life through music over the last 42 years, but it was lovely to do that and the fact that after all this time we had three of the original group. The fact we had been able to go our own ways on different projects but return to the fold made us a strong unit."
Liam Reilly

By now the country had seen an amazing social and economic turnaround. The famed 'Celtic Tiger' was upon us. A country of low unemployment and inflation, solid growth, and low public debt. No other country in the rich world had seen its image change so fast, and Ireland surprisingly became a model of prosperity that other nations looked upon as a template.

A country once known for sending legions of people abroad was now creating work on home soil and amazingly the ferry to England or plane to New York was not the only option. A time when Fianna Fail's popularity under Bertie Ahearne was untouchable and frankly almost unbelievable given the stark contrast of Ireland in the eighties.

We began to live beyond our means. A handful of credit cards, two cars in the driveway, obligatory holiday abroad and new house, or re-mortgage on the old one to free up even more capital. We had struggled to pay our rent; now Irish people were buying property abroad.

Of course, Ireland relied heavily on a property bubble, one that economists warned could bring about a shuddering halt if not kept in check. It may have proved reckless and economists weary but in fairness did we really disagree with Finance Minister Charlie McGreevy when he was announcing budget after budget as Finance Minister between 1997-2004?

Sadly, the crash of 2008 changed all that.

"At the time "Summer in Dublin" was released you could still buy a pint for 47p, a sliced pan was 29p and twenty fags would set you back 55p. The pubs closed for the "holy hour" each afternoon and then closed at 10pm on a Sunday. The low flying jet in "Summer in Dublin" wasn't a Ryanair flight and Aer Lingus had the market to themselves. In 1980 the computer had yet to hit the workplace as it was all typewriters and tipex. If you had to change channels you had to get out of your seat and there was no such thing as recording your favourite programme as even the VCR was a way off. In the midst of Bagatelle's tune, local wannabes U2 played a gig in London in front of nine people. The rare 'oul times? Thanks, but no thanks!
Damian Corless. Irish Independent 4.8.1998

At this point the group would employ a fresh-faced young Robbie Casserly on drums and would prove an excellent addition to the group even though in time it would be a brief stint for Robbie with the band.

"Joining Bagatelle was a great education for me. I was aware of them; I mean who wasn't at that point. They had, and still are, part of Irish music history. I was extremely busy in that time. The group had a punishing schedule but there was a huge demand for Bagatelle out there, so I just went with it." **Robbie Casserly**

Not long after Robbie would become part of the global phenomenon that was Riverdance just after it hit big. Everyone remembers THAT performance in Millstreet, County Cork at the interval of the 1994 Eurovision Song Contest. The success of Bill Whelan's odyssey went worldwide, making a household name (not to mention a millionaire of Michael Flatley) meant Robbie came in around 1997 with the stage show still touring to mass audiences all over the globe.

"I suppose things really happened for me during a Bill Whelan session in Windmill Lane studios. It was around that time Riverdance was setting up a new touring production for the US and Canada. He asked me if I'd be interested ... I was happy to oblige. That nine piece started rehearsals in London in December 1997, followed by performing in Hammersmith Odeon until Christmas. We set off for Vancouver in January 1998 and so began a six-year tour of duty all over Canada and the USA, a thoroughly enjoyable part of my life. Boy I have so many memories from that time."
Robbie Casserly

That six-year stint had obviously limited any further gigs with Bagatelle, though he had remained as faithful as possible to the band playing as many gigs possible. His tenure on drums would obviously be shorter than the departed Wally McConville yet he had played an important part in Bagatelle.

"Though my time with the group was rather short, it was still a wonderful experience. It was great to be part of a band that so many people loved, and I was treated with nothing but respect. I will always be grateful for that. And yes, I had some fun times too. One I remember was chilling out after a gig, sitting down, having a beer when Joe Dolan came through the door. I started singing "It's You, it's you, it's you", to which he sang back "Ah, lads, I don't wanna be your second violin". **Robbie Casserly**

When Robbie could not perform with Bagatelle at certain gigs the drumming duties would be shared with another drummer in the shape of a 23-year-old Dubliner called Paul Byrne.
Robbie and his predecessor Myles Drennan had a span of a couple of years with Bagatelle, but Paul Byrne would be the closest long-term replacement for Wally McConville, spending over 16 years on and off with Bagatelle, longer than McConville's tenure with the band.
His education in his trade would start at an early age but not behind a drum kit, instead he reluctantly played clarinet in one of Ireland's most well known and loved bands.

"I naturally grew up with music and it was part of my life from a young age, singing in the Dublin Children's Choir followed by the Artane Boys Band. I knew all about them and as luck would have it, we ended up

moving to a new house to a home that was literally a one-minute walk from where they practised. My mom enrolled me there but for some reason she didn't want me playing drums, so I began to play clarinet and French horn. That annoyed me a bit, so I would go on the hop from the band when I was supposed to be playing with them five days a week. Finally, Mr. O' Connor, who was the administrator in the band, seemed to notice I was hanging out with all these drummers around town all the time. He rang my mum (which put the fear of God in me when I found out) but basically said "Look, he's on the hop from practice and has no interest in playing the clarinet but he has a huge interest in playing drums. Buy him a pair of sticks and sure see what happens." **Paul Byrne**

A wise decision from Mr. O'Connor.

From there the North Strand teenager decided he'd go the well-worn route of teenage cover band to potential stardom which would end not only in becoming a regular fixture with Bagatelle but as a much in demand session drummer which keeps him occupied and travelling over 20 years after he first joined the band on stage.

"The first few gigs I played was when I joined a school band. We were essentially a heavy metal rock group and played stuff from the likes of Megadeth and Slayer – a thousand miles away from what I was brought up with! I was kicked out of that when I couldn't grow my hair long! But I kept gigging. By the time I was 23 I had worked my way up to playing music semi-professionally for a while. I then left my day job to try go and live the dream and step up to become a professional musician. I worked with Leslie Dowdall and In Tua Nua and Finbar Wright. It was when I got a few gigs with Moya Brennan's band that her bass player Tony had mentioned my name to Darran McGoldrick who happened to be Bagatelle's sound engineer. At the time Myles Drennan and Robbie Casserly had been filling in on drums within the group but I think they wanted someone more permanent. Recommended by Tony, I got a call from Ken Doyle not long after and I ended up joining Bagatelle" **Paul Byrne**

Though three original members remained, they had been lucky to temporarily replace the vacated Wally McConville with drummers as good as Drennan and Casserly. Byrne was well aware of Bagatelle's status. How long they had been around. The hits and the fans that loved them. It was an offer he simply could not refuse.

Taking on this position would mean constant travelling but even at such a young age the Dubliner had put in his hours on the road, sleeping under the stars and gigging till his hands nearly fell off. Ready to Rock & Roll, he gratefully accepted this challenge.

If he had been nervous about joining Bagatelle, then the very first gig nearly pushed him over the edge.

"The first gig I did with Bagatelle was in Strabane in a nightclub called Katie Daly's. A late start (we went on about 11). Their manager said the plan was to meet me at Swords at 7pm and the lads would pick me up. I was a tad nervous when 7pm then came and went! By 8pm I was terrified. Just then I saw this car screaming towards me at 150 mph. Thankfully it was them. We had to run up to Castlebellingham (a small village in Louth) with the tour manager Marty McQuillan and we hopped into his car, tore up the road and arrived in Strabane with about 20 minutes to spare. It was madness. I hadn't met Liam, though he used to come into a piano store and play around which was handy as I worked there, but this was different. And there was no rehearsal. Nothing! Basically, Ken had sent me a cassette tape to listen to as it had Robbie Casserly playing drums on it. The trouble was the tape was only about 20 minutes and to say I was missing a lot of Bagatelle songs was the understatement of the century! I wrote out a few notes that would help me but when we raced on stage to a packed crowd there was no sodding lights on the drums so I couldn't see the notes I had written! The only light I saw was the one practically blinding me as I looked up. The spotlight lit practically everywhere bar the place I had the notes!" **Paul Byrne**

Armed with that old tape cassette of 20 minutes of music, Paul basically winged it. A real baptism of fire that worked out in the end. After that there would be no more cassette tapes, non-rehearsals and tour buses breaking the speed of sound up the M1 to the North as Byrne began to find his groove and got settled in.

One thing the group had always done through the years was to show a charitable side to their profession, often doing gigs for free to help various causes.

1998 would see them come to the aid of one of the most public and horrendous bombings in the history of Northern Ireland.

TEN

ALL THE YOUNG DUDES

"We have played all over Ireland and many countries and continents. All around the world in fact. And that includes playing at Caesars Palace. Well, Caesars Palace in Bunclody!"

KEN DOYLE

A human disaster and a horrifying waste of life on one Autumn morning in County Tyrone would lead Bagatelle into charitable waters again as they helped to heal one of the worst bombings in the history of Northern Ireland.

A car bomb terrorist attack in the small town of Omagh on August 15th, 1998, carried out by a group calling themselves the Real Irish Republican Army would kill 29 people (which would include a pregnant woman with twins) and injure another 220 people. The terrorist group was a Provisional Irish Republican Army (IRA) splinter group who opposed the IRA's ceasefire and the Good Friday Agreement.

The bombing caused absolute outrage both at home and abroad. The North had seen their fair share of tragedies over the 30 years that went beforehand but this was utterly disgusting. President Clinton would visit the horrific site, the main street resembling something from a war-torn foreign country ravished by years of war that you would see most weeks on TV.

Only it wasn't.

This was Omagh. A small town of just over 21,000 people.

The Real IRA would deny that the bomb was intended to kill civilians and apologised; shortly after, the group declared a ceasefire. The victims included people of many backgrounds and ages: Protestants, Catholics, six teenagers, six children, a mother pregnant with twins, two Spanish tourists and others who unfortunately were on a day trip from Dublin.

Bagatelle felt they needed to help in some shape or form.

To do this they put in some air miles. First, they would fly to Gaelic Park in New York to play in a fundraiser for the Omagh Fund which raised over $60,000. Aer Lingus would provide the flights for free. Break to the Border (an Irish taxi firm) took care of transport and accommodation for the band and several companies sponsored the stage set and sound details. A superb gesture from all involved.

After the gig, the boys then flew back to Dublin and travelled to Omagh to take part in another concert for the Fund which was a huge success. That took place at the Silver Birches Hotel and the charity, Omawest, who had been at the forefront of fundraising for the Omagh Fund and the Tyrone County Hospital, were the beneficiaries.

And hope would come from despair.

The bombing strengthened people's resolve. It would spur on the Northern Ireland peace process. Never were the residents in Northern Ireland more determined to rid the country of "these vile and evil people" as Tony Blair would call them.

In 1999, the last year before the end of the century, the group received huge recognition by being presented with an 'International Irish Award' in London for their extensive tours from Asia to America, Ireland and England and everywhere in-between. To receive the award for playing to thousands upon thousands despite not having the chart success on the International market was testament to just how popular Bagatelle had become in this, their 21st year.

That year the group toured relentlessly around the globe. So far away from Ireland that it prompted a few promoters to stop getting in contact with manager Jim McQuillan, thinking the group had actually called it a day!

"Just when you think they'd gone and packed it in you find out that Bagatelle have actually been touring the world to audiences which would explain their absence here! Yep they've been gigging in places like Hong Kong, the Middle East, America and England! They put in so much hard work which should be the forerunner for a new Bagatelle album!"
Anglo Celt 29.9.1999

"It's beginning to look a lot more like Bagatelle might easily become the new 'exiles' from their native country as each passing year sees them continuously tour abroad. In the last 14 months alone, during which time they celebrated their 20th anniversary as a group, they spent over three months in the USA in total. In addition to that there were trips to Hong Kong, the Middle East, Scotland and England to boot." **Sligo Champion 10.11.99**

The group's charitable side again came to the fore in 1999 when they contributed to Ireland's Children in Need single "Piano Man" which topped the Irish Charts. The immediate reaction from the group to get involved with such worthwhile charities went over well with those involved. If there was a need to find a group or personalities to help such causes, Bagatelle could always be counted on.

And the group kept finding new places to play, astonishing as they had toured practically every year since 1978. Places like the Castlecourt Hotel in Westport. The Kilmurry Lodge in Limerick and the wonderfully titled

Scooby Booze in Cavan. The tabloids at this point would refer to Bagatelle as a 'Supergroup'.

Life on the road again became second nature as Bagatelle entered a new millennium. To round off the last century they had played a number of high-profile gigs in 1999 including Vicar Street, Cork Opera House, the INEC in Killarney. However, there would be a significant change on millennium eve 1999.

"We played this place that looked like it was a vintage hall from the Fifties. The whole night was a comedy of errors (though I can laugh about it now.) Big kettle of tea and ham sandwiches. I felt sorry for them but also for myself as I was absolutely dying with the flu. It was the millennium eve 1999. The place looked like it had just been opened after 40 years just for that gig!" **Ken Doyle**

A new century. Still with three of the original group standing and of course the "blow in" Paul Byrne.

"I suppose I was the blow in with Bagatelle, yet despite it, the other three members Ken, John and Liam, never made me feel like that. Yes, even by 2000 I was the new kid on the block and these guys had an absolute wealth of experience, but I was always made feel like I belonged in the band. It was hard work, but good work and I enjoyed it. I've been incredibly lucky in my life. I mean playing "Summer in Dublin" on stage and looking out at the crowd singing it back. Playing in sold out venues, standing room only, that will always be a highlight for me with the band. That was a song that would surely have been a worldwide hit in the hands of an internationally known artist, it was just that Bagatelle at the time had been limited to Ireland." **Paul Byrne**

However, Bagatelle would be forced to alter their line up over the next year and an influx of youth would shape the group line-up for the foreseeable future. After decades of *"us old fogies"* it was time for those *"young dudes to do their stuff"* in the words of John O'Brien. Far from disrupting things, it would favour the group in the long run and give them a new vitality.

There would be sporadic gigs in Ireland but an extensive US summer tour in 2000 saw the group concentrate on things stateside. This time the East Coast was targeted, with over 20 gigs booked. The locals loved it. The Irish lapped it up.

It was that audience that had stayed faithful to Bagatelle. In the year 2000 there were 29 million Irish in the land of the free and the home of the brave, nearly 70 million if you count Americans with an Irish lineage or ancestry they could trace back to the Emerald Isle.

We, the Irish, were important in America. You see if you go back over the history books, we've had a few Irish American musicians over different decades. The Maguire Sisters had Billboard Chart success in the fifties (Ruby, the last of the trio passed away in December 2018.) Big band leader Tommy Dorsey, Rosemary Clooney and Eddie Cochran were Irish American along with the founder of Rock & Roll Bill Haley. Even Bing Crosby had lineage here which goes back to his great-great-grandfather who was born in West Cork. You could even throw in cinema giants like Robert De Niro, Tom Cruise and Meryl Streep to that list!

"It may have only been a song or two but just for those 3 or 4 minutes it brought you back to Ireland. Maybe an Ireland when we all emigrated to find work here, but it was still your native country. Still your roots and as good as things may have been here (for most of us anyway) it brought out that bit of melancholy in us" **Gary Kennedy who emigrated from Waterford in 1996.**

By this stage Bagatelle would be propped up by the Celtic Connection record label under the eye of the late Dave Kavanagh. A fan of the group Dave had over 40 years' experience in the music business and was well known and respected. At one point he was the Irish agent for the Boomtown Rats and U2 back in the day when both groups were starting out.
He became a well-known promoter and managed Clannad during a highly successful 14-year period (1982-1996) as the band garnered international success.
One of the biggest successes Dave had was forming the Celtic Heartbeat label in 1993 with U2 manager Paul McGuinness. The label was set up to capitalise on the growing interest that had been shown in Irish music in America.
Another successful venture was putting together The High Kings, a Irish ballad group who have been going strong now for over a decade.
He was responsible for setting up both Claddagh & Liffey Records, but in 2004 he acquired the Celtic Collections label which to date has proven a huge success. It was with this label he would back Bagatelle. Sadly, Dave had been battling cancer for several years and passed away in April 2018.

"Dave was always a superb guy who backed us. He bought into Bagatelle, our history, and what we could achieve. You need backing like that in this crazy industry. To him, we were still a valuable asset that could sell records. He was aware of what we had done. Some other labels might have thought we were a risk, being around for so long, that we were outdated, but he never thought that way. His belief in us was very reassuring and for that we were so grateful to him." **John O'Brien**

"Dave was such a lovely guy. There's not many in this crazy industry but he was one of the good guys. He was fantastic to work with. We had been around some 25 years to this point, but he still felt us, Bagatelle, were still relevant. We all loved him. Sadly, he passed on before his time, but he was held in high esteem by the music industry in Ireland, so much so Bono spoke of him from the pulpit at his funeral. We will always be grateful to him." **Ken Doyle**

2003 saw another release. This time a *25th anniversary* CD again detailing the finest Bagatelle had recorded since they started (which officially was August 14th, 1978 if you want to be exact about things.) The cover (though and early 1980 snap) would still include the departed Wally McConville and although most of Bagatelle's hardcore fans knew the drummer had left, the Dundalk man will always be associated with the highly successful first ten years with the group and the successful reunion comeback of 1992. Ties may be severed but that fact remained.

Despite some music critics deriding the group for a lack of more new original songs, the 25th Anniversary still made solid sales and money.

To promote it the group went on an extensive tour which naturally took in all of Ireland and England and indeed the USA, however most of Europe, Asia and Australia were also included.

As usual their live set earned rave reviews, especially at home.

"Summer temperatures were sent soaring when Bagatelle came to town and sent the Bridgeford rocking. After wowing the full house, lead singer and composer Liam Reilly handed the reins over to bass guitarist Ken Doyle who sang a medley of covers including "Rockin' All Over the World", "Ghost Riders in The Sky" and "Daydream Believer" among others. Liam let it until last to sing "Summer in Dublin". When he started to sing it was apparent his voice had not changed in the 25 years since the group started and the song which went to Number 1 in the Irish charts. With John O'Brien on lead guitar, harmonica and vocals and Paul Byrne on drums, Bagatelle gave a powerful encore that included an overture of their much-loved hits" **Drogheda Independent 8.15.03**

Though Paul Byrne was Bagatelle's permanent drummer now there would be times he was not available. Even today he spends time gigging between Ireland, Europe and even Australia and New Zealand. In his absence the band relied on a new recruit in Dave Keegan.

"I was happy to be involved with Bagatelle. Coming from a musical background, I was aware of the band beforehand, as I knew the big hits they had in the eighties. It was mid-2002 when Ken Doyle asked me if I was available to do a few shows on their current Irish tour that year. Oh, and the gigs started three days later! I had some serious homework to do as we didn't get any rehearsal! My memory of the first gig was that it was a good show!" **Dave Keegan**

Keegan had, like Paul Byrne, worked his way up to becoming a professional drummer with many Irish artists be it in recording, touring or TV performances. A keen photographer to boot he had documented his life on the road as well as performing with a host of bands.

Dave's drive, can-do attitude and talent had given the group a youthful look and energy and the drummer was heavily involved in the group's 2002/2003 tour of Ireland.

"It was a privilege being part of Bagatelle, right from that first gig of mine with the band in Letterkenny in Donegal. I recall there being a lot of shows in that part of the country. The band proved extremely popular in that area. We were constantly on the road, so you would be up and down all over Ireland gigging, and there would also be shows in the UK and indeed the USA as well as parts of Europe. **Dave Keegan**

Dave had been welcomed into the family Bagatelle, spending another seven years (on and off) with the group deputising when Paul Byrne was not behind a drum kit. His love of photography extended to a host of photographs of many bands in his life taken during his time on the road. Bagatelle were no exception and there are many superb photographs of the band in this book which I am truly grateful for.

Despite now almost 50, Liam Reilly still felt as youthful and vibrant as the young awkward boy from the Fatima council estate in Dundalk who got up on stage with The Boulder Band way back when and introduced himself to what would become Bagatelle.

"Yep, they were good times. Back in the day I was a good-looking fella. I still had hair and teeth. Everything! I took life handy. Didn't care about anything. I was listening to Bowie, Tom Waits, Springsteen, the Beatles and Elton John. I was very introverted at the same time. Everything I saw I wrote down. I had songs coming out of my ears and I still get the odd royalty cheque or two. It's been a while since those first days of hardship but I, and the band remain relevant." **Liam Reilly**

The relentless touring continued with Reilly branching out to do his own solo gigs every so often. With solid sales from his 1990 album *Throwing Caution to the Wind* it was thought the Dundalk man would eventually follow up on that. To date that still hasn't happened.

The 25th *Anniversary* cd sold well. Released in August of 2003 it held its own against a host of fresh new acts like Avril Lavigne, Jessica Simpson and Destiny's Child and fellow old-stagers like The Rolling Stones, AC/DC and Rush.

There would be a strange start to 2006. For the first time ever, Westlife sold more singles than U2. The fact they charted at No.1 in the UK with a cover of Bette Midler's "The Rose", giving them their 14th Number 1 and only just behind Elvis and The Beatles in terms of chart toppers was probably an even more depressing status.

At home we saw emerging acts like David Kitt. Damien Rice, Bell XI, and Damien Dempsey all selling well while the awful juggernaut that was The X Factor took up teenage, and sometimes adult, viewing on Saturday nights, making a star (briefly) of Shayne Ward. However, the Irish album charts had a distinct lack of Irish acts for most of the year. Bar Westlife, only Mario Rosenstock's "Gift Grub" occupied the Top 20 for a few weeks. After a successful summer tour Bagatelle launched *The Irish Connection*. Released on the Celtic Connections label. this 2006 compilation would be produced by Gavin Ralston, a man soon to become a more hands on member of Bagatelle with the eventual departure of John O'Brien. But for now, he stayed behind the mixing console.

Above left, The late Gavin Ralston. Picture copyright of Dave Keegan photography. Right, Sean Devitt on drums. Both would become valuable members of Bagatelle in recent years.

Born in Rathfarnham to an Englishman and a Kerry woman steeped in Irish Trad music, Gavin attended an all Irish school, Colaiste Mhuire, before going to Maynooth college but became a full-time musician before he had a chance to complete the primary degree course.

"I started playing in original bands around Dublin before studying traditional Irish music on guitar with Steve Cooney in 1991. That helped me travel around the world gigging with various artists like Eimear Quinn, Sharon Shannon and rock bands like The Waterboys, Revelino and Picturehouse. That was a great education and I progressed from there to opening my own recording studio in 2002, Silverwood Studios. It was here I had the honour of producing a Bagatelle album."
Gavin Ralston

The Irish Connection took on a more traditional theme with an obvious nod to the Irish American market with a whole host of emigration songs. Reilly's most famous songs of emigration "The Streets of New York", "Flight of the Earls" and "Boston Rose" where included together for the first time but "Bainbridge Avenue", "Farewell", "Going Back to Ireland" "Galway" and "Tipperary" were obviously in the same vein, making it a unique collection that Irish fans at home and abroad would adore.

Top; Bagatelle on UTV Life with presenter Pamela Ballintine. Middle; Happier days prior to Kurt Schefter leaving the band in 2019. Bottom; Ken, Conor and Jim McQuillan lark about on a break whist touring. Right; "The man in black" Conor McGouran relaxing with Liam Reilly.
Picture credit; Dave Keegan Photography.

Above, A Presentation at the Irish Embassy in Riyadh.
Paul Byrne, Gavin Ralston, Ken and Liam with outgoing
Irish Ambassador for Saudi Arabia Niall Houlihan.
Below: Conor McGouran, Ken Doyle, Miriam O'Callaghan, Liam Reilly
and Dave Keegan after performing on her RTE show in 2011.
Photo copyright of Dave Keegan Photography.

Above; At the ACE Café in London.

A Sunday World Lifetime Achievement award for Bagatelle in 2016. Even 38 years after they first burst onto the scene the group still proving they were as popular as ever.

Above; The short lived Mid Atlantic Rhythm Section. A band that featured (l-r) Robbie Casseroles, Robyn Robbins, Phil Donnelly, Ken Doyle and John O'Brien. Called M.A.R.S. for short, the group lasted between 1996/97. An experienced band, Robbins even played with the Bog Seger Band. Sadly, Philip Donnelly passed away in November 2019. He had played with such notable names like Emmy Lou Harris, Townes Van Zandt, Don Williams and the late John Prine. He was also a superb songwriter and penned "Living in these troubled times" for Crystal Gayle. A true gentleman who will be missed on the Irish music scene. Pic; Copyright Evening Herald.

Left; An Ireland's Own front cover from 2014. Cover courtesy of Shea Tomkins.

Top, Dave Keegan, Liam & Conor McGouran in Central Park, New York after a Fest gig in 2007. Picture courtesy of Dave Keegan Photography. Middle; Ken and Liam at a Q&A session for IMRO in 2019. Bottom: It's A Secret. An 80's short lived group. L-R; Howard Wilson, Mark Redmond, Ger Doyle, John Kelly and Ken Doyle. John Kelly would later join Ken Doyle in Bagatelle.

Above; A few drinks and a break between touring in New York 2007. Back Row (L-R) Steve MacFarlane, Dave Keegan and Liam Reilly. Front row - Jim McQuillan and Ken Doyle. Picture copyright of Dave Keegan Photography.

"I loved working with the band in the studio. You have to remember that the lads recorded their initial albums in the late 70's & early 80's really without any computers so it was a very long, careful and painstaking process. When the guys arrived at my studio and saw how the place was operated with the minimum of fuss they were delighted. Gone were the long days and nights in the studio. We set up live and did 2/3 songs each day which was a joy to do. Before you know it, the album is finished."
Gavin Ralston

"They have a unique brand of music. When you think "Summer in Dublin" finished third in the Best Irish Song Ever poll behind "Fairy-tale of New York" by The Pogues and "One" by U2 it shows how popular they are. And those songs are tunes heard across the world. Fans gear up the second they hear the intro to a song like "Summer in Dublin." It is an alternative national anthem sung with such gusto that it almost drowns out the band completely. This collection will please Irish fans home and abroad." **Fermanagh Herald**

For the first time the group would venture into the Christmas single market with "The Next 12 Days of Christmas" a festive tune full of cheer wrote by Ken Doyle. They like it so much that they also recorded Liam Reilly's "Another Christmas Morning" backed by the Saint Joseph's school from Dundalk. Well, is it not obligatory that every band produce a Christmas single however corny? And Jesus there's been some bad ones hasn't there? The festivities of 2006 soon gave way to a New Year. Bagatelle were booked solid on the back of a new release with dates home and abroad. Quickly closing in on 30 years as a group. It should have been a time of celebration.
John O'Brien would feel entirely different.
Tired of touring and admittedly a shadow of himself.
The fire, determination and will to succeed that drove him to make the group successful by now meant little.
Bagatelle's founding member had enough.
The Bray native wanted out.
And this time there would be no turning back.

ELEVEN

STOP THE WORLD, I WANNA GET OFF

"Never look back unless you intend to go there. Dylan once said that. If it was good enough for him then it was good enough for me."

JOHN O'BRIEN

Bagatelle had been lucky to have John O'Brien. The founding member of the group had been well versed in the music business long before he helped form The Boulder Band, a forerunner to Bagatelle in the mid-70's. Even by that point John was almost 40 years old.

He had travelled to London at an early age and by the time Bagatelle was formed in 1978 he was an old hand, and more importantly an experienced father-figure to the band.

Having experienced some wonderful times in his profession throughout his life, and music, Bagatelle's elder statesman called it a day in 2007.

"I am so thankful for what music has brought to my life. But by now I was tired of the whole rock & roll circus. The success of Bagatelle and the money didn't matter to me. I was happy just playing my music. I left in my sixties and am now 77 so I have put my time in on the road. It was just too repetitive. Was it a major decision to quit? You may say it was, but you know I never regretted it. Not for one single moment. "Never look back" as Bob Dylan once said. And he even made a movie called that! Never look back unless you intend going there. If it was good enough for Dylan, then it was good enough for me." **John O'Brien**

"At that point John had arthritis for some years and was on strong medication. John also had ten years up on myself and Liam and of course was our founding father. Yes, there was a demand for Bagatelle, but poor John was starting to suffer health-wise at this point. We knew he couldn't go on like this with the tour schedule. When he didn't have to travel, he didn't have to take medication. That helped I suppose to a degree, but I think John was just tired of the road and everything that went with it. He had, after all, been doing it a lot longer than us." **Ken Doyle**

"I was very sad about John's departure. I think he just got disillusioned with the whole thing. We were staying in a hotel after a gig. I was having

a drink at the bar and he came up to me and said – "You know what, I don't care about 'Raining in Paris". I don't care about "Love is the Reason", I just don't care. I'm going to have to leave Liam." I could tell how much stress the whole situation had been for him. Sadly, that was the end for John." **Liam Reilly**

"John was our mentor. So, leaving Bagatelle was a huge blow for us. The constant gigs we had, you could see he was more and more unhappy. We decided to carry on, which was a brave call as we had now lost half of the original group. So, we carried on, but yes, we missed him. A lot." **Ken Doyle**

"Back in the day we seemed to be breaking up at least once a month. Even Oliver Barry's head was done in over us! Though we never really meant it. Liam used to go away for periods of time, like to America and we wouldn't know what to do. Money matters didn't help things either. I thought for some it took precedent over the music. We had a blast, but it changed for me as the years progressed. That made me sad. Do you know how many times I got on stage, played our songs and looked out into the crowd genuinely wishing I were somewhere else? That should have been heart- breaking for me but by then it was going through the motions." **John O'Brien**

So, the inevitable happened and John O'Brien left Bagatelle.
And then there were two.
At first the thought of calling it a day with Bagatelle entered both Ken Doyle's and Liam Reilly's head. They were heading for their 30th anniversary and still tirelessly touring. Maybe it was time to end it all. With Dave Keegan and Paul Byrne filling in on drums the group now turned their attention to John O'Brien's replacement on guitar.
The obvious choice had been Gavin Ralston.
Having produced their 2006 Irish Connection album, Gavin would step into the considerably large shoes John O'Brien had vacated and started gigging with Bagatelle.

"As an avid young fan of the radio I always loved "Second Violin" when it came on as it was one of the first song titles that caught my ear as a 13-year-old because of the connotations of what a 2nd violin meant. The guitar riff is also unique and a personal favourite of mine to play live. A great friend of mine Karl Breen asked me to stand in for a few gigs with Bagatelle while he was unavailable to during the summer of 2006. That's how I hooked up with them. I had just finished a big American tour with Michael Flatley, so it suited me perfectly as I was available. Obviously I had my own studio by then and one of the first things I did with Bagatelle

was record a new version of "Summer in Dublin" at the request of the record company to create some publicity which was really fun to do but the public understandably preferred the original." **Gavin Ralston**

But the band restructure did not stop there. Keen to have a back-up guitarist, Bagatelle signed up Dubliner Conor McGouran, another superb young musician. Again, Doyle and Reilly had opted for youth over experience within the group. By that stage three decades in and extremely knowledgeable both men did not see the need to add a journeyman guitarist. It would have been impossible anyway to replace John O'Brien with someone of the same standing, knowledge, and drive. The group now had a youthful vitality and swagger about them. It was a shot in the arm that revitalized the group.

"I started at an early age. Ten to be exact. My older brother had a guitar and I would sneak into his room to play it when he wasn't there. He eventually gave it to me as he realised, I had a knack for it. I acquired my own first guitar at 12 which was a 1982 Squier Stratocaster that my dad got me. I still have it. My household had music playing all the time, so it was everything from The Beatles to Steely Dan, Joni Mitchell, Thin Lizzy, Yes, Deep Purple, Jimi Hendrix and even classical music which I loved deeply. Those were my broad range of influences. In my teens I was heavy into Metal, Jazz and Progressive Rock but nowadays I enjoy anything that has an effect on me emotionally." **Conor McGouran**

From a fans point of view the neat thing about Bagatelle was they travelled and toured so much that you rarely missed a chance of seeing them in your hometown.

It seemed they went to every corner of the island. That summer Bagatelle played (wait for it) Bundoran, Dungarvan, Ballyfoyle, Nenagh, Tullamore, Plumbridge, Westport, Kilyclogher, Trim, Cootehill, Balymote, Dungannon, Creeslough, Carrickmore, Ballyroan, Port Laoise, Claremorris, Ballina, Boyle, Enniscorthy and Killorglin.

It meant the fresh faced McGouran was thrown in at the deep end, rapidly playing night after night but the newbie took it all in his stride.

"I joined when I was contacted by their manager Jim McQuillan who received my number from another guitarist that I had recently toured with and was also playing a few shows with Bagatelle. I had known of Bagatelle my whole life. "Summer in Dublin", "Second Violin", and "Leeson Street Lady" were songs I was already very familiar with. Oddly enough, a childhood band that I was in featured Wally McConville's (Bagatelle's original drummer) son on drums. What a strange coincidence."
Conor McGouran

Though the venues became second nature to hardened veterans like Reilly and Doyle to the likes Keegan, Ralston, Byrne and McGouran it was a slight step into the unknown. Bagatelle played venues both big and small. It could have been a sell-out show in Vicar Street or a function room in Roscommon. Their accessibility was key. And the size didn't matter. Bagatelle always drew crowds to the venues they played in. Jim McQuillan would regularly have a headache trying to please promoters up and down the county, trying to find a free spot in the calendar. Bagatelle remained booked up. A reassuring fact now thirty years later.

"You accepted that you played to big crowds when you were part of Bagatelle. It seemed their popularity never waned. By the time I joined the lads had already clocked up nearly 30 years on the road. Not many original members of a group achieve that." **Paul Byrne**

"I think the first gig I played with Bagatelle was near Christmas 2006 in a venue that was up north. I was quite nervous as I had to learn the set in the car on the way up. I'm extremely blessed to have perfect pitch, so I was able to make notes and memorize it. Ken Doyle was so kind to me and coached me too. He treated me like a son. I'm still grateful for that. I earned my nicknames early on. Ken called me "Satan" as I was a rock/metal fan and Jim called me "Tesco" as I used to play a lot of notes all the time, so he said it was like getting two guitarists for the price of one!" **Conor McGouran**

A Bagatelle *30th Anniversary* album (on Celtic Connections) was brought out in 2008 to co-inside with another tour. It was a label manager Jim McQuillan was happy for the band to be part of.

"I must make a mention about Sharon Brown, who bought into the whole marketing value of Bagatelle in my early days with the band. Nothing was really happening at Polygram (now Universal Music) and the band was heading towards its 25th anniversary. I needed to get the band a more active label and Sharon, then the head of Celtic Connections record company, got it straight away and offered the band a really good deal. She was later to be instrumental in putting together Celtic Woman (which is huge in America) and then shortly after she put Celtic Thunder together, proving just as popular. Celtic Connections of course would later be taken over by the late Dave Kavanagh (Dave had previously managed Clannad.) It was a great deal for the band." **Jim McQuillan**

The 30th Anniversary album again was produced by Gavin Ralston. Half of the album would be recorded live at the Millennium Forum in Derry and so offered a new version of Bagatelle originals. These recordings and the 30 songs in total gave it a different edge though many will still see it as a *"Best Of"* album.

Greatest Hits. I have a few in my collection; The Eagles being the biggest culprits with no less than five different versions of their classics. Though it has to be said their *Greatest Hits 1971-75* album has clocked up sales of 38 million and counting! Only Michael Jackson's *Thriller* has currently sold more.

Traditionally Christmas is the *Greatest Hits* season. Bagatelle's competition that 2008: English indie gods Radiohead, Birmingham's finest UB40 and retro acts The Doors, Lynyrd Skynyrd and Petula Clark along with country artist Tim McGraw who sold extremely well in Ireland as we love a bit of country over here (except the residents around Croke Park when there's a Garth Brooke's show in town.)

Bagatelle 30[tj] Anniversary Collection with 30 songs making it the groups biggest collection to date held its own but not in the league of the Platinum selling *Gold – The Best of Bagatelle* from 1985. That group highlight would never be equalled or even surpassed.

It was a time when more and more music fans were using online outlets like iTunes, Spotify and Deezer for music. Now you didn't even have to leave your bedroom as you could download your favourite tracks without your head leaving a pillow. The compact disc, which had revolutionized the way we listened to music in the mid-eighties, making the tape cassette obsolete, was now in sharp decline. In the UK just 26 million CDs were sold in 2019 - almost 100 million fewer than in 2009 and record stores like HMV became the most high-profile victims of the online revolution with mass closures.

"There were many great shows and their fans always treated me like I was a full-time member. Like any band, there were a couple of bad shows as well, but Ken's positivity always helped as I was the one who could be quiet self- deprecating about my own performance. He taught me a lot in dealing with those kinds of issues. I really enjoyed touring at the time. I played all over Ireland numerous times, and England, Scotland and the US with Bagatelle. Of course, travelling, lack of sleep and fatigue didn't help but it never derailed a show. Not when I was there anyway. I was just happy to play. It was a great experience as I was still in my early 20's when I began playing with them." **Conor McGouran**

"Travelling the country is a double-edged sword really: great to be playing Liam's songs night after night and meeting the loyal and attentive fans but the long trips especially arriving home at 5 or 6am really does take its toll on your body. Also, the guys liked a drink so that had its drawbacks as well. It was a thing that just heightened the mood at the time. We've had many great nights. I remember places like the Firtrees Hotel in Strabane where we'd stay up chatting to the fans and

enjoy the craic but when we were on those long trips the loneliness kicks in and it brought out the unhappiness but that's not unusual. It was part of the deal." **Gavin Ralston**

"The early days of my time with the band were extremely busy and a lot of driving, so you had to be match-fit! When you travel in close proximity with any one group for a long time, it's important to have your own space to make sure you put in a good gig, and there were some magic nights onstage due to the fans being so loyal and giving you back a great response. I enjoyed the experience and got to play and perform in so many lovely venues and countries. Even though I don't work with the band anymore, we all still keep in touch with each other and when we get to catch up socially, we'll always have a lot to talk about from our adventures on the road!" **Dave Keegan**

In 2009 Bagatelle teamed up with a host of other well-known Irish acts to bring "The Best of Irish" concerts to the nation. The lads shared the stage with the likes of Johnny Fean of Horslips, the Dublin City Ramblers and Brush Shiels with comedian Big O on hand to add a few laughs as host in what proved a unique and very well attended set of shows.

However, there would be a health scare for Liam Reilly at the closing ceremony of the annual Enniscorthy Strawberry Fair on the first Sunday in July as Reilly collapsed unconscious on stage.

Concerned band members rushed to his side to aid him, and within minutes an ambulance was at the scene. Though Liam was well enough to walk to the ambulance and even waved to the crowd as he left the stage, there was still a concern as when he was seen in Wexford General Hospital it was announced that the singer had suffered a seizure, not only on stage but also in the back of the ambulance. Following blood tests, it was revealed that the cause of the epileptic fit was due to a low level of potassium. The Dundalk man spent some time in the hospital before checking out with a clean bill of health days later.

The group were thankful to the emergency services and the Strawberry Festival committee for the way they handled this incident.

It was around this time that an idea to do an album of covers was floated. It would seem the natural route to go as many artists and bands had produced an album of covers none more successfully than Rod Stewart who recorded three albums of *The Great American Songbook,* selling nearly seven million copies in the process. Bagatelle were a band of striking originality, so nobody was about to accuse them of jumping on the bandwagon, cashing in and running for the hills. It also brought the band back into the studio.

Somewhat of a different departure, the band went in search of a dozen or more songs to put on their first ever album of covers. Picking the songs wouldn't be easy. The band had a list of favourites that came to 500 which had to be cut down to just 16.

The album listing would finally read.

Piano Man (Billy Joel), The Way It Is (Bruce Hornsby) , Make Me Smile (Steve Harley), Old Time Rock & Roll (Bob Seger), Daniel (Elton John), Walking In Memphis (Marc Cohn), Changes (David Bowie), Missing You (John Waite), Maggie May (Rod Stewart), Hope That I Don't Fall In Love With You (Tom Waits), Walk In The Room (The Searchers), Take It Easy (The Eagles), Bad Moon Rising (Creedence Clearwater Revival), Addicted To Love (Robert Palmer), Whiter Shade of Pale (Procol Harum), Sunny Afternoon (The Kinks).

Under the Covers, a fresh take on old classics proved a wise move and many songs were slotted into the Bagatelle set-list when they toured in 2010. Buoyed by its success Jim McQuillan was dealing with even more fresh new bookings in Europe and America. A whistle-stop tour of new venues in Europe and old favourites along the east coast of America, with extra dates on the west, were arranged, but the volcanic ash that summer ended that idea. You would wonder how the eruption of Grimsvotn, Iceland's most active volcano, would cause so much trouble but it brought most of the European and trans-Atlantic flights to a standstill for a while. Over 10 million people were either stranded or had their flights cancelled and airlines lost close to a whopping €2 billion euro. It would be low-cost airlines, like RyanAir of course, who were hit badly, and I recall Michael O'Leary being a less than happy man that summer.

President Mary McAleese invites Bagatelle to her humble abode! An indication of how well Bagatelle were thought of. She's a big fan!

Bagatelle have had a number of accolades throughout their career but possibly the most prestigious was bestowed upon them in 2011: an invitation from then President Mary McAleese, to come to Aras an Uachtarain for her annual Garden Party event. This was a million miles away from gherkin sandwiches and stale steak & kidney pies in a van. A whole different ball game from playing to 15 people or a pub owner collecting a whip around for the band at the end of the night.

It was an invitation the band gleefully accepted. The event would be hosted by television personality Kathryn Thomas with around 350 invited guests who represented groups from DSPCA, PSNI and Rehab Care.

By this stage Paul Byrne had been drumming with the band a number of years.

The former Artane Boys Band member had stepped in at the start of 1997 and though his appearances tapered off from 2010 on, he still gigged until finally leaving in 2013.

Similarly, by 2010 and the release of *Under the Covers*, Dave Keegan had finished a 7 year stretch between 2003-2010 with Bagatelle having shared those drumming duties with Paul Byrne, though Conor McGouran and Gavin Ralston remained on guitar.

A vacancy had opened up again on drums. A search began and Bagatelle's move for a more permanent drummer would lead them to Sean Devitt, who in 2020 remains Bagatelle's main drummer. Brought up in Harolds Cross from an early age he was influenced by his father who was a huge jazz fan. Miles Davis, Duke Ellington and Charlie Parker would fill the halls of his house from an early stage.

"Obviously with a house full of music I was influenced so early in life and my choice of instrument became the drums. My dad bought me a second-hand kit when I was 14 and I practiced like crazy every single night from our house in Harolds Cross. I haven't looked back since" **Sean Devitt.**

His first proper band would be an outfit called No Buckets which he joined in 1976. The group played an instrumental mix of jazz and rock. The band moved to Holland in July 1977 for a year before returning to Dublin. However, Sean would become well known and gigs wouldn't be a problem for the young man. During the 1990's he would spend extended time across the water Stateside with Irish group The Devlin's who were making a name for themselves at the time. The Indie Rock band were expected to breakout bigtime, their first album Drift receiving a four-star review in Rolling Stone, however mainstream UK success eluded them.

"I spent about six years on the road with The Devlin's. That was quite an experience. A long way from messing about as a 14-year-old with the friends on the block in Harold's Cross! We toured all over Canada and North America supporting people like Sara McLaughlin, Sheryl Crow and Tori Amos. I had also played with Paul Harrington, Mary Black and Mary Coughlan, along with Horslips. Great experience. The lads in Horslips were fun and that gig was a blast." **Sean Devitt**

Backing Sheryl Crow meant Sean got to play Madison Square Garden with The Devlin's. Crow had just broken in America. Her album *Tuesday Night Music Club* would sell 4 million copies. If ever there was a time to be an up and coming support act to the L.A. chick this was it.

The touring abroad meant Devitt would only get to see his wife every three months. The money may have been good, but the absence of heart meant Sean missed his home life. Those long nights with sleep deprivation can take its toll and if you were a family man it can hurt even more.

"I enjoyed touring, especially with The Devlin's. They were a superb group. Because I had to spend time in America with them as they tried to crack it, it meant a long time away from my home and wife in Bray. But I suppose that kind of goes with the territory and I wasn't a newcomer to that. As a drummer I'd been used to life on the road. It has its ups and downs. You learn to adapt. If you can't this crazy business is not for you." **Sean Devitt**

Sean's first contact with Bagatelle came through Ken Doyle who needed a drummer for a Sligo gig. It was a gig Sean would have adored and not want to turn down, however the elements had something to do with it!

"It was a pleasure joining the band. I knew Ken Doyle from the early eighties as I lived in Bray. He called me to ask if I could do a gig in County Sligo at a moment's notice. The problem was it was the year of the heavy snow. So heavy that if you remember we had two big snow drifts that year. The bottom line was I couldn't even get out of my driveway, let alone drive across to the other side of the country to Sligo. I felt I may have missed my chance but to be fair to Ken he called me a while after that, just to fill in. The boys were doing well so I started to become their regular drummer from then" **Sean Devitt**

Though joining Bagatelle meant working with a former Eurovision runner up in Liam Reilly, Devitt did play with a man who went one better than Liam in that same competition in 1994.

"I've been lucky enough to play in a lot of bands along the way, but my longest stint had been with my good friend Paul Harrington. He had just won the Eurovision in a landslide with "Rock & Roll Kids" with Charlie McGettigan of course. That was a great time to be an Irish musician and a great act to be involved with". **Sean Devitt**

Owing to a radio campaign with Will Leahy from 2FM, the much-loved song "Summer in Dublin" was used for the official launch of Ireland's Summer 2013. And so, the number one chart topping single (that wasn't number 1 but was!) had re-entered the Irish charts AGAIN 33 years after it was originally released proving it is a timeless classic loved by all generations.
Boy is there no end to this song!

It was a summer bassist Ken Doyle was happy to see. In July his motorbike had a blowout while travelling on the M50 near Dundrum. A "very near miss" in his own words.
Losing all control; he fell off and was knocked unconscious. Ken was rushed to St Vincent's Hospital with suspected head injuries and had to undergo a brain scan but mercifully was given the all clear. Shortly after

that he was taken back to Vincent's Hospital with a suspected heart attack and breathing difficulties. Co-incidentally the same ambulance man who attended to him after his bike crash was surprised to see Ken again so soon.

Bagatelle's bass player treats the ordeal with humour. *"Thankfully it wasn't a heart attack but was related to my earlier accident. My heart is good and a good heart these days is hard to find,"* he laughs loudly while channelling Fergal Sharkey.

Naturally, he remains indebted to the staff who helped save his life.

Much to his relief he got all clear and after undergoing a number of tests was released later that morning.

Then he hopped in the car, drove to Donegal and played an open-air gig with Bagatelle to 4,000 people. Rock & Roll baby... Rock & Roll.

The band saw the departure of Gavin Ralston in 2013. Gavin would leave the fold to bravely fight an ongoing personal battle with cancer which meant he was unable to tour with the band. Not only a key member of Bagatelle, Gavin had produced three of their albums in a time he enjoyed very much.

His participation in Bagatelle's lifetime had been extremely important.

"I look back at my time with the lads as really informative and a window to an era when bands were told that they were going to change the world. I was with The Waterboys for a few years and they also came from the same mindset which is really remarkable. They believed that music was really going to make a difference to society so as such really took their job seriously, especially with the song writing.

I ended up being a professional in the 90's when music was starting to lose its magic touch for people leading to what it is today: a simple form of entertainment which you can access for free without any real depth associated with it.

Bagatelle were the first Irish band to talk about Irish place names and things (take that now famous 46A bus route) which gave us all immense pride at the turn of the 80's. We hadn't really heard any Dublin references on radio before apart from the Dubliners and other such ballad bands. Working and writing music with Liam certainly was a high point for my career. Whatever about his eccentric behaviour watching him write and nail a lyric is really something remarkable. It really is his most productive zone" **Gavin Ralston**

In 2006 Conor McGouran, who had been rocking out on lead guitar, would leave but without a single regret from his time with the band.

"I can only speak for myself. I thankfully never had an argument with Liam, Ken, Paul (Byrne), Dave (Keegan) or Gavin (Ralston.) I had a lot of respect for everyone involved. Particularly Jim, as he was the one that

kept the show on the road. As Ken Doyle used to say to him, out of affection, "Manager...Manage!!" I eventually joined a UK band called Xerath in 2013 and became a full-time member of that outfit. Unfortunately, I was not able to fill in on further Bagatelle shows at the time but have helped on the odd night since then. Because of my experience with them I'd do it again anytime if needed."

Some of my happiest memories were with Bagatelle. Ken Doyle was like a father figure to me and we were always in tears laughing. Liam had an incredible dry wit and was a serious intellect. He could talk about anything. He is also one of the greatest songwriters Ireland has ever produced and I was proud to share a stage with him. I'm glad I never took that for granted. I learned a hell of a lot as a musician as well. What to do and most importantly, what not to do. I'm so pleased to see them being stronger than ever and long may it continue."

Conor McGouran

Yet again the band were looking for a guitarist, however this time they stuck with just one, recruiting the latest member from overseas.

In Kurt Schefter they found a musician with some serious chops. Schefter had played with a host of fine musicians, but his big break came when he joined the Alannah Myles band.

The Canadian Grammy award winner broke into the mainstream in 1989, going all the way to Billboard Number 1 with the huge selling "Black Velvet" a song that also went on to receive an ASCAP Millionaire Award for over five million radio airplays by 2000. The resulting debut album would sell in excess of six million copies.

Nice work if you can get it.

The Toronto born Myles would refer to Schefter as "My co-conspirator guitarist" on many occasions. The lead guitarist was a sought-after session musician and also played with the likes of Tim Roland, The Jitters and Bob Wiseman.

"I was happy to join the band in 2013. I knew Bagatelle and instantly I enjoyed playing music with Liam. His songs and indeed his talent inspired me! I was very excited and committed to the group."

Kurt Schefter

Aside from their normal indoor gigs Bagatelle would play a number of outdoor festivals. Events like the Clancy Brothers Festival, the Belfast Nashville Songwriters Festival, Temple Bar Trad-Fest, and the Nobber Fair Festival were all events Bagatelle rocked at the start of 2014. Demand for the group was high, indoor or out, but the group revelled in the great outdoors, a step back to when they first played Siamsa Cos Laoi in Cork under the guidance of Oliver Barry.

There would be yet another trip to meet the President, this time Michael D Higgins in 2016. A prestige invitation to be at Áras an Uachtaráin once in a lifetime but for Bagatelle to meet two Presidents on two visits showed how highly the group were, and still are thought of. The group also flew Stateside to pick up another prestigious honour.

"We didn't know that "The Streets of New York" had been adopted by the NYPD as their anthem. We knew the song went down well with the Irish in America, but this was something extra special. They told us this song has always meant a lot to them and the firefighters but since 9/11 it means a whole lot more. They flew us over to New York for a presentation on the site of the Twin Towers, which was incredibly moving." **Ken Doyle**

2016 also saw Bagatelle receiving a Lifetime Achievement Award at the Sunday World Entertainment Awards. It was an accolade the group deserved for being part of the fibre of Irish music over five decades. The group of course now consisting of Ken, Liam, drummer Sean Devitt and guitarist Kurt Schefter gleefully accepted the award.

Yet it felt bittersweet. Yes, it was superb a tabloid like the Sunday World had bestowed this honour upon them, but it was also coming at a time when the band had enough of the road, late nights, too much beer, too much whiskey, too much of the lifestyle that they accepted back in the day. Both Liam and Ken were 61 and 62 years old. From here they savoured each gig like it was the last with retirement seemingly just around the corner.

The group would ramp up the sentimentality with a sold-out gig at Bray's Royal Hotel. The homecoming stirred up much emotions. After all this was the place the group had started, way back in the days when they were jamming at 100 Sugarloaf Crescent. Where an unsuspecting Liam Reilly had popped along to audition to an even more surprised Ken Doyle and John O'Brien. It was a place Wally McConville excelled both as a musician and songwriter.

It was here, in the Mississippi Rooms, Bagatelle packed them in back in the late seventies, a sentiment not lost on Bray natives Doyle and O'Brien. Proud men indeed,

A group that had shared the stage with such artists as Bob Marley, Don McLean, Glen Campbell, Van Morrison, U2, The Boomtown Rats and Jose Feliciano and had albums produced by Gus Dudgeon and Phil Coulter.

And though that had meant the world things had changed.

It was now 38 years on the road.

Bagatelle's two original members were tired.

Too damn tired.

TWELVE

ONE NIGHT IN VICAR STREET

"I was married once for two years. Oh well, you can't be happy all your life!"

LIAM REILLY

Leaving the road after almost 40 years on it was not a decision the group reached over a cup of coffee. There had been so much to take in. For Reilly and Doyle, they had lived out their dreams each night, entertaining hundreds of thousands and travelling the world in that period. Number 1 records, platinum albums; success they could hardly have dreamt of when they piled into the back of a battered van in 1978, eating mouldy sandwiches, earning £40 a gig in a rundown hall in remote rural Ireland or a pub you couldn't swing a cat in or see the 14 people in the crowd through a haze of billowing smoke.

This would be an emotional decision.

In the end the head would rule the heart.

"We decided by that point we were going to check out. 38 years on the road, on and off, was enough for us. While I still enjoyed playing to live audiences, which can make the hair stand on your head sometimes, I, like Liam, was just weary. Weary of the road, travelling and what went with it. I had never missed a gig and travelled far and wide, bringing our music to audiences in Europe, America, the Middle East and China, and of course our hectic schedule at home. But I was 62 now. I wasn't getting any younger" **Ken Doyle**

"There was a lot of thought put into the decision for us to call it a day. There were a lot of good memories, but we felt it was right. A lot of fine chapters but now we were closing the book of Bagatelle seemingly forever." **Liam Reilly**

With the decision to call it a day made, manager Jim McQuillan talked to the band and persuaded them to do a "Final Year Tour."

"I asked them (well I persuaded them really) to do a "Final Year Tour" rather than a few gigs over a few weeks. This way it would give them the opportunity to do those final gigs all across the country. North, South,

East and West and then stop. If they wanted, they could take breaks between gigs. I didn't know what to expect but this proved to be a huge success for the band. Sold out shows all over the place. And that included venues like Vicar Street, the Olympia, Ulster Hall, Belfast, the Cork Opera House and the Millennium Forum in Derry." **Jim McQuillan**

One of the highlights would be a final date at Vicar Street on Valentine's Day 2016. A superb and much-loved venue by the band – this was the gig to go out on a high.

Vicar Street, first opened in 1998, was and still is one of Dublin's best live music venues and practically hosted a who's who of music artists, both Irish, European and Worldwide in the last 22 years. Bagatelle had always found it a superb venue, which they sold out regularly, even now in a new century: 38 years in as a band. Tickets went on sale early and were quickly snapped up for the sold-out show. If Bagatelle were finally calling it a day their fans both in Dublin and nationwide were not going to miss it.

It would be an emotional time for the group. On the band's social media pages there was an outpouring of sentiment from the people who had followed the band often over five decades. They shared stories of when they first saw Bagatelle or heard "Summer in Dublin." Or how they met their partners at a band gig and younger fans who shared photos of their parents who introduced them to Bagatelle but are sadly no longer with them.

The night kicked off with a rousing rendition of "Is it Raining in Paris Tonight?" which got everybody rocking from the get-go. "Love is the Reason" follows. "Baby's Looking Good Tonight" keeps the mood up-tempo.

Liam Reilly breaks away from group mode with his trilogy of emigration songs, "Streets of New York", "Boston Rose", "Flight of the Earls" and "Somewhere in Europe", his solo success that should have crowned him a Eurovision winner.

The mood softens with "Leeson Street Lady," the song inspired by a "Lady of the night" from Appian Way in Ranelagh. "Jersey Girl" and 2,000 "Sha La, La's" sung back with vigour then "Johnny Set 'Em Up Tonight", a song which would become more poignant over the years having been dedicated to those loved and lost by the band.

By the time "Trump Card" brings the set to a close the crowd have been whipped up into a frenzy , determined to enjoy every last second of every last song and so drenched in sweat the clothes that had been loose and dry at the start of the night were now stuck to their skin.

In all, Bagatelle performed 22 songs in the set which includes three encores.

They finish on the masterpiece. The trademark. The timeless classic.

Liam clears his throat, trying to disguise the emotion in it.

"Take me away from the city and lead me to where I can be on my own."

The rollercoaster of emotion almost gets too much as the band bow in unison for one last time. One last lingering look out at the sea of heads all jammed together like sardines in a tin.
Devoted. Still devoted after all this time.
And it is that emotion that weighs heavy on Doyle's mind as Liam hugs his friend and the band embrace for the curtain call, waving into the night to the very people who had put them where they were. On a pedestal. On a perch they refused to be knocked off even after 38 years.
One last intake of breath. A smile. A nod of appreciation. And then farewell.
The band left the stage.
The roadies went to work.
The end of the night and an era.

"Coming towards the end of the tour and seeing such a large turnout wherever the band went, I think everybody was trying to get them to change their minds about quitting. Of course, the answer was always a resounding "NO!" at the time. They were stopping and that was it. There would be so many emotional gigs on that tour, but I think Vicar Street was the best, yet worse (if you know what I mean), on that tour. It was at that gig that all the band's family and friends were there. It was definitely a tough one but amazing at the same time."
Jim McQuillan

But then a funny thing happened.
The office phone rang. And rang. And rang. And rang.
In fact, it never stopped.

"From the very next day, and indeed right over the next few weeks I was getting calls and offers from all over the place. They wanted Bagatelle but I was saying to all the callers "Sorry, but they've finished. That's it." But the offers just kept on coming! Venues and promoters were insisting that I put them on a list in the chance that the group changed their minds. They all knew that they had been on that Final Year Tour and that it had finished but they didn't care. They just wanted the band! So, for at least a month I go near the lads, didn't call them, nothing Eventually I did pick up the phone and call them. When I did, I asked, "Why not do a one off or occasional gig at your leisure?" By this stage, typically, the band was already restless from doing practically nothing. Everybody who knew them (especially their musician friends) kinda thought that's exactly what would happen!" **Jim McQuillan**

Even after nearly 40 years the group seemed to have outdone itself. A wonderful feeling of nostalgia still existed for Bagatelle. Sometimes you can be at a loss to explain how a bunch of young men who started to make music in a tiny two bedroomed house in Bray with no money, no job and original music that nobody knew could survive such a cutthroat business, adapt to their surroundings and produce songs that have stood the test of time despite being loathed by the critics ("They are so middle-of-the-road they'll be run over the minute they manage a miniscule of success" – wrote one review) and land a major recording contract with one of the biggest record companies on the planet.

Bagatelle didn't make music to prove the critics wrong. They did it to prove their fans right.

The group were now getting great offers. Offers they could not really turn down, long after they had finished the Final Tour farewell. Pretty soon the band found themselves on familiar ground again. Absence seemed to have made the heart grow fonder.

A rethink was in order.

"We all thought it was a good idea. To me, the whole thing about getting back on the road, was like going for a few drinks. You don't know how many! And in this case I really didn't have a clue how many! So, we went with "One for the Road" with certain selected gigs across the country and it proved to be a huge success. Since then the band has completed 40 years in the music biz (which incidentally they celebrated with a 2018 gig in Glasgow with long-time friends Smokie.) We had definitely made the right call" **Jim McQuillan**

"We never suspected that people would still want us after that tour. To see us again. To bring their friends, cousins, sons, or daughters to see us. It was amazing but very humbling. Over the years when we meet our

audience, they would tell us their own Bagatelle stories of the Sunday drive, the cassette popping into the machine and everybody singing along to our songs. They now come along with their adult children and their young children and tell us what the songs have meant to them over the years. They talk about deceased family members who were big fans of Bagatelle. And when they come along to the shows, I light-heartedly rib them about being the infectors and the children they have infected. Blessed are the infected for they shall inherit the earth. These were the people who had put us on the map, stayed with us on that "final tour" and now wanted to see us doing it all again. Obviously at this point it was something me and Liam had to consider, having been with the band all these years but we found a way to make it work." **Ken Doyle**

The band took to the road again. Like they had never been away from it. Maybe the idea of coming off the road when there seemed to be a demand as big as their eighty's heyday was a bad idea. So that decision to add some extra gigs for a "One for The Road" tour to finish off in style was taken. That was three years ago.
They are still playing!
Amazingly there was no end to the amount of bookings Jim received. There seemed to have been an outpouring of love for the group that astonished the band, even after nearly 40 years.
At a March gig in 2017 in Strabane, Ken Doyle and Liam Reilly surprised promoter Joe Gallagher with a very special award. A platinum disc was handed to the popular music promoter from the last remaining original members of Bagatelle and their record company Celtic Connections after a sold-out gig in Strabane. It was a well-deserved award for all his endless hard graft working on behalf of Bagatelle over the years.
Joe started off as a DJ, "many, many, many, years ago" and first came across Bagatelle in the Knocknamoe Hotel in Omagh just as the group seemed to have taken over the Irish airwaves.

"After my stint as a DJ, I started off the promotions side of this job in the late eighties and I will share one particular story with you. I first booked Bagatelle in 1992 when they had got the original band together again. From there I booked them for places like Lurgan, Omagh, and a couple of dates in Donegal, working closely with Jim McQuillan who was managing the band then.
The date I remember well. The Aghyaran GAA club, near Castlederg, County Tyrone – a Friday night. At that point the GAA Club was the centre of attraction. A real hub of activity. So, they asked me to book Bagatelle, which I did. However, around that time the local parish priest was moving from the town to pastures new, so we had to cancel the gig. We had to reschedule the gig which was the evening of Tyrone playing

Derry in the 1992 All-Ireland Senior Football Quarter-Finals (which they lost) and naturally this affected the crowd. It was sparse to say the least and there wasn't enough money to pay the band. Feeling slightly embarrassed I gave the band the small amount of money that we got on the door. It was a kind of take it or leave it effort. It was then I realised this promotion racket wasn't all of what it was cut out to be." **Joe Gallagher**

Joe would go to pastures new again as a DJ. Not Derry, Down or Donegal. In fact, Denmark! It was here, through a series of unfortunate yet amusing mishaps that brought about his first and only squabble with Bagatelle.

"Yes, I headed off to Denmark and was doing a few gigs as a disc jockey there and I got a letter to appear in court. I wrote back saying there was no way I could make any court date and could a repayment structure be put in place for the money owed to the band from the GAA gig but my letter never made it to Ireland or the court as there was a postal strike that started the day before I sent the letter. I thought this will sort out any problems with the band, yet there wasn't the hope of anything I wrote down getting back to Ireland, let alone Bagatelle! Years went by and ten years ago I was asked to book them again. Any money owed was then sorted thank God. One night we were in Derry, I met Jim, we sorted our differences and now we are the best of pals." **Joe Gallagher**

The friendship has seen Jim and Joe chat every evening, sometimes two or three times a day.

Gallagher became a successful promoter in the North, touring concert acts like Jools Holland, Bryan Adams, the Beach Boys, Van Morrison, Tom Jones, Smokie, Hot Chocolate, Ronan Keating and Michael Flatley's wildly successful "Lord of the Dance." Most worked hand in hand with Joe.

He would also successfully put Bagatelle & Smokie on the same bill for some sold out shows in 2018. Even though he was dealing with two bands with nearly 80 years' experience between them, Gallagher still knew both could pull a crowd, especially Bagatelle.

"Does it surprise me that they have lasted 40 years? Truthfully, no. Address it any way you want but Bagatelle were more successful than U2 at the start of the eighties. Their success was amazing. It was a brave step to take; play original music and persevere with it. You also have to take into account it was a time many bands in this country survived by doing covers. Playing gigs for money with songs the people would know. There was also a thriving country scene in Ireland. That would never change. There was a dance hall scene where you'd hear covers all night, and there was a pop scene. Falling back on covers was the easy solution. Bagatelle never fitted that box. That is what made them so unique."
Joe Gallagher

Fury at plans to alter iconic 46A bus route

OVERHAUL: Locals oppose change

In July 2018 an iconic bus route, made famous by Bagatelle, was changed in a radical shake up that was made to Dublin's bus network. The 39 to Blanchardstown was the first popular route to stop but it was the humble 46A to Dun Laoghaire that angered many.

Of course, it was the 46A that a young 23-year-old Liam Reilly had hopped on 40 years ago in 1978 as he was stopping off to pick up his guitar. It was there he met a drunk on the bus that told him how to get rich.

Liam was glad he wasn't going too far.

That 46A which runs from Dun Laoghaire to the heart of the city centre had been in operation for over 66 years of unbroken service. The plan was to rename the route to E2 but the sentiment hadn't been lost on the local residents. If you mention the 46A to Dun Laoghaire to Dubliners of a certain age you can be sure most will smile back and attempt a few lines of "Summer in Dublin."

It wasn't the first time the Bus Route was subject to change. In the summer of 2010, the 46A route was to be altered and angry residents took to the streets. This was because the Monkstown Farm area would be bypassed and no longer part of the route. A residents meeting was called in which over 200 concerned residents took to the street which was followed by a protest march days later. At the time local Fine Gael Councillor Mary Mitchell O'Connor was absolutely livid about the situation.

"I cannot believe this. Bagatelle might have sung about jumping on a bus to Dun Laoghaire, but nobody from Monkstown Farm will be able to do so regularly from now on thanks to this disgraceful decision." **Evening Herald (August 31st, 2010)**

That decision had been made as Dun Laoghaire had been hit badly by the recession. Over 66 shops had closed in the two years between 2008 and 2010 as the realisation dawned on us all we were up a certain creek without a paddle.

For many the route conjured up the sweltering summer of 1980 an Ireland is recession and Bagatelle's breakout song that made the 46A bus famous. Never one to miss a PR opportunity, Ken Doyle made sure the papers snapped himself and Liam standing outside the 46A bus to Dun Laoghaire they had made famous way back when.

It was that Doyle knack of spotting a promotional opportunity that led them to revive another iconic piece of Bagatelle history in early 2019 when the band took a wonderful stroll down memory lane thanks to the revival of a much-loved Dublin service.

A step back in time to almost 40 years ago and a landmark the group will always associate themselves with.

The Number 11 Liffey Boat that the band stood on way back in 1980, posing for the cover of their debut album was the same boat that used to ferry passengers up the Liffey back in its heyday. It had gone out of commission for an age but was reintroduced in a lovely nostalgic turn in 2019. "Cross the Liffey in a Jiffy" the highly popular ferry service last functioned in 1984 when it headed to the North Wall where along this quay now stands the National Convention Centre.

At the time the ferry was actually an important link for commuters. It became known as "the Dockers taxi" for workers on the docks who constantly used the ferry but the completion of the East Link Bridge would see it decommissioned, however the Dublin Port Company bought and renovated the vessel, spending around €300,000 on the restoration and in a wonderfully nostalgic turn it was launched again in January, 35 years after it last carried passengers up the Liffey.

Despite writing a dismissive lyric of how Dublin's river stunk like hell way back when, Bagatelle were on hand to officially launch the Number 11 boat on that freezing January morning. Memories turned to a sizzling summer's day in 1980 when O'Brien, Doyle, McConville and Reilly posed on the boat as they started out as a budding Irish band full of hope and determination. Two familiar faces remained, braving the elements on the coldest day of the year trying to persuade the assembled crowd that it was in fact Summer in Dublin.

You see Rock & Roll never forgets.

Never.

"It was really nostalgic but really freezing! I was staying across the road in the Hilton so walked down to where the boat was. We were supplied with lots of drinks as we took this step back down memory lane. You think back and remember it's been a full 40 years since the four of us posed on the boat. Hard to think it's been all that time. But I'm delighted the organisers remembered us and included us for the relaunch of the boat" **Liam Reilly**

President Michael D. Higgins and his wife Sabina having a chat with the boys on their 2016 visit to Aras an Uachtarain. A feat that very few Irish bands have had the pleasure of achieving.

THIRTEEN

JOHNNY SET 'EM UP TONIGHT (IN HEAVEN)

"Sometimes the illness got him down, but John never wanted sympathy. We have lost our brother. There never would have been a Bagatelle were it not for the creative ideas of our founding father."

KEN DOYLE

In 2019 Bagatelle got some well overdue praise from IMRO.

The Irish Music Rights Organisation are the body that administers the performing right in copyright music in Ireland, basically on behalf of singers, songwriters and publishers. An important organisation. You could not play copyrighted material unless you were paying for it with a fee to them. And I'm talking even at Uncle Joe's 5th marriage or Grandad's 96th birthday! IMRO's other function was to then collect and distribute all royalties to artists involved.

On Wednesday January 30th IMRO's hosted a special event at their head office in Dublin to celebrate Bagatelle's 40 years of original music. Before the actual gig, Ken Doyle and Liam Reilly sat down and over the course of an hour chatted about the band's songs, success, ups and downs over the past 40 years. This was followed by a special presentation to the band.

"As grateful as I was to make a living from touring with Bagatelle, I was delighted I had Ann from the start. She got used to the long nights away, touring up and down the country. It didn't matter at the time if we played in front of 50, 500 or 5,000 people, I was still away. However, if you look at it from the point of a bass guitarist in this band, I may have been away all weekend but from Monday to Thursday I would be back at home in Bray because we only gigged on weekends. Our relationship has stood the test of time. Blessed are the cracked because they leave the light shine in." **Ken Doyle**

"I was married once for two years. Well you can't be happy all your life! She was well aware of my travelling but also the money I was making from it. When the marriage broke down, she came out of it well. She got my house. For someone who was wed for just two years and wanted the relationship ended then, she had done extremely well. You learn a lot from relationships and being on the road and I'm a wiser man for it" **Liam Reilly**

However, in February guitarist Kurt Schefter would leave Bagatelle. He had been an integral part of the group in more recent years, giving them an edgier feel leading up to their 40th anniversary but long nights on the road began to take its toll and he would quit shortly after Bagatelle teamed up with another old favourite, Smokie for special a gig in Glasgow.

On April 26th John O' Brien, founder member, elder statesman and the driving force behind Bagatelle, sadly passed away. The fact that he had left the group years before meant nothing. It was still a crushing blow. Without John there would have been no tiny house at Sugarloaf Crescent to pile into and practice. No name. No record contracts. No-one of his knowledge and motivation for the band to succeed at all costs.
Long before the limelight John had cut his teeth with showbands including Pat McGuigan and the Big Four, New Blues, Ranchers and Tumbleweeds. Of course, there was the Elastic Band, the Boulder Band and Ground Zero, but also groups like Blue Swede News, and The Roof Rabbits.
Been there. Done That.
That phrase was meant for this one man.
A friend and a mentor to Liam, Ken and Wally, John O'Brien's place in Irish music was cemented by his peers long before he shuffled off this mortal coil for the great gig in the sky.
A highly intelligent man yet very quiet and caring. He had grafted as a tube driver on the London Underground during his time in the capital, playing gigs at night. Above all John was musically gifted and could turn his hand to any instrument and make it sing.
In his 77 years he had packed a lifetime of musical memories. Even in his

last few weeks he was steadfast in his beliefs, never wanting sympathy for his ailing ill health and though he knew his time on this earth was short he never regretted what went before him.

"Some people get angry at certain conditions or predicaments that lead to such moments in their life and say, "Why me?" I know I'm ill. I've accepted the hand that I have been dealt. I like to think I have remained modest about what I achieved with Bagatelle. I never took it too seriously. The success of the band was irrelevant in my eyes. I was surprised we lasted that long, and that I had stayed the course for as long as I did. I look at my guitar in the corner, an instrument that has been my profession. I can't play it anymore. That hurts, as does my pain but I remain philosophical. It is easy to let anger overcome you. There are not many things I would look back on and say, "You know what, I should have done that a different way." And for that I am grateful. It made the road I did take a lot easier"
John O' Brien

"I remember John in his playing days with the Boulder Band with Bree Harris and Paul Fairclough, Ken Doyle and Marian Byrne years before Bagatelle was even thought of. Since then, we have travelled the world, and have co-written songs with him and Ken. I feel stunned and sad. I really do. John was a guitarist, songwriter, banjo and harmonica player, who lived and breathed music. We have lost an inspirational energetic man. The world has lost a gentleman and musical genius." **Liam Reilly**

"It was an honour to be in such musical company. I think back to the two years of the Boulder Band, the disappointment when it dissolved but John telling me about this new venture that would become Bagatelle. I always trusted his instincts and he was determined to have me in the band. Looking back, that was a big compliment, I guess. We kept in touch and I would often pop up to him, share an Indian takeaway and chat. Sometimes the illness got him down, but John never wanted sympathy. We have lost our brother. There never would have been a Bagatelle were it not for the creative ideas of our founding father." **Ken Doyle**

A large crowd filled the Victorian Chapel at Mount Jerome Cemetery to commemorate John's life. Bray's brother shall be missed.
Sadly, just a short few months later in September Gavin Ralston, the former guitarist and producer of Bagatelle, lost his long battle with bowel cancer at the age of 49. In his short time on the planet he had performed not only with Bagatelle, he had toured with the likes of Sharon Shannon, Clannad, Picturehouse and The Waterboys, cramming this in and gaining no less than 25 years' experience in the music business.

Gavin was diagnosed with bowel cancer in 2014. Without knowing what the future would hold he signed up for an optional critical illness cover when taking out his mortgage in 1999 and forgot about it until 15 years later when he was sadly diagnosed with stage three bowel cancer.

That pay-out would help Gavin recover and rest from the treatment and surgery for a number of years. On April 1st, 2019 the Gig for Gav, a Vicar Street fundraiser for Gavin as well as raising awareness for The Sarah Jennifer Knott Foundation took place with artists like Mundy, Mary Black, Paul Harrington and The Waterboys played at. His passing was met with an outpouring of love from those who knew him best.

"At the time Gavin had just been diagnosed with a tumour so I immediately enquired was it benign, but he told me it was active. I remember thinking "Oh No." Gavin was a fine 6"3 good looking guy. A very talented young man on many fronts and a nephew to the wonderful Irish accordion player Seamus Begley so he had music flowing through him. He was highly intelligent and had a great sense of humour. He played for us for around three years and you couldn't help but love him. We all did. As he used to say "Don't mind me. I'm just a big child." We follow where you go Gavin "Fingers" Ralston. Rest in peace in the Free World." **Ken Doyle**

"Ireland lost one of its most talented guitarists and producers today. If you ever worked with Gavin Ralston, then you know we have lost a very special man. I am utterly heartbroken. My condolences to his family." **Jim Sheridan**

Gavin Ralston was not just a great guitar player and beautiful guy but the spirit with which he fought his illness was an inspiration to me and I'm sure the many others who were lucky enough to know him. He lit up the room. Rest in peace Gav. Xxx" **Joe Chester**

Perhaps the most poignant came from Mike Scott of The Waterboys. *"Our pal is gone."* Gavin. P. Ralston 26/2/1970 – 23/9/2019.

With the departed came a tribute.
"Johnny Set 'Em Up Tonight", Liam Reilly's touching composition, would take on a new meaning. Played in the set-list the song, now 38 years young, sparks a sad sentiment of the departed O'Brien and Ralston. Much loved and much missed. One who had brought his knowledge and leadership to the group, the other added a youthful vitality that was infectious to all. A song of sadness that has also become an ode to other Irish artists who had passed on like Big Tom McBride or Dolores Riordan.

A sad but fitting farewell to friends.
The latest addition to the group would be guitarist John Kelly, joining the

veterans in 2019. A lead guitarist who looks like a cross between Roger Walters and Richard Gere. In short, a real good looking' sonofabitch! The Bray native has fitted seamlessly into the fold and though new to Bagatelle, Kelly was a seasoned campaigner and just right for the job.

"My mum is a good singer and throughout her life has sung in choirs and musical societies, so I get that background from her, I guess. My father loves music but he's not musical. When I was growing up, he would listen to Irish ballad music which filled the halls of our house. That along with rock & roll music from the likes of Elvis and Billy Haley & the Comets."
John Kelly

Born in 1965, Kelly pinned down the type of music he was influenced by early on which led to him starting on the magical mystery musical tour that would bring him, over four decades later, to the house Bagatelle built!

"I took my influences from the bands of the 1960's and 70's as I grew up listening to them. I was particularly fanatical about Led Zeppelin during my teens. That made me take up the guitar when I was about 17 because really all I wanted to do was play Zeppelin's stuff. To this day their music stands up and I've always been a big fan of Jimmy Page. Outside of them I could point to people like Gary Moore, Steve Vai, Richie Sambora, Eddie Van Halen or Steve Lukather of Toto. That became part of my background when I decided to start out playing."
John Kelly

Slightly a later bloomer, Kelly started playing in bands when he was 20. Cover bands were much the order of the day but in the mid-eighties John would join a Celtic Rock group called It's A Secret, a band which featured none other than another Bray native called Ken Doyle! Ken's brother Ger would also be part of the short-lived group (though their Celtic rock vibe and background would have made them a big hit these days) before they disbanded. Ken had Bagatelle to fall back on whilst John took a different path.

"That was my first music experience with Ken. Little did I know I would hook up with him again over 35 years later in Bagatelle! After It's a Secret I joined a rock band called Angelheart. That was an enjoyable time of my life and we stuck it out for around five years, writing our own material along the way. Unfortunately for us the whole Grunge thing had taken off around the same time, took over the charts and brought in a new style of music so we sort of suffered because of that in the end. Our sound just wasn't in demand anymore by then. After that I played with a three piece covers band with my brother Breffni and a singer named

Donal Burton. We called ourselves Dog Ruff and we managed to play together for almost 20 years (2000-2018) Sadly that project came to an end when Donal fell ill and passed away in July 2018." **John Kelly**

Kelly would be called up as a direct replacement for the departed Kurt Schefter but had ironically played with Bagatelle, very briefly, on a couple of gigs in the 1990's and had been part of It's A Secret, a short lived breakaway Irish rock group which featured Ken Doyle.

"I had actually subbed for John O'Brien on a couple of gigs in the Nineties when John couldn't play because he had injured his back. In 2018 Kurt took some time off for a holiday so again I subbed on lead guitar with the group. I finally landed the gig full time when Kurt left the group in 2019. It's a privilege to play with Liam, Ken and Sean although I was nervous for the first few gigs. They are such a well-established band and excellent musicians. Bagatelle's music is iconic, and Liam has written some real classics." **John Kelly**

For many Bagatelle began in the hot sticky summer of 1980 and an iconic song launched on an unsuspecting public, but the groundwork had been put in years before. It catapulted Ken Doyle, Liam Reilly, John O'Brien and Wally McConville from a two bedroomed flat in Bray to modern stadiums and thousands of fans. A radical shift, one they embraced but also knew the burn out ratio that could follow them, like many a band.
Friedrich Nietzsche once said, "Without music, life would be a mistake."
Liam Reilly and Ken Doyle could not agree more.

Left: Celebrating the relaunch of the Number 11 Liffey Boat in 2019, nearly 40 years after they first stood on it.
Right: Ken Doyle, Sean Devitt, Liam Reilly and John Kelly...Bagatelle 2020.
Picture courtesy of Roadie TV

"The enjoyment we have given people and the enjoyment people have given us over the years has been incredible. We were just a band, playing a few songs with no plan and no real expectation. We just got together to play a few tunes and drink a few beers because we like music. Our success? Well to be honest over the years it's been a series of happy accidents. A friend of mine, who gives inspirational seminar talks to corporate people, said it's called synchronises and it's something he always used in his lectures. I told him it sounded like a sexually transmitted disease to which he laughed loudly and said that it simply means to get out of your own way and just let things happen. His name is Olly and I thank him for that perspective." **Ken Doyle**

"I remember coming back from a gig and there was a small steak & kidney pie left on the dashboard from a few nights before and we'd have to split it four ways. One night we ended up eating gherkin sandwiches as that's all we had to eat. We were starving musicians, but I still knew this is what we'd be doing for the rest of our lives." **Liam Reilly**
(interview courtesy of Catherine Murphy, Irish Independent)

Liam Reilly & Ken Doyle with their Outstanding Achievement to Irish Music award. Still rockin' in the free world! 42 years later. Picture copyright of Dave Keegan Photography.

EPILOGUE

42 years.
504 weeks.
15,330 days.
A lifetime of gigs.

An audience of millions and what seemed like an eternity on the road.
By August 2020, the band had come full circle. Two original down. Two original still standing.
Celebrating 42 years in a cutthroat business like this, it was an outstanding achievement.
Music is spiritual. But the music business is not - once wrote a wise man.
Every band starts out with a set of goals. Some just to entertain friends, some who want it as a living. Some dream of more lofty ambitions. Gold records. A paid off mansion. Trophy wife and mistresses to booth.
Original music by an Irish band in the shadow of cover version dancehalls - it was almost unheard of. Yet Bagatelle pitched their tent, declared their intent, and stuck by that ethos, even though in 1978 it may have looked foolhardy.
Days of anticipation giving way to nights of dingy bars, seedy backrooms, a fistful of fivers and a crowd you could count, ever optimistic that things would get better. That a break was only a handful of gigs away.
Sometimes your hardest times often lead to the greatest moments of your life. So, you keep going. Tough situations build strong people in the end.
Persistence. Patience. Perfection.
Bagatelle aimed for nothing less.
In the end there was no real secret to success. It was the result of preparation, hard work, and learning from failure. Bagatelle had put in the groundwork and lay the foundation for a career that dictated they wrote and recorded original music.
Have they been given the plaudits they deserve? In some quarters yes. In others, no.
Did it matter? Probably not.
Reviews don't buy records. The public do.
A group that backed their belief and sang their message to the Irish diaspora in every corner of the globe and maintained a connection with those who dreamt of their homeland yet had moved to pastures new. In doing so it produced a melancholic memory, sometimes of a sad nature, as to what life would be like back in Ireland had years and years of oppression, unemployment and emigration not taken its toll.
Have there been regrets? Of course.
A fairy-tale ending would have probably seen Doyle, Reilly, O'Brien and

McConville taking a curtain call 42 years later in a career which garnered success across the water, a UK chart hit, obligatory video and a slot on Top of the Pops. Even now, mentioning what the group had missed out on will bring an exasperated sigh of what might have been.

For Reilly, the frustration was heightened. Had it not been for a Cypriot jury and some questionable voting, the Dundalk man would have walked away the King of Europe. Does it come to mind every time "Somewhere in Europe" is on the playlist?

Maybe.

But there is much to look back upon and be fiercely proud of what Bagatelle has achieved in this time which I had detailed among these pages. Gold and Platinum albums, a plethora of hit singles, superb live shows. 30,000 people at Dalymount singing "Summer in Dublin" in unison as Bob Marley looks on.

There have been good days.

As they limbered up backstage for an early 2020 Waterford gig at a sold-out Theatre Royal there was an air of expectancy for Seat 42 Row G.

I was seeing my band again.

A band that when I was 11 years old on July 15th, 1980 had the number 1 record and album in this country.

A band who I have seen countless times with one-night stands, bad dates and free chicken and chip dinners for the entry fee.

The women came and went. The music remained.

For good times and bad Bagatelle, mostly by some quirky twists of fate, have been part of my life.

Not just mine. Many.

Ken Doyle, Liam Reilly, Sean Devitt, Brian Kennedy (author), John Kelly and manager Jim McQullian.

Ken Doyle and Liam Reilly presented with keys to the city by the NYPD and FDNY for Liam writing "The Streets of New York" at The Guinness Oyster Festival in New York.

POLYGRAM RECORDS
congratulate
BAGATELLE
On going gold in Ireland with their debut album 'BAGATELLE'

New single 'TRUMP CARD' now available in the U.K.

BAGATALES

(A section of memories from friends & fans)

BRIAN DARCY

Music in the 60s and 70s in Ireland was, on the whole, dominated by the Showband phenomenon. At its peak there were over 600 professional bands playing throughout Ireland North and South. Dancing thrived, in the cities at least, seven nights a week.

Most of the bands drove up and down the country a minimum of five nights a week. Roads were poor, signposts non-existent, vans were of their time. These musicians played to huge crowds with little glamour through low amp 'crazy-boxes.'

Towards the middle of the 70s the entertainment industry began to change. It had to. It's an industry that, of its nature, must change or die.

A more sophisticated audience was looking for a warmer and better atmosphere than many of the huge concrete ballrooms could supply. They wanted to socialize in comfort, enjoying a drink and a chat. They turned away from massive ballrooms, where men thronged along one side and women on the other. They wanted more intimate venues; it wasn't enough to dance the night away with nothing more than a mineral bar and a cloakroom for comfort.

In the early 70s the ballad scene was becoming more popular. People could relax in a relatively comfortable lounge even though they still had to endure thick smoke and loud, loud music from bands and ballad groups.

Tastes in music were changing too. The younger generation was becoming more comfortable in their own skins. They wanted to express themselves through more global musical tastes. They wanted to write their own songs and take their proper place on the international music scene.

On the home front the Rock scene was mushrooming, eventually peaking with the arrival of U2. Before that though, in 1978, one of the most talented bands ever to play in Ireland was being put together, based in Bray, Co. Wicklow. The origins were in The Boulder Band where Ken Doyle and John O'Brien cut their teeth.

Sadly, John has recently left us; he was a gifted guitarist, songwriter and musician.

He was an experienced musician before then because he played with Pat McGeegan and The Big Four (i.e. Pat McGuigan father of Barry McGuigan). He knew what the entertainment industry was all about.

Others will tell the story of how Bagatelle finally came together, but when I got to know them it was Wally McConville on drums, John O'Brien guitar,

Ken Doyle on bass, Liam Reilly on keyboards and vocals. The band grew into a talented rock band and no wonder, for they were as individuals, extremely capable musicians.

They went on to become one of the most successful and most entertaining rock bands in these islands. I have never attended a Bagatelle show that wasn't enthusiastic, uplifting, and unique in their sound and their songs.

What makes Bagatelle great is not only the sound, but the incredible original songs associated with them – "Second Violin", "Summer in Dublin" and "Lesson Street Lady" to name but a few.

It's well accepted now, and I'm sure fully documented elsewhere in this book, how they influenced other musicians to have the courage to take their place on the world stage. Most famously they significantly influenced the path U2 took.

One of my favourite albums is *The Best of Bagatelle and Liam Reilly*. It regularly accompanies me as I traverse the countryside. It's like a soundtrack to my life.

Bagatelle came to prominence at a difficult time in Ireland, economically and politically. Before 1975 music was the great unifier in Ireland. Nobody cared much whether you were from the North or the South. The bands played all venues. There was no border in music.

However, in 1975 with the murder of three members of the Miami Showband, freedom in music died.

Thuggery and violence devastated a music scene which brought nothing but joy, friendship and self-expression.

It took many years to overcome the divide that was so cruelly placed between North and South after the Miami massacre. The frontman was Fran O'Toole, a near neighbour of Ken Doyle.

Bagatelle was one of the first groups to bring back the good times to people on both sides of the border. Their music, especially the brilliant song-writing of Liam Reilly, was appreciated throughout the island. For that we must always be eternally grateful.

I remember when I was helping to arrange the funeral of Fran O'Toole how important he was to the people of Bray. It is only right and proper that another band from Bray should have taken up the mantle of greatness from the legend that was Fran O'Toole.

As long as music is played, the songs of Bagatelle will endure. In time others will re-do and rearrange their music but it will always be the music of Bagatelle, the most enduring rock band on this island.

Like the 'good book' says, they have endured the trials of life, they have overcome the obstacles; they have fought the good fight; they have finished the race; they have kept the faith.

And, more importantly, we still believe in Bagatelle.

CHUCK FISHBEIN

I can honestly say that I could not have enjoyed the level of success that I have achieved as a Cinematographer, had it not been for the members of the band Bagatelle, and more specifically, the group's guitarist John O'Brien.

I met John in 1972 when he was guitarist for Irish act Glen Curtin, Lola and the New Blues in an Irish dance hall in the Bronx NY called the Red Mill , and that meeting was the beginning of an epic journey with Bagatelle and Ireland , that would eventually lead me to working with U2, Francie Conway, The Corrs, Foo Fighters Garth Brooks and even Harley-Davidson.

The first time I visited John in Ireland he was rehearsing with a group called The Boulder Band which appeared to be gaining some popularity, but on the next visit, he had a new band called Bagatelle and they were already hugely successful. Their records were flying off the shelves.

On my next visit, I drove for hours right across Ireland from Dublin to Castlebar to see them perform at a venue where RTE was recording for a future broadcast.

The crowd was absolutely mad for them, singing along and demanding encores of "Summer in Dublin". It was sheer lunacy. I loved it!

In the fall of 1986 the late Jack McNeice, President of Harmac Records, asked me to photograph the band, as well as create a commercial, which eventually evolved into their first music video for "Cry Away the Night". It was actually my first music video, and I was a bit terrified at the time, but the experience totally changed the direction of my career.

The original members of the band had a unique dynamic. Liam had established himself as a vocalist and musician and had penned the groups most successful tracks. The simplicity and consistency of Wally and Ken's backline would drive the band, while John's unusual, bluesy guitar style somehow homogenized the sound.

Over the years I watched the band and their music evolve, witnessing breakups, restructuring and eventually the reformation of the original members.

I created several music videos with Bagatelle during those years, as well as a documentary that ended with a sold-out performance at the Olympia Theatre in Dublin. It was absolute madness. Everywhere they performed the crowds were filled with nostalgia singing songs like "Trump Card" and "Leeson Street Lady", often overpowering the band.

As a photographer and filmmaker, working with Bagatelle was an experience that will always live in my heart. I will always be grateful for their friendship, loyalty and trust.

I have kept a cassette copy of their first album on my desk for over 40 years!

LOUIS WALSH

Bagatelle have been rocking ever since their first hit in 1978, although they never gained the international fame they deserved. It started in Bray, Co. Wicklow, August 1978 and even today they remain a hugely popular band in Ireland. The hits "Summer in Dublin", "Second Violin" and "Leeson Street Lady" are still heard on the radio while tunes like "Boston Rose" and "The Streets of New York" are hits covered by numerous Irish bands/ artists making Liam Reilly one of Ireland's greatest and most famous song writers, his songs are timeless.

U2 have given credit to Bagatelle for their influence in U2's early days. With a few line-up changes Bagatelle are still rockin' in the free world. Here's to the next 40.

MICK McCONNELL

When I was asked to write this segment of the book, I was genuinely taken aback and as I write this I feel truly honoured to make this contribution for a band who have managed to combine success and longevity in the very fickle business we call music.

I first came across Bagatelle many, many years ago, but in recent times, Bagatelle have shared the same stage as Smokie on several occasions, so I have gotten to know them not just as a band, but as friends too. Of course, in true rock n' roll fashion, we have also shared a drink or two in the hotel bar!

Over 40 years in the music business is a long, long, time, and if you can add success to that too, then in my mind you have truly made it!

Bagatelle are one of the few bands that can say they stood the test of time, continually touring and bringing their brand of Irish influenced music to their loyal fans and followers. However, that's the easy bit! Doing it with enthusiasm and finesse is a different matter altogether! These guys are true professionals, always giving 100%, always delivering their unique brand.

It's a credit to them that they celebrate over 40 years in the business, something they should feel proud of and I'm delighted that they can share their exploits, trials and tribulations in this book. Their fans will no doubt revel in the details and inside stories; what happens behind the music, what makes this band tick. This book is a long overdue opportunity to delve into the wonderful world of the great Bagatelle. Lads you should be proud of what you have achieved. Myself and the other members of Smokie wish you well and hopefully you've got a few more years left in you yet!

None of this happens by accident of course. Liam's inspired song-writing, flawless musicianship, endless touring and a work ethic that would shame most of us, has resulted in simply stunning live performances which ensure that the legend is kept alive.

They are unique and thank God we still have them.

HARRY O'DONOGHUE

I met Liam Reilly sometime in 1982 I believe. I had a band called Terra Nova and we were gigging between Philadelphia, Wilmington, Delaware, Los Angeles, St. Louis, Houston and points in between. The band members changed regularly but in 1982 it consisted of Trish Rogers, Triona O'Mahony and me - Harry O'Donoghue. Trish knew Liam from Dundalk I believe. We met in Philly where Terra Nova had a large following and in the Fall of '82 we had orchestrated our first recording.

It was funded by folks who came to see us regularly (what one would nowadays call a Kickstarter or Go Fund me campaign) which was great. Liam, as I recall, was over to 'clear his head' after the explosion of Bagatelle on the Irish music scene. I certainly knew who he was. I was a fan of the band and actually saw him one time in the Cellars bar in Drogheda, my hometown, before I left Ireland. He was passing through I assumed, but he made an impact on the customers that evening by just being there.

In Philadelphia he was playing piano part time in a bar close to where we recorded; Third Story Recording Studio. The studio was owned by John Wicks and we arranged recording time with Liam at the helm. I cannot remember the monies involved with respect to Liam, but it was per track, a couple or three hundred dollars; to include Liam as producer, arranger, musician and vocalist. It was my first recording and so I was extremely nervous.

I remember the atmosphere as being easy going, friendly, encouraging and very productive. Liam changed hats with considerable ease, and I was in awe of his talent and know-how in every area of the process. This studio experience would be repeated three more times... a second Terra Nova album and two of my solo projects...all with LR at the helm.

The second Terra Nova album was again recorded at Third Story. These sessions were not as harmonious unfortunately. Liam felt that some of the material wasn't ready, especially the original songs and at least one other, but him being a professional, he soldiered on and finished the recording. He then went on to help by having John Woods at Polydor Records in Ireland who listened to the finished album and we got signed!

The record came out on Polygram in late 1985 and they even released a single...a rocking version of the "Wild Rover."

By this time Mr. Woods had retired and the new heads at the record company really didn't show an interest in us. It would lead to the band (a duo by then) breaking up around '86 –'87. By then we had moved our goods and chattels down to Savannah, Georgia (in 1984) and were well settled in Kevin Barry's Irish Pub where we were considered the 'house band'.

Liam had also moved to Savannah, but I can't put a date on that. He played late afternoon piano in Kevin Barry's for a while. It was late '87 into '88 when I recorded my first solo project 'Another Misty Morning'. Liam again produced and arranged and played multiple instruments and added backing and harmony vocals. He and Phil Hadaway, who owned the studio, made a terrific duo and again I remember that time with great fondness. I continue to work with Phil to this day, but unfortunately when Liam left Savannah in 1990, I never did get to work with him again.

When looking through the original material for my first solo album I had disregarded a song. Liam asked why and I told him that the powers that be in Philadelphia, where I did some demos, said the song wasn't nearly up to par. He asked to listen to it and then pronounced that I had written it from the heart, it did have a good core and we were doing it! The song is called "Pray for the Darkness."

He re-arranged it, had me change some lyrics, and we were off to the races. Interestingly, it's one of my very favourite original songs, and when it came time to put a solo into it, Liam said "Let me try something really quick'. He did and then used that for guidance and played about eight or nine different solos to try and improve on the first, but what you hear on the finished track is that first solo he played. It's a beautiful part, he nailed it first time. Pure magic.

We did have some laughs in the studio though. I was recording a version of Eric Bogle's "And the Band Played Waltzing Matilda", which is a long piece. We had almost finished after many hours and I was trying for a main vocal. Everything was going well until the last verse when I heard a voice in my headphones going "vroom, vroom, vroom, vroom."

I was startled and looked through the booth window up to the control room, saying "What the f***!" Liam pressed the talk button and said,

"It's porch Harry. Sit on my porch...not in my Porsche!"

We laughed for a while!

Another time, same album, he stopped me again saying "Ah, Harry it's THE reason I left Mullingar, not DE Reason. Put the H back in will you!"

Another memory is of us taking a dinner break during recording. Liam and I sat in a restaurant called Applebee's, at the bar. The bartender was a fetching young girl but not the sharpest blade in the drawer. She was friendly and inquisitive, mainly due to our accents. At one point she said, "You boys ready for another cold beer?" to which Liam replied, "Is a frog waterproof?"

This completely flummoxed her, and she paused for a second or two before replying, 'I wouldn't know but do you want a couple more beers?'

My father came over to America once, my mother came four or five times. I introduced Da to Liam and we sat at the bar one afternoon. Dad was mightily impressed meeting Liam and was all inquiries. He asked of Liam's girlfriend Sylvia "Where is she from Liam?" to which Liam replied, "Stuttgart in Germany Tom." The conversation stalled, then after an awkward silence Dad said "Germany Liam. She wouldn't be Catholic then would she."

"No Tom. She's a Lutheran, about as much use as an ashtray on a motorbike". My father nearly fell off the stool!

Bagatelle certainly took Ireland by storm. I must admit, because I wasn't writing music at the time, I was blissfully unaware that the band wrote, (mainly Liam), their own songs. It didn't take long for me to realize that Bagatelle were a music tour de force and took me even less time to understand that Liam Reilly has a huge talent as a musician, arranger, songwriter and producer. We recorded a live album in 1989 upstairs in Kevin Barry's. All Irish folk songs and ballads. Liam played piano, guitar (and maybe accordion) and sung backing vocals. He arranged it on the fly, the evening was great fun and the album *Live and Well* is probably my best selling of the sixteen that I have released.

One of Liam's last projects in Savannah was to produce a record for Joe Dolan. I was playing that week in Kevin Barry's and Liam would drop Joe down for a jar after the studio session. I got to know Joe pretty well over those couple of weeks.

We never told him that Danny Doyle was playing the next week and we orchestrated that Joe be at the bar when Danny arrived. It was magic, seeing these two Irish stars interact and tell stories of the Irish music scene.

Liam never came in on any of those nights. He was producing Joe's album and he thought it wholly unprofessional to imbibe when he was at the helm of an important project.

VIVIAN O ROURKE

I had started work with Pye Records back in 1969 with John Woods when he was the MD. Pye closed its doors in 1971/72 so John then went to take over at Polydor. He was great to work with. Absolutely superb. I gained so much knowledge from him and worked with him until he decided to retire in the 1990's.

We always had dealings with Oliver Barry who had this new group, Bagatelle, under his wing. I remember seeing them first in the Stella in Mount Merrion on a Sunday and the place was jam packed. You simply could not move. Not long after that they were signed by Polydor Records. I had known them as The Boulder Band before then, as they had carved out a reputation for themselves.

I spent a lot of time on the road as a sales rep for Polydor and only back in the office on Friday afternoons. My work kept me extremely busy. It was during this time "Summer in Dublin" was released. It was on every radio practically everywhere. It was such a huge hit. We were very happy.

TOMMY MANGAN

"I joined Bagatelle as a session keyboard player in the early eighties, just after the release of "Summer in Dublin". In the three years that I played with the group I had many great times with Liam, John, Ken and Wally. We toured everywhere and always got a great reception wherever we went. The band were big time. There would be a couple or articulated trucks following us around on tour, full of equipment.

I first met Liam when I was working for Yamaha at the time. He would come into the shop, play the piano for a while and we would chat. To this day he remains a very good friend. I learned so much from him in regard to his keyboard skills. The most memorable gigs would have to be Siamsa Cois Laoi, the National stadium and the RDS.

I also had success with Allies, another Irish group, with a song called "Half the World Away" which had won an Eastern European version of the Eurovision Song Contest. It was won in Bratislava in the Czech Republic. The currency we won it with was worth nothing to us. Anywhere we went! I remember being in Russia with 20000 rubels in my pocket and it was useless. I remember this worker asleep next to me and I put the money in his jacket as it was no use to me. I would have loved to have seen his face when he woke up! Mind you, we were well stocked in vodka though!

Some years later I joined Liam again when he was doing his solo career and the release of "Somewhere in Europe" doing concerts in the Gaiety Theatre. How that song didn't win the Eurovision that year is still a mystery. Even when he made a rough recording of it on my old reel to reel recorder in my house, I thought the song was destined to win it.

I now tour with Nights on Broadway; a Bee Gees tribute band and I can actually see a resemblance between both The Bee Gees and Bagatelle – two great groups, very popular, who probably didn't get the full credit that they deserve.

JOE BOLLARD

I first met John O'Brien after a gig I was doing in the Royal Hotel in Bray. I remember him coming up to me, introducing himself, and we got chatting. We agreed to meet up again some days later for coffee and another chat. We enjoyed each other's company and became close friends from then on. I was surprised one day when he told me of his intentions to form a band consisting of bass guitar, drums, keyboard and guitar and would I be interested.

At first, I said no. I was a solo artist and was happy that way, but John had great powers of persuasion! It interested me that this group was going to rely mostly on original material with some popular tunes thrown in.

He was going to name this band "Bagatelle" which he explained meant a musical nothing. So, I agreed to join. He told me there would not be much money in it to start with, but we would build up our own following, so after agreeing to give it a go we started rehearsing.

So, we had a few gigs. John brought in a female vocalist, and the core of the group Bagatelle was now in place. If my memory serves me right, I remember John saying the band was going to release a single. After a while however I got a little disillusioned with things. The group began to play a lot of rock numbers (certainly not my scene) so eventually I told John I was leaving the group. He was extremely disappointed and asked me to reconsider but I was adamant about leaving, so I did.

I went back to doing my own thing, picking up a regular gig in a hotel in Dalkey where John would often pay me a visit. He would keep me informed about how the group was getting along. He always had great drive and determination so I knew he would make it work. I had no regrets about leaving Bagatelle and was delighted with the success the group had.

PETER BARDON

My first contact with Bagatelle came through John Woods who was the Managing Director of Polydor who had just signed Bagatelle for both Recording and Publishing. Bardis Music administered the then Polydor publishing company called Raglan Music. When the Raglan rights expired after 10 years, Bagatelle asked Bardis to take over the management of the publishing.

"Trump Card", which was produced by Gus Dudgeon, put down a marker as one of the first local pop records with an international quality production which made the local industry sit up and take notice of the band.

"Summer in Dublin" was a superb song and everyone marvelled at how Liam included a reference to the 46A bus. It's unique. Like all great songs it stands the test of time and is as popular today as it was when first released in 1980.

Liam is a great wordsmith and his emigration songs like "Streets of New York" and "Flight of Earls" perfectly captured the experience many, many young people were going through at that time. Oliver Barry, Bagatelle's manager, who also managed the Wolfe Tones, gave them the songs and they recorded wonderful versions of them.

We all know Liam is a creative genius. I give great credit to the laid-back Ken Doyle and the late sadly missed John O'Brien along with Jim

McQuillan with keeping the Bagatelle brand alive for so long.

At the end of the day it's all about the great songs and the memories they created for that generation and Bardis is delighted and proud of our role in protecting the full Bagatelle publishing catalogue.

PHIL HADAWAY

I met Liam one evening in 1985. A mutual friend brought him by my studio and introduced us. We immediately developed a friendship, and he was very interested in some of the new technology that was evolving and that I was using.

He told me he needed to record a vocal for a demo that he had received. I had no idea who he was or his history. Remember, this was Savannah, Georgia, and it was way before you could use a search engine!

We recorded the vocals, background vocals, and a couple of synth tracks for a song called "Hurting Inside." He sent my mix off, and that was that. More later.

We started hanging out a bit more and Liam had written this song called "Savannah Serenade." With the help of Vic Power, the owner of Kevin Barry's Irish Pub, we recorded the song and they shot a promotional video. It was a beautiful piece, and again with the technology, we were able to get great sounds on just eight tracks of tape!

In 1987, Liam and I co-wrote a song called "Christmas in Savannah," with all of the sales proceeds going to a local charity. It's still played to this day! By that time, my studio had moved and had grown to sixteen tracks and a lovely English console.

We formed a production team and started making records for several Irish singers.

Among them were: Harry O'Donoghue, Frank Emerson, Cahir O'Doheity, and Tom O'Carroll. Liam was a great producer and was able to handle all of the keyboard duties while I played bass, guitar, percussion, and did all of the programming.

Liam and I began working on a record for ourselves in 1988, "Savannah Souvenirs." This was my studios' first 24 track project. We flew to Atlanta to mix it with a young engineer, Brendan O'Brien. We had a blast working with him. Little did we know that he would go on to become one of the biggest producers in the world. Brendan has since won two Grammy Awards and sold over 200 million records.

Some of the artists he has worked with include; Bruce Springsteen, Pearl Jam, Train, Stone Temple Pilots, Rage Against the Machine, The Black Crowes, AC/DC, Matthew Sweet, Michael Penn, Korn, Aerosmith and about a million more. I would later go on to work for Brendan as both a

Producer and Engineer for his record label on Epic Records.

As a side note, when we went through security at the airport, we asked that the tapes be hand searched. They were not very cooperative, and Liam commented, something about a bomb. Needless to say, he missed his flight! We did meet up later for a Paul Carrack release party at the recording studio where we would be mixing.

Joe Dolan approached us about producing a record for him in 1989. I knew a little about him and it seemed like an exciting project. Joe wanted a little more "American Sound" to this record. He flew to Savannah for three weeks, and we cut the basic tracks and vocals for the "*Always Loved You*" album.

Joe returned home while Liam and myself completed the record. I wound up playing all of the guitars while Liam played the keys and did background vocals. On the night before we were to fly up and mix, we had a choir scheduled to come in and sing backgrounds on "Tell It Like It Used to Be." They refused to sing it because it was not a gospel song. WOW! I sent my assistant engineer out to scour Savannah for people who could sing. About 1:00 AM, four people were dragged in, and somehow, we managed to record a drunken choir. We flew up to Atlanta the next day and mixed the record in 4 days. That was a close one!

By 1990, Liam had resigned with Polydor, and he asked me to come over and produce his solo album "*Throwing Caution to the Wind*." He had recorded most of the basic tracks, and I brought a few tracks that we had been working on together. I got to work at Westland on Lombard Street and had the pleasure of recording Davy Spillane. The first song I mixed was "Somewhere in Europe," which was to be the single after the Eurovision debut. I felt it was a superb tune but unfortunately politics seemed to come into play, and Liam came in 2nd on the night.

While I was there, we went and surprised Joe Dolan. I've never had a hangover like that!

So, back to "Hurting Inside." I am at the airport in Dublin and walk into one of the shops and see *Bagatelle Gold* on CD and purchase it. I get home, put it on, and guess what? The rough mix I sent to them is on the CD, precisely the way I sent it. I didn't even get a credit. That's just the way it goes!

Meeting Liam was a great stroke of luck! He, directly and indirectly, influenced my career and made me a better Producer, Engineer, and musician!

TOMMY SWARBRIGG

It was a sweltering hot summer and I was heading somewhere in my car, when this record came on the radio. It was "Summer in Dublin" by

Bagatelle and I stopped the car to listen and to find out who it was. I've done this only twice in my life (the other time was when I heard 'Sultans of Swing' on the radio). Liam Reilly's amazing voice and writing talent defined that year for me. I can still hear the power and pathos in his voice. Other great tracks followed, 'Trump Card' and 'Second Violin; etc... I heard Bagatelle recently and they still have the ability to transport me back in time to that magical Summer.

JOHNNY HERO

Most acts can only dream of having the same kind of impact as Bagatelle. Their songs have woven themselves into the very fabric of Irish society to such an extent that we now have three generations of fans who will get ready to sing their heads off when the opening riff of "Second Violin" swirls from the speakers. It used to be said that every Irish household had a picture of JFK and the Pope, add to that Bagatelle's Gold album and you begin to appreciate what a national treasure they have become.

DARRAN McGOLDRICK

I was working country wide as a freelance sound engineer and also had started a sound rental company in 1995 which meant doing shows with rock bands of the day such as Something Happens ,An Emotional Fish, My Little Funhouse etc. I got a call in roughly 1996/7 from Jim McQuillan on my mobile cell phone (all the rage at the time) looking for a vender to work with Bagatelle, so away we went to our first show in Dungarvan, Co Waterford where we did our thing and got on with all the lads.

I had not played drums in about 5 years and was happily mixing the shows and generally looking after everything technical. Robbie Casserly was the drummer at that time, and he was (and still is), one of the country's best so my admiration and attention was always focused on his playing. He would regularly play the first half of the set with one hand effortlessly and eat his burger and chips with the other!

Then one New Year's Eve we were playing in Waterford. The crew got their work done, sound-checked every instrument , as the lads did not soundcheck or carry any of their own kit, when out of the blue Jim rushes up to me, telling me Robbie cannot make the gig. It was Ken who then suggested myself as I knew Robbie well. We always sat together, travelled together on the road and flights, and got on well plus I could play so I was slotted in on drums. The problem however was not playing the gig, it was how just two of the crew could mix the show to a full crowd in a large venue as neither were trained sound engineers! But we made it work. I'm sure we had done alright as I got paid TWICE that night!

A few months later Robbie was given the drumming gig on the Riverdance tour, so I took over on drums for a while. It was a nice fit. I was already in the camp and knew the songs and had bought the existing drum kit from Robbie so literally nothing had changed as that kit was still in the back of the truck.

I soon got to see how in-demand Bagatelle was. The guys were extremely popular, and the hotter spots were always up North and down South. We averaged three shows a week for about 40 weeks of the year. The old reliable haunts being returned to every 12 or 14 weeks. Jim ran a good ship and we hit many rural festivals and one-off places that normally could not afford a big band like this, but they would put up marquees in farmyards or school grounds as such. The lads would never look down on what was often ramshackle venues.

The party always happened by hook or by crook. I was also an electrician so often had to construct some creative temporary fixes to get the amount of equipment needed while functioning on little more than a domestic extension reel but it never bet me, we always got there.

I loved playing with the band. When in America we used to do a small Irish club in the Bronx called The Fireside Pub which I think was on Katona Avenue. It was your average Irish American pub but the reception and hospitality the lads received there was great. I think it was run by a man called Tom who was a big fan. The most memorable gig was the official gig in Omagh as a fundraiser after the bombing. The Irish Foresters Hall was very close to where it all happened. It was a mixed audience of all religions and sections, and we had gigged in it many times previous but there had been a gap of time after the bombing. We sat downstairs eating the obligatory biscuits then when it was show time, we headed for the stairs to be stopped by security as there was someone about to do an introduction. It could have been the local peacemaker priest but I'm not certain. He said a few words then says, "Welcome on stage, Bagatelle."

The place erupted and the floor and stairs were moving. I always walked at the back onto the stage, but I froze for a minute with the hairs standing on my body. There was a lot of emotion in that room that night, but the lads played out of their skins and it was definitely a very memorable gig for me. I was on a show in Omagh last December and walked by it and went in to have a look around. It has not changed at all but doesn't run shows any more. After it we did a similar Omagh gig in Gaelic Park Chicago. That was special as well.

And we travelled quite a bit. Mainly, Stateside – the East and West Coast as a drummer initially but then as a one-man crew combined with drums. After that it was harder to get big dollars and everything became more efficient. But I still made money: being paid to drum, supply the PA, supply the backline along with driving the van. At the time I bought my own PA and stored it in a friend's warehouse in Brooklyn. In the end I would end up working in America three months of the year and once or twice would finish with gigs with the lads.

In New York I would hang around doing freelance mixing to start with and ending up working with The Wolfe Tones or another Irish act.

I did the Macau Trip with Bagatelle which was a great experience and a definite highlight. It was sort of strange as well as after the gig we were paid in Northern Irish sterling by the dodgiest festival promoter I ever came across. But I would have done the gig free just for the experience. It was my first gig in that part of the world.

The UK was always fun and the Galtymore in Cricklewood was always my favourite.

I got on well with the band in the seven or eight years I was with them and consider them friends. John was an absolute gentleman, and nothing was ever an issue. You could tell him his guitar amp was after blowing up, but we have done a temporary fix to get him through the night and he would be happy out and play on regardless. I always held him in high regard.

Ken was funny. He could be late and scruffy when travelling but he always put the show on seconds after landing in the venue like a pro. He was great craic.

We always travelled together and often met in Bray and go out with our wives on occasions. Liam is a very talented songwriter and performer and obviously penned some greats.

I still run my own company and employ three full time technicians. MG Audio. We support corporate clients, looking after all aspects of staging, lighting and video and transport. I still like to do music gigs and tour occasionally but only for short periods.

STEVE HOGAN

It was Paul Byrne who recommended me to the lads in Bagatelle as I played drums. To that point I had been basically freelancing with different bands, getting lots of experience, doing sessions and television work.

I grew up in Kimmage in Dublin. The first drum kit I ever owned was a Maxwin Kit by Pearl. So, I joined the band, and I remember my first gig with Bagatelle was in the Garda Club in Harcourt Street on a Thursday night. I was running in from an earlier gig so set the kit up earlier in the day. A baptism of fire!!

I really enjoyed my time with the band. Lots of travelling around the country and even a few trips over to England. There was never any stress and it was great fun.

OLIVE DALY

I grew up in a small village called Doon in County Limerick and used to listen to the radio a lot. 2FM had just started and they played so much new pop stuff. It was there that I first heard "Summer in Dublin". I love a huge range of music, but this song stood out the first time I heard it over the airwaves. In 1980, my older brother Tony moved to Dublin for work. That was his first summer in Dublin, the reason why the song related to him.

One weekend Tony arrived home with Bagatelle's first album on cassette. Naturally, I played it until it was nearly worn out. Yes, it had "Summer in Dublin" but I also discovered great tracks like "Trump Card", "Leeson Street Lady" and "City Lights", however my favourite was "Rock & Roll Fantasy".

Soon after my brother got myself and my sister Norah tickets to go see Bagatelle in concert at the Savoy in Limerick. I can even remember the date. May 22nd, 1981.

I was 17 and this was my first concert, and the first chance I had to see Bagatelle. Needless to say, they were superb on the night and travelled the country to see the band perform.

I was busy studying for my Leaving Cert when Bagatelle's second album was released. School priorities were put on hold and the only studying I was doing was listening to the groups new music and learning the lyrics! By the end of the summer I had worn out the album.

We had just got a big new stereo system in our school hall and my friend and I were in charge of playing the music at lunch time. It was a big hall, and everyone used to be up dancing, but I just wanted to play "Second Violin" over and over again!

It was a pity my speciality subject was not Bagatelle because I would have definitely got an A! It was great when they played in more local places like Dromkeen in County Limerick or Dundrum in County Tipperary. Mind you, if the band were playing within a 90-mile radius of Limerick I was the first to know and the first to go!

Of course, my love of the group meant I had to be front row centre when Bagatelle played a gig, screaming the lyrics back to the band and hopping around like some mad possessed woman. By this stage the whole of Ireland had bought into Bagatelle. One of the highlights of my time as a fan was watching them play Siamsa Cois Laoi in 1982 when they played to over 40,000 (they returned again in 1983 and 1984 to which I went.)

Self-Aid would also prove to be a memorable moment - sharing the stage with the likes of Paul Brady, Van Morrison, Thin Lizzy and U2.

With their popularity at an all-time high I was delighted that the group kept churning out singles and albums at a rapid rate, meaning I didn't have long to wait to buy that next Bagatelle album or single from my local record shop.

The level of song writing was superb. Their third album proved no different to the first two. You take songs like "Raining in Paris" and "Don't Play A Sad Song" that are now almost 40 years old but still sound superb. I loved the cover of "Jersey Girl" but my favourite was "Midnight Child", so much so anytime I went to see Bagatelle, I would ask Ken to sing it for me.

Years passed and I moved to Dublin. Yes, there was a temporary change in band personnel in the late Eighties, but I saw their reunion gig in the Spa Hotel in Lucan where Ken, Liam, John and Wally, got back together again. The band were so nice to me on a personal basis, especially Ken. I remember seeing the band in the Shelling Hotel, Raheny. I met Ken just before the show started and he told me, "I have your song tonight". I just could not believe it! Although it took 18 years of asking, he finally sang "Midnight Child" for me! It was amazing and I am so thankful to Ken for that memory which I will never forget. Mind you I saw them a few weeks later in the Submarine in Crumlin and guess what...Ken sang it for me again!

We all know those wonderful songs that followed throughout the 1980's. Tunes like "All Fall Down Philadelphia", "Can't Get You Out Of My Mind" and "Cry Away The Night" to name just a few and I have all of their various compilation albums too. I cherish my almost fully complete collection of Bagatelle records, cassettes, and CDs.

I was totally devastated when I heard that Bagatelle were doing their Final Year Tour but thankfully that hasn't been the end of their story. When you see them perform and pack out venues like Vicar Street and the Olympia even after all this time you see how special the group still are to thousands of fans.

I am delighted to have my thoughts on record of my love for the band. I would like to thank them for giving me so many good times (with a special mention to Jim McQuillan.) They have been the soundtrack to my life, and I am so glad I can still see them play, many, many, years after I first got a £5.99 cassette of their first album from my brother!

TONY TONER

Ken is a fellow motorcyclist, a horizon chaser like me, who takes their motorcycle out of the garage and goes for a spin, not knowing where they are going, just looking to interact with the countryside and the weather in a very real way. Motorcyclists don't need a reason, they need an excuse, and in that mind-set, Ken and I are kindred spirits. The journey is more important than the destination.

I knew of Ken since the formation of Bagatelle, but in 2004 a mutual friend introduced us, as Ken wanted to ride Route 66, (4,000kms, Chicago to Los Angeles). I had just completed my second tour down Route 66 in aid of Temple Street Children's Hospital and was preparing for our 2006 return. From that first handshake we were bonded – we are family.

I was 19 and arrived in Donnybrook in 1973. My foot patrol beat and the area I lived in introduced me to Appian Way, Leeson Street, the open-backed bus that was the 46A and everyone at that time had to endure the smell of the Liffey at low tide. When "Summer in Dublin" subsequently hit the airways it immediately resonated with me, the connection as real today as it was in 1980. Liam Reilly's ability to knit words with his unique voice elevates him to a musical storyteller supreme. I cannot remember how many times I have seen them over the years prior to 2004, but it was many and since then the friendship with Ken, Liam and manager Jim is personal and precious.

My own experience of artists is that whilst they may look like us ordinary folk, they are wired completely different. I learned many years ago to never try and fully understand them – it is much better to accept their idiosyncrasies and relish their interpretation and capture of life and living. I have cried laughing with Ken Doyle, his ability to be 18 again in a blink of an eye. Ken's love of Bray and walking the beach in gleeful wonder at what the tide has left behind is an indication of his boyish inquisitiveness and his innate understanding of how our world really works. Ken's eclectic persona changes as soon as Bagatelle take to the stage, when every note and beat is literally on song, his harmony with Liam welded without seams. Liam Reilly is a musical storyteller, who captured the marriage of time, place and mood into music. Bagatelle's music is as relevant today as it was on the first day of its airing. It doesn't age because it relates to the person listening from its essence. Ireland has had many writers of note, the words of Liam Reilly and the music of Bagatelle deserve to be acknowledged in the four decades that is now in their mirrors and a secure future, where generations to come will relish the recounting of the everyday of yesterday as if it were today.

DECLAN LYNCH

Bagatelle first came to my attention in 1981. What made them stand out is the fact they were writing and recording original music at the time. Very few bands were doing that. I began to follow and became interested in them. I immediately went to buy their first album which was recorded a year earlier. They had started to record it on January 29th, 1980, which also happened to be Liam Reilly's birthday. In time I had the pleasure of getting to know Liam and the band. The first time I ever met Liam was outside the Glenavon Hotel in Cookstown. He was very kind and told me to come backstage when the gig was over for a chat.

A ticket from a Bagatelle gig in Gaelic Park Stadium, New York that John O'Brien gave Declan.

Naturally, I was a fan and have seem them countless times since. Places like The White Horse Hotel in Cavan. The Ardhowen Theatre, Enniskillen. The Hillgrove Hotel, Monaghan. The Pulse in Letterkenny and the Europa Hotel in Belfast and saved most of my VIP tickets from these events. And I am really naming just a few, trust me!

The energy and dedication to their gigs hasn't changed. They have always been superb live. I recall one particular gig in the Ardhowen Theatre in 2003, which was probably my favourite.

John O'Brien was a wonderful man and it was my pleasure to get to know him. We became great friends. I live in Fermanagh on the border, about one mile from Clones where John was living at the time. His sister also lived in Clones as well and John had played with The Big Four which of course featured Pat McGuigan – father of Barry McGuigan the boxer. Even by then he was an experienced musician. Along with this his was very articulate and highly intelligent.

You could have a conversation with him for hours.

I have kept hundreds of newspaper and gig clippings of Bagatelle over the years. As I speak, I'm looking at the cassette of *Bagatelle Gold*, their biggest selling album.

It's been a pleasure to know the band personally and live my life through their music since the got together in 1978. I am so thankful for Bagatelle in my life.

MICHAEL McPHILLIPS

As a young cub in the early 1980s a lifelong interest in music began with me listening to the likes of Radio Nova, one of the great pirate stations of the day, and later to 2FM which featured the one and only Larry Gogan, God rest him. He did so much to launch many, many Irish acts over the years and no bigger fan or friend of Bagatelle than Larry.

It was an incredible time for the pirate stations and homegrown music. Here in Fermanagh we couldn't get the great Dublin stations like Sunshine and Nova so myself and a friend Brian Sheridan sat down one day and designed a wooden frame aerial that you mounted 50 yards of copper wire on and a tuning switch in the centre and yes (don't laugh) but when it was put beside an FM radio it boosted the signal and we had wall to wall pirates come into rural Fermanagh that not another resident had! I often thought had these aerials been seized by the cops there would have been a lot of questions asked in Fermanagh in 1980!

What was so unique about these ghassans (to use a South Armagh term for those who hailed from Louth and Wicklow), was that they were pumping out all original material, something unheard of at the time, when most bands were doing covers so this alone was one of the first attractions for me to Bagatelle. As a 14-year-old cub my brother bought me that now famous cassette simply entitled Bagatelle with a sleeve cover of the lads on the Liffey Ferry in Dublin. What an album. "Summer in Dublin", "Trump Card", "Leeson Street Lady", "Rock & Roll Fantasy". I played it so much that it wore away and had to be replaced. Thinking of "Leeson Street Lady" many years later I had the pleasure to photograph the co-writer of that track Walter Peter Mc Conville , the original drummer in the band, standing at the Leeson Street sign just around the corner from Appian Way my god those names bring such memories back.

There second album in 1981 was also a classic. "Love Is the Reason" was, and still is, one of my favourite tracks which John O'Brien co-wrote with lead vocalist Liam Reilly. One of those old songs that was always introduced as the slow set in a nightclub. Jesus I'm showing my age! "The Slow Set" (most of you can remember) was all about running across the floor to get that good looking girl you thought you could see through all the dry ice and sweat in hope she would dance with you.

Times were tough here in the North in those days of the early 1980s but we always had the release valve of a Bagatelle gig to go to and lift the spirits as the band churned out hit after hit and built a massive following in Ireland. Venues like the Knocknamoe and St. Enda's GAA complex in Omagh, the Astoria in Bundoran, the Kilmore in Cavan, the Hillgrove in Monaghan and Kellys of Mohill all come to mind. As a boy of 16, still underage to enter licensed premises, I experienced my first "Live Show" with Bagatelle 38 years ago.

My brother Jimmy promised to bring me to a gig on the Christmas tour of 1982. Jimmy and 3 friends Brian Sheridan, Debora Swift and Christine Wilson and myself headed out of a terrible frosty night to the Kilmore Hotel in Cavan, 18 miles from home and it feels as if it was yesterday. I could still tell you the set-list and every aspect of the show that night. It was the first of many gigs for us four lads. Tour after tour came along and when I was the age to drive and got my first car there was no stopping me. Ironically my brother Jimmy, who ran the family grocery shop at home in Newtownbutler, today is Parish Priest of Lisnaskea in Fermanagh so almost 40 years ago he was responsible from bringing the "Holy Gospel" of Bagatelle and the 4 wise men into my life!

Bagatelle never cracked the British charts but in Ireland there was nobody better. I think of people associated with Bagatelle over the years like Peter Smith of Ballyhaise who managed the band for years and tour managers like Billy Madden and Val James and sound men like Alan Nolan come to mind. Many a night I was escorted into a gig free of charge and right up to the changing rooms to get a chat with the lads before they hit the stage. Peter Smith with that strong Cavan brogue on many an occasion would ring me up and say "Mickey I have a delivery for ya" and it would be the new album to be listened to and critique. I remember saying to him once "Peter if it was happy birthday the group recorded, I'd say it was class!" He was a real gentleman and friend in those Bagatelle days.

I became good friends with the lads from those early days and I used to enjoy the craic when friends always said I was the 5th member and at school, as Liam Reilly often tells at gigs, I was known as "Mickey Bagatelle". My mother bought me a new leather school bag starting back to school one year and in the woodwork room one day I sharpened a chisel and carved the work "BAGATELLE" into the front of the good leather bag. I was as proud as punch, well till I got home and my poor old mother looked at the expensive leather satchel with not too pleasant a greeting, but it was my trade mark and she often would say I was a Bagatelle fanatic. I now make a public confession but in those early days I used to tape the shows on a little cassette recorder in fact many a night Alan Nolan would set it up for me, but I have to say for legal reasons it was just for my own personal use as many a man said to a judge about cannabis if they were caught!

In 1987 I met up with Ken before a show one night in Monaghan and he played me a selection of songs they had recently recorded for the forthcoming Cry Away The Night Album. He came to a song called "Heartache Street" which he played and asked my opinion on. I told him I liked the original better. To his amazement I explained I had a recording of a show from several years earlier and they had done a version of the song which was a lot different than the one he played me. I had the cassette in the car and loaned it (yes loaned it) to make sure it was kept safe and returned to me. When the new album came out low and behold the version that I had given Ken was on it so that is my claim to fame on "Heartache Street". In those days the band would throw out a few tracks to see the reaction of fans and many never made it to albums, but Heartache Street did.

Over the years I met many fellow fans of Bagatelle and to this day they are friends, something which I'm proud to say - and that's from every part of Ireland and the United States. Declan Lynch from Magherraveely just a stone's throw from my home. Gerry Mc Govern and his wife Noeleen from Hearsdale New York via Ballinamore Co. Leitrim, and Ballycastle County Mayo the late Martin Melarkey from my home town of Newtownbutler the Crudden family of Aghadrumsee to just mention a few who all soldiered alongside me over the years through rain, hail and many a night of heavy snow never to be beat and turn up at a gig. To quote Martin Luther King ``As long as we live, there is never enough singing."

Asked what was the best gig I ever attended was a hard question to answer but one that stood out would have to be the Carrick Springs in Cavan at the end of Are We Keeping You Up Irish Tour in 1982. It was a night of craic where all involved were coming to the end of a long tour and everyone was on a high and as the notes of" Leeson Street Lady" was played on the piano by Liam, I think it was Billy Madden or Val James, just strode onto the stage dressed as one of those ladies clad in a black bin liner and fishnet stockings and done a twirl and Liam, Ken, John and Wally just fell around the place laughing! The craic was ninety! I think the best venue in the country had to have been the St. Enda's GAA complex in Omagh in fact I think it held the record crowd at a Bagatelle gig in Ireland.

I took up the art of video production and film work and in 2013 I was so honored to produce Liam Reilly's Christmas single "Another Christmas Morning" filmed with the children of St. Josephs National School in Muirhevnamore in Dundalk. What fun filming on a hot summer's day, clad in Christmas woolen jumpers and holly wreaths all around to give the impression of Christmas and then the launch in the Marches shopping centre in Dundalk and hanging out of a cherry picker 50 foot about the courthouse on a cold frosty night filming the kids on the square! Great fun and great to be working with the kids and Liam.

In the late 1980s the Troubles were very prevalent in the North and many people like me and many friends would socialise south of the border in Monaghan and Cavan where we felt safe.
But there was always the exception.
That would be the Christmas GAA gig in Omagh.
I loaded the car and headed for the venue. After the gig, around 3am, we

were ready to make our way home after the regular sausage and chip from a local chippy. I turned the key of the car and there wasn't a kick.

The last vehicle in the car park and 40 miles from home.

Sweet Jesus.

What were we going to do? I made a roar at Peter Smith and ran like hell back to the complex and was so happy to see the familiar Citroen reg still sitting at the side of the building. He was still there.

I knew Peter would be travelling through Newtownbutler so our lift home was sorted. About 3 miles north of Newtownbutler we rounded a bend and up ahead we could see flashing hazard lights, so we all got ready to be stopped by British army or RUC. But as we slowly rolled up to the scene, we could see a car sitting on top of a hedge and a girl was lying on the grass verge and a man walking about in a daze. As it turned out it was a lad from Cavan that Peter knew called Paul who had crashed on his way to bringing his girlfriend home in Lisnaskea. We all bailed out in the dark and started to comfort the girl in the pitch dark and I took off my coat and put it under her head.

She had broken her ankle. As we talked and asked questions all of a sudden, she stopped talking and said, "It that you Mickey?" to which I answered yes. As it turned out she was a friend of Deirdre from Lisnakea who I knew. We couldn't stop laughing as we sat on the side of the road.

As I went back to see Peter and Paul, I could suddenly hear the sound of clicking all around us. I told them not to move or say anything and within seconds a flare went up into the sky and lit the scene like daylight. Then several dozen heavily armed RUC soldiers rushed us and shouted to get our hands up. I knew the clicking was the safety catches of guns been released and had an idea who was around us. We were quite shaken by the reaction of the police but when they moved in and seen the injured parties they immediately radioed for an ambulance and lowered their guns. They believed they were going to be ambushed and had slowly surrounded us preparing for an attack but thankfully all worked out but I have to say this stood out as one of those momentous night after a Bagatelle gig I never will forget.

As Martin Luther King once said "I had a dream"- well yes, I did. It was a dream of all four original members of Bagatelle playing again but that dream died on the 26th of April 2019 and the loss of our dear friend John O'Brien.

To finish I will quote Bono and early groupie of Bagatelle who once said "Music can change the world because it can change people."

GERRY McGOVERN

I first time I got to meet the lads from Bagatelle was in the Kilmore Hotel in Cavan back in 1980. I was living in Ballinamore, County Leitrim at the time and doing an Engineering Degree at that point.

As for the first time I saw them perform live, that was at the Carraig Springs in Cavan, which would have been around late 1979. It was a pleasant surprise to find out the group played almost all original material.

Ken Doyle, Gerry McGovern and Liam Reilly hanging out in Gerry's Bar.

I saw the band play lots of times up until August 1984 when I left Ireland for New York. Unemployment was rife at the time. There were no jobs in Ireland.

In New York I worked in numerous places for the first five years and in 1989 started my own business. I have been lucky ever since. I have seen Bagatelle play Irish Festivals in Boston, New Jersey, Maine, Philadelphia, and of course flying from Dublin to Killarney in a toy plane for a New Years Eve gig at the Gleneagle Hotel.

Another special gig was The Guinness Oyster Festival in New York, where the lads were presented with keys to the city by the NYPD and FDNY for Liam writing "The Streets of New York." I was lucky enough to work with the band as their sound engineer in America for the last four or five times they have been over here.

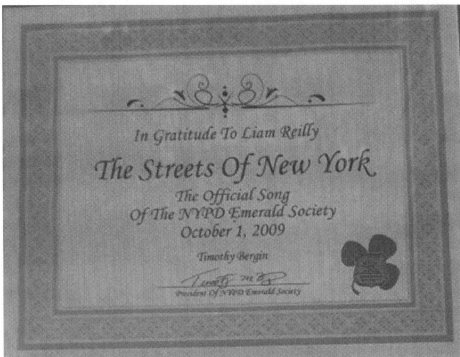

In Gratitude To Liam Reilly

The Streets Of New York

The Official Song
Of The NYPD Emerald Society
October 1, 2009

Timothy Bergin

President Of NYPD Emerald Society

Top; Liam Reilly poses with Gerry McGovern's Mercedes with its
Bagatelle licence plate Above; The special award presented to Liam
Reilly as "The Streets of New York" is chosen as the official song of the
NYPD Emerald Society.

40 YEARS

40 years of music,
And songs that touch the heart,
Original and timeless,
Right from the very start.
Songs hold a special meaning,
In a word or verse or phrase,
That trigger many memories,
That time cannot erase,
There are songs for the broken-hearted,
Or when new love hits the scene,
And for quieter reflective times,
And occasions in between.
I've had the best of times and the worst of times,
And found songs to see me through,
From "Trump Card" to "Boston Rose"
And then "Bainbridge Avenue"
Of course, I've sang "Outrageous"
When I've drank far too much wine,
And "Throwing Caution to the wind",
I've played time after time,
Not forgetting those who have left our shores,
And were feeling all alone,
A song or two from Bagatelle,
Made them feel far more at home,
We've had 40 years of magic,
And stories told in song,
A truly amazing talent,
To have lasted for so long,
It's the gift that keeps on giving,
And it really has been a pleasure,
I'm sure there's no denying,
Bagatelle - a national treasure.

MARGUERITE POWER

ABOUT THE AUTHOR

Brian Kennedy is a Waterford born author. To date he has somehow managed to write 13 books in the last 15 years and still keep his sanity, which he puts down to the use of several legal drugs and copious amounts of Jack Daniels.

In 2011 his book *"Just Follow the Floodlights; The Complete Guide to League of Ireland Football"* was shortlisted for the William Hill Irish Sports Book of the Year and went to Number 1 in the Amazon Best Selling Football League Chart.

A football fanatic he is tormented on a weekly basis by Exeter City Football Club and to a lesser extent Arsenal and writes a column for his local League of Ireland Club Waterford FC.